Orr Scharf
Thinking in Translation

Studia Judaica

―

Forschungen zur Wissenschaft des Judentums

Begründet von
Ernst Ludwig Ehrlich

Herausgegeben von
Günter Stemberger, Charlotte Fonrobert,
Elisabeth Hollender, Alexander Samely
und Irene Zwiep

Band 94

Orr Scharf

Thinking in Translation

Scripture and Redemption in the Thought
of Franz Rosenzweig

DE GRUYTER

ISBN 978-3-11-076415-4
e-ISBN (PDF) 978-3-11-047689-7
e-ISBN (EPUB) 978-3-11-047527-2
ISSN 0585-5306

Library of Congress Control Number: 2019934968

Bibliographic information published by the Deutsche Nationalbibliothek
The Deutsche Nationalbibliothek lists this publication in the Deutsche Nationalbibliografie;
detailed bibliographic data are available on the Internet at http://dnb.dnb.de.

© 2021 Walter de Gruyter GmbH, Berlin/Boston
This volume is text- and page-identical with the hardback published in 2019.
Printing and binding: CPI books GmbH, Leck

www.degruyter.com

לֶכְתֵּךְ אַחֲרַי בַּמִּדְבָּר, בְּאֶרֶץ לֹא זְרוּעָה (ירמיה ב׳, ב׳)
לשירה באהבה

Contents

Abbreviations —— IX

List of Tables —— XI

Acknowledgments —— XIII

Introduction —— 1
- Redemption —— 2
- Translation —— 3
- The Bible —— 5
- Exposition —— 6

Chapter 1: Redemption through Philosophy? —— 8
1.1 Rosenzweig's Relative Relativism —— 9
1.2 Rosenzweig's Economy of Ideas —— 14
1.3 Failed Messianic Hopes —— 20

Chapter 2: Between Intellectual Homelands (1): Germanic Revolution —— 31
2.1 Critique of Pure Idealism —— 34
2.2 Hegel Revisited —— 42

Chapter 3: Between Intellectual Homelands (2): Hebraic Redemption —— 50
3.1 Absolute Difference —— 52
3.2 In Search of Bridges —— 55
3.3 On the Threshold —— 72

Chapter 4: "Eternal Life in Our Midst": Bible, Translation and the Bridge between Transcendence and Immanence —— 75
4.1 Divinity —— 77
4.2 Time —— 91

Chapter 5: *Im Angesicht Gottes bewährt:* From Truth to the Divine Face —— 107
5.1 From the Truth to God —— 110
5.2 From Thinking Into Life —— 120
5.3 In Life Itself —— 132

Chapter 6: Redemption through Translation: *Die Schrift* as the Culmination of Rosenzweig's Quest — 133
6.1   The Redemptive Potential of Translation — 134
6.2   Redeeming Words, Redeeming Worlds — 147
6.3   "Curiosity Abounds and Knowledge Proliferates" — 164

Conclusion — 167

Bibliography — 171
  Primary Sources — 171
  Primary Sources — 173
  Jewish Sources — 173
  Translations of other Jewish sources — 174
  Other Primary Sources — 174
  Secondary Sources — 177

Index of References — 189

Index of Names — 191

Index of Subjects — 194

Abbreviations

Arbeitspapiere	*Franz Rosenzweig. Der Mensch und sein Werk. Gesammelte Schriften IV: Sprachdenken 2. Band. Arbeitspapiere zur Verdeutschung der Schrift.*
Bavli	The Babylonian Talmud
Briefe	*Walter Benjamins Briefe I–II*
BT I & II	*Franz Rosenzweig. Der Mensch und sein Werk. Gesammelte Schriften I: Briefe und Tagebücher. Band I: 1900–1918; Band II: 1918–1929*
GS	*Walter Benjamins Gesammelte Schriften*
Guide	Maimonides, *The Guide of The Perplexed* (English translation)
Illuminations	Walter Benjamin, *Illuminations: Essays and Reflections*
Judah Halevy	*Franz Rosenzweig. Der Mensch und sein Werk. Gesammelte Schriften IV: Sprachdenken. 1. Band. Jehuda Halevi. Fünfundneunzig Hymnen und Gedichte, Deutsch und Hebräisch mit einem Vorwort und mit Anmerkungen.*
Kokhav	*The Star of Redemption* (Hebrew Translation)
Life and Thought	Nahum Glatzer. *Franz Rosenzweig: His Life and Thought.*
Moreh	Maimonides. *The Guide of the Perplexed* (Hebrew)
On Jewish Learning	Franz Rosenzweig, *On Jewish Learning*
Reflections	Walter Benjamin, *Reflections: Essays, Aphorisms, Autobiographical Writings*
Tagebücher	Typescripts I–III, 14 December, 1905 – 4 March, 1908; Typescripts IV–V, VII and Notebook, 6 March, 1908 – 13 September, 1922. Franz Rosenzweig Collection, AR 3001, Series II, Subseries I. Leo Baeck Institute, Center for Jewish History, New York
Scripture and Translation	Martin Buber and Franz Rosenzweig, *Scripture and Translation*
SE/SR	*Stern der Erlösung/Star of Redemption*
SW	Friedrich Wilhelm Joseph Schelling, *Sämmtliche Werke*
Theological Writings	Franz Rosenzweig, *Philosophical and Theological Writings*
Yerushalmi	The Palestinian Talmud
Zweistromland	*Franz Rosenzweig. Der Mensch und sein Werk. Gesammelte Schriften III: Zweistromland: Kleinere Schriften zu Glauben und Denken*

List of Tables

Tab. 1.1: Daniel 11:14 —— 17
Tab. 3.1: The Guide of the Perplexed in The Star of Redemption —— 63
Tab. 4.1: Isaiah 25:8 in the Star of Redemption —— 81
Tab. 4.2: Jonah 2:3–4 and the "sea of God's inner physis" —— 83
Tab. 4.3: Exodus 3:14 —— 89
Tab. 4.4: Numbers 28–29 and the Liturgical Calendar in the Star —— 97
Tab. 4.5: mikra kodesh – Exodus 12:16 —— 103
Tab. 5.1: Biblical Citations in "Buber's" Star of Redemption —— 112
Tab. 5.2: Jeremiah 10:10 —— 118
Tab. 5.3: Maimonides and Rosenzweig on Jeremiah 10:10 —— 118
Tab. 5.4: פנים in Translation —— 124
Tab. 5.5: Rosenzweig's Vision of the Temple and Parallels in Hekhalot Literature —— 130
Tab. 6.1: Exodus 19:1 —— 158
Tab. 6.2: Exodus 4:15 —— 162
Tab. 6.3: Exodus 12:49 —— 162

Acknowledgments

Thinking in Translation: Scripture and Redemption in Franz Rosenzweig's Thought is also the title of my dissertation, which I completed at the University of Haifa's Department of Philosophy in 2014. Prof. Paul Mendes-Flohr agreed to supervise my dissertation of out the pure kindness of his heart. He not only taught me the craft of scholarship, but what human dignity and genuine care for the other look like in real life. As our meetings grew longer, he insisted on dedicating more and more time to conversations about family, mine and his, and any other topic that was relevant to my personal life at the time. Prof. Daniel Statman had no good reason to become my supervisor either, as modern German-Jewish thought is not exactly a natural complement to the many areas of his research and expertise. But once he agreed, Prof. Statman became an enthusiastic reader of the evolving dissertation and a sage advisor on all matters academia.

Vivian Liska, Professor of *Germanistik* at The University of Antwerp and Hebrew University has been an unfailing source of support and an incredible source of inspiration. Prof. Nitza Ben-Dov, head of the Cultural Studies M.A. Program at the University of Haifa, my academic home, became my guardian angel. If it was not for her, *Thinking in Translation* would not have completed the transition from dissertation to book. No words will suffice to express my indebtedness to her encouragement, practical advice, and above all her inexorable *Menschlichkeit*. Stuart Schoffman, my mentor and dear friend, has been teaching me for many years what Thinking in Translation is and can be. My dear friend Dr. Avital Davidovich Eshed has been a rock-solid source of support and insight.

This book has undergone a long gestation. As a fresh Ph.D, Prof. Guy Miron generously invited me to the Open University of Israel where I spent two wonderful years as a post-doctoral fellow. Since we first met Prof. Ora Limor has been an avid supporter and edifying interlocutor. My stay as Ruth Meltzer Fellow at the Herbert D. Katz Center for Advanced Judaic Studies, Philadelphia in Spring 2017 has been a true eye-opening experience. Center Director Prof. Steven Weitzman proved to be not only a gracious host, but also a wonderful conversation partner on all matters Rosenzweig, generously sharing his expertise in Bible scholarship and general erudition. At the Center I have also greatly benefitted from the friendship and advice of Natalie Dohrmann, Anne Albert and Arthur Kiron, as well as from edifying conversations with Lihi Ben Shitrit, Emily Cooper, Menachem Lorberbaum, Vered Sakal, Claude Dov Stuczynski, Vasileos Syros, Philipp von Wussow, and most of all Lois Dubin, whose insights about life and abiding friendship influenced me even more than her consummate scholarship. My thanks also goes to Bonnie Blankenship, Sam Cardillo, and Elizabeth Martin for their warm welcome and helpfulness.

I am thankful for the reader at De Gruyter for his forthcoming feedback and uncompromising corrections. Prof. Michael Morgan read my dissertation and responded both encouragingly and critically. Prof. Zev Warren Harvey generously agreed to read the chapter on Maimonides and provided invaluable comments and suggestions. Cass Fisher has been a partner-in-crime to the study of Rosenzweig's life and thought. Nassima Sahraoui, Caroline Sauter and Paula Schwebel gave insightful comments and helpful references on Walter Benjamin's work. Albert Baumgarten, Michal Bar-Asher Siegal and Jonathan Ben Dov accepted me to their study group on Jewish Culture in Antiquity. In the realms of ancient history I also owe deep thanks to Tessa Rajak, Martin Goodman and Andrea Schatz of the AHRC Josephus Project at Oxford University. My thanks is due to many other fine scholars: Paul Franks, Antonios Kalatzis, Ron Margolin, David Myers, Hindy Najman, David Ohana, Benjamin Pollock, Ishay Rosen-Zvi, Ada Taggar-Cohen, Claudia Weltz, Christian Wiese and Ynon Wigoda.

At The University of Haifa, I would like to thank Prof. Gur Alroey, Dean of the Faculty of the Humanities for his wonderful responsiveness and encouragement. Cedric Cohen Skalli and Amos Morris-Reich were fantastic testing ground for new ideas and their genuine help for my career is deeply appreciated. Riki Snir-Zusman, the Cutural Studies Program's indefatigable coordinator has contributed enormously to the final stages of the book's preparation with advice and encouragement.

Over the years, this project has enjoyed generous material support. My thanks goes to the Graduate Studies Authority at the University of Haifa, the Memorial Foundation for Jewish Culture, the Leo Baeck Institute in Jerusalem, the Lakritz Foundation at the Hebrew University, and the JNF Israel-Switzerland Fund.

I would like to extend a heartfeld thanks to the wonderful team at De Gruyter, especially to Alice Meroz and Katrin Mittmann for their consummate professionalism and patience.

I cannot begin to thank my family for their love, and most of all for the reassurance that I am doing the right thing. My mother, Batia Scharf and her partner Ephraim (Miki) Peisik never tired of asking questions and asking for a taste of the ideas and arguments in my work. I am especially thankful for raising me to believe that I should always follow my heart. My wife's parents, Moshe and Dalia Halfon are a second pair of parents of my own: loving, warm and helpful beyond explanation. My uncles and aunts, Nili Gold and William (Billi) Gold, and Moshe Zeidner and Eti Zeidner, took exceptional interest in my work and generously shared their time, advice and love whenever the need arose. My brother Yoav and his wife Michal, my sisters in-law Einat Halfon and Miranda Murray, and my sister and brother in-law Elad and Vered Halfon, always make me feel that I'm doing the most important thing in the world. Gilad Efrat and Rotem Balva, my siblings by fate rather than blood, are always there for me with sage advice, rock-solid support and endless love.

This book is dedicated with eternal love to my wife Shira, and to my children, Avigail, Eitan and Ella. None of this would have been possible without Shira, who is a perpetual inspiration with wisdom and God-given gift for practicalities. Her faith in me and her abiding love gave me the strength to see this project through. Avigail, Eitan and Ella came into this world as my Rosenzweig project was begotten: first as a dissertation and later on as a book. They made me realize each time anew with their smiles, joy and energy why this project is so important, and why having things in life other than this project is even more important.

Introduction

Franz Rosenzweig's life has become a model of spiritual resilience and intellectual inspiration. The son of an assimilated Jewish German family, so the biographers, who approached the threshold of the baptismal font, decided in a moment of rare courage to devote his life to probe the depths of Jewish faith. He realised his calling in ways as diverse as writing a highly complex work of philosophy, *The Star of Redemption*, founding and directing the adult education centre, the *Freies Jüdisches Lehrhaus* in Frankfurt, and when his rapidly-atrophying body afflicted with amyotrophic lateral sclerosis (ALS) left him bedridden, paralysed and mute, he dedicated his remaining years largely to the translation of the Hebrew Bible. What Rosenzweig's biographers tend to overlook is the continuity in his intellectual universe, which first came to expression in the *Star of Redemption*. In fact, few are the studies that approach Rosenzweig's intellectual legacy at all its stages as ideationally cohesive. The dramatic changes in his intellectual development—beginning as a medical student, writing a dissertation on Hegel under Germany's leading historian, Friedrich Meinecke, deciding to become devoted to the renewal of Jewish spiritual life, serving in the German army in the First World War, publishing academic studies on German Idealist philosophy, the *Star*, and then dedicating his writing to all things Jewish—rendered it difficult to discern a centre of gravity for all of these disparate activities. Indeed, it is far from a trivial task to identify a common intellectual thread for *Hegel and the State* and the exquisite translations of and commentary on poems by medieval Jewish thinker Yehudah Halevy; or for the beautiful, idiomatic German prose of the *Star* and the startling Hebraisms of *Die Schrift*.

Reflecting on the path his life had taken, Rosenzweig wrote to his cousin, Rudolph Ehrenberg, two years before his death:

> What in 1913 I realised and in 1919 wrote down in the third part of the *Star*, is the beeline [*die Luftlinie*]. What I have done, already in writing [it] down and in publishing [it], and then everything that followed: academia, the *Lehrhaus*, my home, Yehudah Halevy, the Bible, lies to the right of the beeline and precisely so little of it may be construed in detail from the beeline as much as what the Zionist does to the left of it (*BT* II, 1133/*Life and Thought*, 157–158).[1]

The beeline, Rosenzweig tells his cousin, is the imaginary straight line that Theory delineates, from which the paths of life [*die Straßen des Lebens*] deviate in different degrees, to the right and to the left. The aim of this book is to present the

---

1 Translation altered.

Hebrew Bible as Rosenzweig's "beeline", and the concept of redemption and the practice of translation as the pathways that led him into the Bible and back into modern secular life.

Redemption

Rosenzweig's engagement with the concept of redemption (*Erlösung*) tapped into an extensive and elaborate discourse in German thought. The confluence of Catholic, Lutheran and pietistic theologies with philosophers' quest for absolute truths in early modernity produced strong redemptive undercurrents in the thought of philosophers such as Leibniz, Hobbes, and Spinoza (Taubes, 125–130). With the emergence of German Idealism, these undercurrents rose to the surface of philosophical discourse, culminating in the work of Hegel and Schelling. By the turn of the 20th century, philosophy, science and theology, which Hegel and Schelling had sought to unify within an all-encompassing system, faced an unprecedented danger of fragmentation. The emergence of historicism and epistemological relativism threatened to tear asunder the presuppositions of these disciplines, while thinkers were impelled to respond to the acute sense of impending cultural crisis.[2] The First World War and its debilitating consequences stimulated redemptive discourses with a decidedly political dimension in Germany.[3]

In "Multiple forms of Redemption in Kabbalah and Hasidism", Moshe Idel identifies six redemptive tropes in medieval and early modern conceptions of redemption in Jewish mysticism. Some of these tropes bear resemblance to ideas Rosenzweig develops in his work: noetic redemption actualised through the intellect, redemption of the individual soul through performing the commandments (Idel 2011,31), as well as the concurrent redemption of the nation and of the *Shekhinah* (33). One may also find in Rosenzweig's work brief references to the other themes that Idel enumerates—astrological calculations for the coming of the Messiah (31), redemption as the overcoming of cosmic evil (32), and political redemption(33)—that Rosenzweig considers untenable. The chief contribution of Idel's model, however, is its accommodation of these disparate tropes within, "a constellation of Jewish messianism" (27, 36, 38, 66). Idel contends that by viewing them as interconnected within a single, elaborate constellation, a "language of crosscurrents, syntheses, tensions and controversies will become a vital part of the intellectual

---

[2] Cf. Bloch; Spengler.
[3] Schreiner. On Rosenzweig's reaction to the early stages of this crisis see Meineke; Mendes-Flohr 1991.

apparatus of Kabbalah scholarship" (38).[4] This complex of ideas divides into two primary categories, redemption and messianism, which can exist either separately or overlap (30). Rosenzweig's definition of these concepts differs from Idel's; nevertheless, the basic dynamic between these two categories is equally fundamental to the redemptive scheme of the author of the *Star*.

In Rosenzweig's thought, messianism, i.e. collective salvation brought about by the acts of a person entrusted with the task, is acknowledged as an important trope in the Jewish religious tradition that has a primarily symbolic function: as the image of the Son of David who is the counterpart of man created in the image of God (SE, 341/SR, 307); and as a personification of redemptive yearnings expressed in the liturgy (SE, 349/SR, 314–315). For Rosenzweig, it is the praying community that functions as the prolepsis of redeemed time. But when it comes to the actualisation of messianic ideas, Rosenzweig is wary of their destructive dialectic between allure and disappointment (SE, 373/SR, 336). Famously, he grounds the impossibility of concrete messianic events in the ontological claim that the Jewish people exists outside of history (SE, 331–342/SR, 298–308). Bereft of land and state, so Rosenzweig, the Jews are free to fulfil their spiritual calling of drawing eternity into the present by practicing liturgy (SE,342–364 /SR, 308–328). Idel's distinction between two basic categories—redemption and messianism—and his insistence on their mutual inclusiveness in Jewish tradition is conducive to a more nuanced understanding of Rosenzweig's redemptive scheme.

The current book will showcase the evolution and dynamics of redemptive ideas in Rosenzweig's work: beginning with the early search for personal and intellectual redemption from the perplexities of the crises of relativism, engendering profound doubts about the promise of modernity, culminating with his commitment to what he regarded as the rich redemptive possibilities of the act of translation. Simon Bernstein's observation that *Die Schrift* proved to be Rosenzweig's personal fulfilment of redemption (Bernstein, 20) is an important reminder for this dynamic.

Translation

Gershom Scholem's admiration for Rosenzweig's work, as well as their disagreements on the nature and practice of translation are well known. It is a much less known fact that Scholem was invited to translate the *Star* into Hebrew in the late 1920s, or early 1930. In a letter to Martin Buber written shortly after Rosenzweig's

---

4 See also Idel 1998, 17.

death, Scholem confesses that he will not be able to accept the undertaking due to the insurmountable difficulties it poses.⁵ David Biale describes Scholem's reply as reflecting his finding "… a magical, even demonic connection between the work and the spirit of the German language which made the *Stern* both untranslatable and incomprehensible" (Biale 1977, 167).⁶

Scholem and Rosenzweig agreed on the impossibility of translation, and on the necessity of translation in spite of, and in the face of, this impossibility.⁷ But instead of demonic powers, Rosenzweig saw tremendous potential in the act of translation to unleash redemptive powers. This view has surprisingly close affinities with Walter Benjamin's conception of translation. One crucial difference between their respective views is Rosenzweig's approach to translation as philological in essence, while Benjamin does not mention this aspect of the craft whatsoever. In this sense, Rosenzweig was much closer to Scholem's understanding of his own discipline, the study of Jewish mysticism:

> Indeed, history [Geschichte] may be fundamentally an illusion, but an illusion without which insight [Einsicht] into the essence [of things] in temporal reality [in der Zeit] is impossible. With a miraculous prism [Im wunderlichen Hohlspiegel] the philological critic can show people today, for the first time and in the purest way through the legitimate discipline of commentary, the mystical totality of the system [jene mystische Totalität des Systems], whose existence vanishes precisely when projected unto historical time.⁸

The application of philological analysis in an attempt to capture the ever-elusive content of religious lore, and relying on its conclusion in the construction of a systematic totality is precisely what Rosenzweig does in his translations. Yet, the most obvious site for investigation of this observation—*Die Schrift*—is a late stage in a long evolutionary process that began in Rosenzweig's early student years.

---

5 Scholem confesses that the translation of Maimonides' *Guide of the Perplexed* is an easier task than translating the *Star*, as Rosenzweig's work contains passages that are untranslatable in the current generation (Buber 1972, 367–368).
6 The copy of Biale's dissertation at the Gershom Scholem archive, the National Library of Israel in Jerusalem is marked throughout with Scholem's comments and corrections. It would be safe to assume that Scholem's refraining from leaving any markings on the passage quoted reflects his agreement with this observation.
7 "Only one who is profoundly convinced of the impossibility of translation can really undertake it" (*BT* II, 698–700/*Life and Thought*, 100–102).
8 Scholem cited in Biale 1982, 156. My translation. Cf. Biale's translation in ibid, 32.

The Bible

Scripture had always intrigued Rosenzweig. A letter he sent to his cousin, Gertrude Frank, not long after his bar mitzvah shows a penetrating grasp of the language of biblical prophecy (*BT* I, 2–3). Later, while still a medical student, he noted in his diary having read Song of Songs in the Greek translation of the Septuagint (54). A few years on, as Nietzsche and Goethe inspired his search for the path to the Truth, he applies a midrash-like reading to Genesis 16:14, using the expression he extrapolates on, לַחַי רֹאִי (*lahai ro'ee*), as the motto of the diary notebook in which this entry is written. In the same diary he notes that he likes to think in "biblical images" (*BT* I, .37). With his growing interest in theology as a viable avenue for reflection on the problems that continued to perplex him, Rosenzweig explored the Bible, developing a special affinity for the Book of Isaiah.

Yet, the most conspicuous manifestation of Rosenzweig's interest in the Bible before he undertook *Die Schrift*, the grammatical analyses of biblical prooftexts in Part Two of the *Star*, far from exhausts the contribution of Scripture to his thought. The Hebrew Bible emerges from the investigation presented here as a repository of eternal truths, the ground of the encounter between humans and revelation, the remedy to the ailments of philosophy and the object of philosophical interpretation, to list some of its roles in Rosenzweig's thought. In this sense, the translation project with Marin Buber provided Rosenzweig with an opportunity to fuse all of these roles together. The rendering of Scripture in German prose and verse thus allowed Rosenzweig to convey those insights with a non-systematic mode of expression.

Rosenzweig's translation of the Hebrew bible in collaboration with Martin Buber is presented here as the culmination of a long evolutionary process; not as a break with his other pursuits.[9] Based on the reciprocity with Rosenzweig's earlier work, the investigation of *Die Schrift* approaches it as a site of excavation in search of the initial, untainted meaning of the biblical text. The excavation is performed by backtracking the layers of readings, interpretation and appropriations that had accumulated in the course of the centuries, in a bid to undo, as it were, the palimpsest that encrusts the words of Scripture. Cognisant of the impossibility of rendering Hebrew Scripture into German, Rosenzweig and Buber pursued it by establishing a dialogue with early readers (the rabbis, the Septuagint) and modern interpreters (Martin Luther), as their philological *modus operandi*. While the collaboration between the translators was close, and the affinity be-

---

[9] Compare: "Rosenzweig made Scripture into a foil for 'philosophy'" (M. Benjamin 2009, 28).

tween their approaches to the project substantial, for the purposes of this study I will assume that *Die Schrift* reflects Rosenzweig's, rather than Buber's, position.

Exposition

Thinking in Translation traces the chronological development of Rosenzweig's ideas and work, albeit not to the point of providing an intellectual biography. The first three chapters trace the development of particular ideas in the earlier part of Rosenzweig's life, whereas the remaining three chapters present analyses of his two major works—the *Star* and *Die Schrift*—by chronological order: chapters 4 and 5 focus on his magnum opus, and chapter 6 on the translation project. This combined chronological-thematic approach aims to substantiate the argument for the cohesion of Rosenzweig's thought, from its nascent stages to its ripest development. It also sheds light on the dynamics between earlier and later ideas in his life's work—some retaining their initial structure, while others are re-examined and changed.

In chapter 1 I follow Rosenzweig's intellectual pursuits between 1905 and mid-late 1913, arguing that they were guided by a powerful redemptive drive to overcome the cultural and intellectual crisis brought about by epistemological relativism and trenchant historicism. The chapter presents a notion that I call "Rosenzweig's economy of ideas": tracing how early experimentations with the translation of biblical verses, and commentaries on Goethe, Nietzsche and Hegel found their way into the *Star*.

Chapters 2 and 3, chart Rosenzweig's two intellectual homelands, respectively: Germanic thought, epitomised by of the Idealist concept of system; and Hebraic Bible exegesis premised on the conception of Scripture as a repository of eternal truths. Chapter 2 opens with a re-evaluation of interpretations of Rosenzweig's thought, proposing a new approach to overcome the tendency to read him as *either* a philosopher *or* a Jewish thinker. The methodological discussion is followed by a new critique of Rosenzweig's interpretation of Hegel. Despite the *Star*'s dismissal of Hegel's philosophy as untenable, I argue that he remained both indetbted to and inspired by the Owl on Minerva. Chapter 3 proposes to understand the synthesis between system and Scripture in the *Star* as inspired by the work of Maimonides, epitomising his Hebraic homeland. This unlikely affinity betwee Rosenzweig and the medieval sage in the *Star* receives an extensive evaluation for the first time in Rosenzweig scholarship.

Chapter 4 explores Rosenzweig's subtle employment of the Hebrew Bible in the *Star*. Subjecting two central concepts within the system to close examination —divinity and temporality—the discussion presents Rosenzweig's reliance on

Scripture in shaping these concepts. In the course of this interpretative act the Hebrew Bible becomes an object of worship that sets in motion the liturgical year cycle, in addition to its role as a repository of eternal truths. Chapter 5 explores Rosenzweig's reliance on Scripture in translation in the transition from the discursive to the non-discursive parts of his system. The discussion is framed by the relation between Rosenzweig's ideas and those of two of his close friends: the concept of truth in Hermann Cohen's *Religion der Vernunft aus den Quellen des Judentums* (*Religion of Reason out of the Sources of Judaism*) and Martin Buber's reflections on the conclusion of the *Star*.

Chapter 6 examines *Die Schrift* as a redemptive project. A comparative reading of Rosenzweig's views on the redemptive potential of translation, alongside Walter Benjamin's is followed by a detailed analysis of Rosenzweig's translation of *torah* and *ruah*—two key terms in the theological vocabulary of both Judaism and Christianity. The discussion presents *Die Schrift* as an attempt to re-appropriate, or redeem as it were, the Hebrew Bible from Christian appropriations, while tapping into the exegetical mindset of the Bible's earliest readers.

★ ★ ★

The abundance of original ideas, sources of inspiration, objects of interest, and avenues of research in Rosenzweig's oeuvre is overwhelming. Shakespeare, chemistry, musical criticism and modern Hebrew literature are only some of the topics he wrote about and which are usually excluded from more "serious", systemic discussions of his work. *Thinking in Translation* attempts to share the richness of Rosenzweig's intellectual universe as much as possible, and to show that it was ultimately channelled to support the attainment of very specific objectives. Though not much of a traveller in the conventional sense, Rosenzweig was probably one of the most accomplished seafarers of his day in the ocean of human knowledge. A passing reference of his to a Buddha, Aeschylus or Isaac Luria is never haphazard; it reflects careful meditation and penetrating intention. This leaves the scholar equally reverent of and frustrated by the encyclopaedic erudition of Rosenzweig's legacy. At the same time, Rosenzweig tended to employ his vast knowledge to confound, and perhaps even manipulate, the majority of readers unable to keep up with his sophisticated argumentation and endless citations and adaptations of works and ideas. When reconstructing his thought, one must thus muster one's utmost intellectual probity and rigor. Surely, Rosenzweig demanded nothing less from himself.

Chapter 1:
Redemption through Philosophy?

> What, however, the age *needs* in the deepest sense can be said fully and completely with one single word: it needs ... eternity. The misfortune of our time is just this, that it has become simply nothing else but "time", the temporal which is impatient of hearing anything about eternity". (Søren Kierkegaard, *The Point of View for My Work as an Author*).

Franz Rosenzweig was born into tumultuous times. The urgent need for eternity that Kierkegaard had declared in the name of his own generation was very much felt in the cultural and intellectual circles that Rosenzweig joined as a young man. Germany had waded through political upheavals (1848) and a ruthless war (1871), while at same time enjoying unprecedented technological progress and economic prosperity. Philosophers and historians were still coming to grips with the bequeathal of Hegelian thought and Kantian rigour. This predicament was all the more perplexing for Germany's liberal Jews. The civil rights they enjoyed as non-Christians came at the price of remaining excluded from the higher echelons of German society; for promising intellectuals like Rosenzweig, the entry ticket to a thriving academic career was baptism (Horwitz 2010a, 83).

The son of a successful Jewish industrialist in Kassel, Rosenzweig was destined to a medical career, and began studying toward an M.D., first in Göttingen, later in Munich, and finally in Freiburg. But his diaries and letters from his two years at medical school (1905–1907) reveal modest interest in his future profession. At 19, young Franz was immersed in the study of Goethe, Nietzsche, Shakespeare, renaissance and baroque art, taking the occasional excursion to contemplate his Jewish identity. What these personal records show from their earliest days, is a sense of urgency. Rosenzweig felt compelled to paint a picture that would be as accurate as possible of Being, in a philosophical sense, and existence, in a practical—cultural, social, historical—sense, as he moved from the aforementioned cultural heroes to thinkers that appeared at first more promising: Kant and Hegel. The shift in his intellectual interests also led to a dramatic career move: in August 1907 Rosenzweig quit his medicine studies and went to Berlin to study philosophy and history, and in autumn 1908 he settled in Freiburg to write his dissertation on Hegel under the tutelage of Friedrich Meinecke (1862–1954), the most celebrated German historian of the day. Rosenzweig commenced his studies still under the spell of German Idealism's promise of a redemptive consummation to take place with the full actualization of Spirit, and completed it in 1912 utterly disillusioned.

According to the commonly held narrative of Rosenzweig's early biography, he initially held relativistic philosophical views and was rather indifferent to matters of faith in general, and to his Judaism in particular. His encounter with Eugen Rosenstock-Huessy (1888–1973) in 1910 sparked a growing interest in religious thought, culminating with a dramatic conversation on 7th July, 1913, known as the *Leipziger Nachtgespräch*. This event, so the narrative, had led Rosenzweig to "convert" from his earlier views to a life of faith, and to Christianity, a decision that he overturned some three months later in favour of a deep commitment to a meaningful Jewish life. Although this narrative is generally correct, it arguably excludes important milestones in Rosenzweig's biography, in light of which the impact of his early intellectual development emerges as much more central to his mature thought than is customarily maintained. The reinterpretation of Rosenzweig's student years presented in this chapter puts forth two claims: (1) despite its dramatic transformations in the course of 25 years, Rosenzweig's thought remained fundamentally cohesive, thanks to a fascination with the notion of redemption; (2) initially diffuse, this fascination gradually led Rosenzweig to place his centre of gravity at the intersection of German Idealism and Jewish thought.

Based on a fresh reading of Rosenzweig's earlier letters and diaries, the "relativism" and "atheism" usually ascribed to Rosenzweig's intellectual youth will be presented here as objects of interest, rather than guiding principles. Thus construed, Rosenzweig's intellectual pursuits between 1905 and mid-late 1913 emerge as an expression of an eclectic, rather than nihilistic tendencies. Rosenzweig's search for inspiration in the legacies of Nietzsche, Goethe and Hegel, which followed a recurring pattern of infatuation followed by disillusionment, joined a growing in interest in the Hebrew Bible and the translation, the earliest record of which dates as early as 1906. The incorporation of some of these youthful experimentations into the *Star* demonstrates that Rosenzweig's originality and sophistication were present from early on, growing deeper and richer as time went by.

1.1 Rosenzweig's Relative Relativism

As with many other historical figures, the reception of Rosenzweig's biography was shaped to a large degree by a seminal account to which all later studies owe a great debt. Significantly, the approach to and substance of the research into Rosenzweig's intellectual development were shaped by the *narrative* as much as by the *sources* and the interpretation on which the narrative was based. Therefore, in re-evaluating what we know and think about the years that led to Rosenzweig's transformation in 1913, we should pay attention to the selection of evidence cited as much as to scholars' commentaries on that evidence; because as we shall see, the sources that figure prominently in most studies, are complemented and even countered by other, less scrutinised sources from the same period, which shed new and fascinating light on the familiar evidence and its customary reception. Contrary to Else Rahel-Freund's designation of Rosenzweig's letters as "merely" introducing their readers to individual thoughts and as making his personality more endearing (Freund, 42–43), the reading proposed here will insist that they are essential for gaining a richer understanding of Rosenzweig's oeuvre, as they attest to an inherent consistency of his early ideas with his mature work.

Franz Rosenzweig's life story was canonised and enshrined by his close disciple Nahum Glatzer (1903–1990), who almost single-handedly introduced the English-speaking world to Rosenzweig. His seminal anthology of selected letters, diaries and writings (Glatzer 1953) offered a first glimpse of Rosenzweig's work in English translation, and was decisive in shaping the reception of Rosenzweig's biography and intellectual legacy.[1] As years went by, however, Glatzer's account of the high drama of Rosenzweig's return to Judaism came under increasing scrutiny as scholars became more wary of the subtle bias in his narration of Rosenzweig's personal and intellectual biography. Most conspicuous in this respect is Rosenzweig's experience of the Yom Kippur service in 1913, following which he decided to remain a Jew and to dedicate his life to the furthering of a vibrant, modern Judaism.[2]

The beginning of the 21st century marked a new phase in the assessment of Glatzer's canonisation of Rosenzweig's biography. Concurrently with the unanimous admiration for his many contributions to the study and reception of Rosenzweig (Sheppard 1994), Glazter's work has also been described as contributing to a "hagiographic impulse" in Rosenzweig scholarship (Gordon 2011, 13). Most recently, Benjamin Pollock has challenged the view that Rosenzweig maintained in

---

[1] Prior to the book Glatzer had published two synoptic articles on Rosenzweig's intellectual biography: Glatzer 1946 (which is itself an English translation of a Yiddish version published in Glatzer 1945); and Glatzer 1952. A more extensive study of Rosenzweig's early diaries appeared in Glatzer 1961.
[2] For a critical assessment of this narrative in the course of five decades see Pollock 2014, 1–14. Earlier skeptical responses to the near-conversion narrative include: Horwitz 2010a and Dagan 2001.

the years leading up to the 1913 transformation a relativist position, showing new evidence that Rosenzweig had experimented with original theological ideas, which Pollock describes as "Marcionist", as early as 1910 (Pollock 2014; 2012a and 2012b). In the same vein, the argument put forth here does not seek to shake the foundations of Glatzer's presentation of Rosenzweig's biography and its intellectual-cultural significance; rather, it aims to posit him as the foremost contributor to the formation of a "grand narrative" in whose light Rosenzweig scholarship has been conducted, and against which a more nuanced reading of Rosenzweig's writings should be proposed.

To make things more complicated, a re-evaluation of Glatzer's own account, especially his emphasis on the abrupt change in the course of Rosenzweig's life in mid-late 1913, is a secondary result of our primary object of critique, an early article, or rather, an article title, by Glatzer's own disciple, Paul Mendes-Flohr.

"From Relativism to Religious Faith: The Testimony of Franz Rosenzweig's Unpublished Diaries", an article Mendes-Flohr co-authored with Jehuda Reinharz, can be said to have been largely responsible for cementing in the minds of scholars of the last three decades an image of Rosenzweig's earlier life as one of an agnostic Jew maintaining relativist views bordering on the nihilistic, who transformed into a religious thinker reliant on a sophisticated conception of faith based on revelation.[3] To be more precise, it is the *reception* of the article that grounded the image that the title reflects, and not the authors themselves. Because as we will see, Mendes-Flohr and Reinharz underscore the ambiguous nature of Rosenzweig's conception of relativism and the redemptive orientation of his engagement with relativistic ideas.

Offering a prudent consideration of Rosenzweig's confession that the *Leipziger Nachtgespräch* had extracted him from his relativism, the authors caution that, "relativism bears many faces, and being bereft of specification Rosenzweig's confession remains somewhat obscure", adding that, "The [early] diaries serve to illumine the nature and depth of the relativism that so intensely preoccupied Rosenzweig and from which *Offenbarungsgläubigkeit* 'redeemed' him" (Mendes-Flohr & Reinharz, 162). The article proceeds to reveal Rosenzweig's dilemma of trying to maintain different forms of relativism, while continuously being drawn to the search for an objectivist point of view, an Archimedean point on which a non-relativistic philosophy may be based. The authors delineate two phases in the evolution of Rosenzweig's "relativism": an earlier consideration of the relation between subjectivity and objectivity, through the study of Goethe, Kant and the dynamics between their positions during 1906–1908

---

[3] See for example, Stahmer 1984, 66; Batnitzky 1999, 525; Hollander 2008, 166.

(Mendes-Flohr & Reinharz, 165–169); and a more mature engagement with the question of historical relativism during 1908–1909, under the mentorship of his dissertation supervisor Friedrich Meinecke and influential teacher Heinrich Rickert (1863–1936).[4] The reading in Rosenzweig's diaries leads the authors to conclude that he stopped considering relativism as a viable philosophical position in the wake of the Baden-Baden conference, held in 1910. Rosenzweig's attempt to "forge a new subjectivity … [which is] a consciousness of the self *qua* subject of the *Zeitgeist*", that is, a subjective consciousness that orients itself to an historical centre of gravity, led to the inevitable conclusion that "God redeems man not through history but … through religion". At this point, however, this conclusion was not yet grounded in faith, but was rather "a philosophical proposition, a logical deduction" (Mendes-Flohr & Reinharz, 173). It emerges that Rosenzweig's conception of relativism, was, well, relative, as it changed in accordance with his shifts of interest and influence. The article's leaps from 1910 directly to 1913 is understandable in light of its stated purpose of reading Rosenzweig's diaries, which end on 22.6.1908 and resume more than six years later, in September 1914. Understandable, but apparently not coincidental. Hitherto neglected documents recently analyzed by Pollock show that Rosenzweig entertained original theological ideas as early as 1910, to a large degree under the influence of his cousin Rudolph Ehrenberg.

For a relativist dilettante utterly disinterested in the religious heritage of his ancestors, twenty-year-old Rosenzweig took matters of religious belief and theological concerns quite seriously. Though far from dominating his intellectual pursuits at the time, in 1906 alone Rosenzweig contemplates sundry matters of religion such as divine grace (Tagebücher II, 20–21), theophany in the Book of Job (Tagebücher II, 2) and the divine element in the human (Tagebücher II, 12), among others. To be sure, these musings were not yet motivated by profound religious faith, but rather were part of the searching process in the development of a young intellectual. Moreover, Rosenzweig expressed a pronounced ambiva-

---

[4] Mendes-Flohr & Reinharz, 170–173. Citing Georg Iggers, the authors present both Meinecke and Rickert as radical historical relativists. Immediately following the cited passage, however, Iggers concludes his survey of Rickert's thought by saying that "[…] Rickert vigorously defends his position against the charge of historicism or relativism […] Similarly [in Rickert's view], any attempt to explain life from life itself, without reference to transcendental rational norms, is absurd". See Iggers 1968, 168. Reflecting this latter view, David Myers pits the influence of Meinecke's relativist *Ideengeschichte* against Rickert's objectivist scientific approach to history, in Myers 2003, 78–79. In this context it is symbolic that Rickert, and not Meinecke, submitted for publication in 1917 Rosenzweig's study, *Das älteste Systemprogramm des deutschen Idealismus*.

lence to all matters Jewish (as Glatzer emphasizes in his commentary in *Life and Thought*),[5] and a certain affinity with relativism. This latter aspect of Rosenzweig's development was taken to dominate his early thought mostly based on his own confession in a letter to Rudolph Ehrenberg dated 31st October 1913. The letter, in which Rosenzweig announced, *Ich bleibe also Jude,* is equally famous for conceding Rosenstock's overpowering argumentation, which "... pushed me [Rosenzweig] step by step out of the last relativist positions that I still occupied and forced me to take an absolute standpoint".[6]

These and other similar statements of Rosenzweig's, which sustain the commonly-held view of his early years, in fact serve to emphasize the seed of redemptive orientation that later ripened in his mature thought. In a certain, narrow, sense this claim reinforces Pollock's contention that Rosenzweig had maintained "a position of faith" some three years before the *Leipziger Nachtgespräch* and hence Rosenstock's victorious argumentation did not convert him from relativistic indifference into religious faith (Pollock 2012, 225–226); but in another, more profound sense, this claim reaches farther back in Rosenzweig's biography, as it not only maintains that the kernel of his search for salvation are to be found much earlier than what is widely maintained; as my discussion will show, Rosenzweig's redemptive orientation survived the transformations of his early years, as some of the themes from the early diaries made their way into the *Star* with little, if any, changes. Most notably, the diaries offer compelling, though scant, evidence for Rosenzweig's appreciation and *utilization* of translation as a hermeneutic practice that is crucial for the development of philosophical ideas when applied to Holy Scripture. Neither the minimal familiarity with the Jewish exegetical tradition at that point in his life, nor the limited scope of discussion, detracted from the depth of Rosenzweig's early hermeneutic exercises.

---

5 E.g.: "Joseph Prager relates: In 1907 we had three months' vacation together for the pursuit of natural sciences and mathematics. Rosenzweig made the following condition for this joint enterprise: there was to be no mention of Jewish problems. 'I don't want to hear about it! I'm not going to be a Zionist!'" Glatzer 1953, 15.
6 Rosenzweig, *BT* I, 133. English translation by Altmann 1969, 32. Pollock convincingly argues that Rosenstock-Huessy's triumph in the *Leipziger Nachtgespräch* owed to the fact that, "Rosenstock modeled for Rosenzweig a kind of Christian life in the world that Rosenzweig had hitherto taken to be impossible" (2014, 72). That is, rather than undermine a sceptic position, Rosenstock offered his friend a positive model for a life of faith.

1.2 Rosenzweig's Economy of Ideas

Rosenzweig appears to have been highly conscious of the usefulness of nearly every idea that he recorded, either to himself, or in letters to others.[7] As we will now see, this awareness of an "economy of ideas" was in place from an early stage in his intellectual development.

1.2.1 Fullness and Plenitude

The two earliest records available of Rosenzweig's hermeneutical engagement with the Hebrew Bible date from September 1906. In the first of the two (dated 6.9.1906), we find Rosenzweig extrapolating an epistemological observation from the Hebrew expression לחי ראי (*lahai ro-ee*), from Genesis 16:14:

> The way for man to carry about human being in the world is —[*sic.*]לחי לראי—to live, to see. Thinking [*Denken*] is for him only a barrier, a shield against the multitude of sights [*die Fülle der Gesichte*]. And so he organises that which he has experienced and seen in drawers, to make room for new ones. But the labels on these pigeonholes are not an end in themselves, but merely a means to keep things in order. The things themselves are what matters![8]

Rosenzweig's misquotation of the original Hebrew (לחי ראי, adding the prepositional prefix ל—to, or for—to ראי), was in all likelihood intentional. As the editors of his *Gesammelte Schriften* note (*BT* I, 56 n.1), his translation of the expression as "*zum Leben, zum Schauen*" ("to live, to see") appears to have been inspired by the opening of Goethe's *Türmerlied* (watchman's song) in *Faust*:

> *Zum Sehen geboren,*
> *Zum Schauen bestellt,*
> *Dem Turme geschworen,*
> *Gefällt mir die Welt*[9]

But the manipulation does not end there. In order for the translation to correspond with Goethe's rhyme, Rosenzweig inverted the meaning of ראי (*ro'ee*)

---

[7] Rosenzweig's cousin, Gertrude Oppenheim (then Frank), told the editors of the *Gesammelte Schriften* that in 1917 Rosenzweig recalled a shared childhood memory. In response to her surprise that he remembered it, Rosenzweig retorted: "I forget nothing". *BT* I, 3.
[8] Rosenzweig, *Tagebücher* II, 24.
[9] Goethe 1984, 340 (Part II, lines 11288–11291).

from the original passive form—he who sees me—to the active רואה (ro'eh) — he who sees; without, however changing the verbal inflection of the biblical verse.[10] The tension between the passive and active forms of the verbal noun is heightened by a tension between the seemingly secular context of Rosenzweig's observation and the revelatory scene in Genesis 16:6–14. Sarai's maid, Hagar, flees her wrathful mistress to the desert, where she encounters God's angel who instructs her to return and suffer under Sarai and that she shall bear a son, Ishmael. The compliant Hagar calls in God's name, אַתָּה אֵל רֳאִי (16:13; *ata El ro'ee*) which literally means "you are the God who sees me". The place of the encounter, a well, is then named in the following verse בְּאֵר לַחַי רֹאִי (*be'er lahai ro'ee*).

Offering a secular-theoretical reading of the above diary entry, we may say that Rosenzweig is suggesting that the calling of humans is to exercise an existential outlook by letting their vision serve them as the unmediated ground for encountering the world, rather than hiding behind rational categories and preoccupying themselves with classifying their experiences. And yet, under the surface of this reading, the tension with the revelatory quality of לחי ראי remains. The ordering *Denken* that Rosenzweig criticizes, likely a reference to the Aristotelian system of classification, corresponds with a diary entry written nearly five months earlier, on 1.4.1906, in which following August Horrnefer (1875–1955),[11] Rosenzweig posits the fundamental reliance of *Griechentum* on *Wissenschaft* as the polar opposite of the reliance of *Judentum* on revelation. In the 1st April entry Rosenzweig confesses that it is too early for him to define the difference between Greek thought and Jewish thought[12]; yet by September of that year, he outlines, if obliquely, this very difference. That this association of the existential dictum marks an attempt to break away from rational classification with its Hebraic source, is confirmed by the cover of Folio III of Rosenzweig's handwritten diary, one which the enigmatic, pithy expression לְחַי רֳאִי is inscribed as a motto as it originally appears in Genesis 16:14 (*Tagebücher* III, cover).

Yet, Rosenzweig's most penetrating move in the diary entry of 6th September is his designation of the full existential engagement as *die Fülle der Gesichte*.

---

10 Rosenzweig was probably encouraged to neutralise the passive inflection by Zunz's translation of רֳאִי in the preceding verse, Genesis 16:13: אתה אל ראי, as *Du, Gott der Erblickung* (You, the God of beholding). On the importance of the Zunz Bible at the Rosenzweig household see Glatzer 1953, xxxvii.
11 Rosenzweig wrote this entry after attending a lecture of the philologist (Glatzer 1961, 148). In a letter to Hans Ehrenberg dated 6.7.1908 (*BT* I, 84–85) Rosenzweig recommends to his cousin Horneffer's *Nietzsche als Moralist und Schriftsteller* (published 1906).
12 "I see that I am not ready yet [*noch nicht reif bin*] to attempt an answer to this question – *Griechentum und Judentum*". Rosenzweig, *Tagebücher* II, 1–2.

Both nouns have several overlapping meanings: *Fülle* connotes fullness, and may mean abundance, multitude or plenty; *Gesichte*, rendered here as "sights", means visual information, and is often used similarly to the English "visions", i.e. in a miraculous, mystical or religious context. And indeed, Glatzer translated it as "the crowd of visions" (1953, 12). But the reappearance of this very idiom in the *Star* indicates that Rosenzweig had chosen it for designating in his diary the vastness of sensory-empirical experience, in order preserve the revelatory quality of the dictum that he extrapolated from לחי ראי.

Die Fülle der Gesichte first appears in *Star* I:2 in successive sections entitled *weltliche Ordnung* (worldly order) and *weltliche Fülle* (worldly plenitude) (SE 45–50/SR 42–46). Rosenzweig posits the multitude of sights as the manifestation of the world's ever-renewing nature, opposite to God's static, eternal essence, and to the self-imposing logos/thinking that "pours into the world as a system of rationalisations" (SE 46/ SR 43). Precisely as he did in his diary, Rosenzweig separates being from logos/thinking as a system that he may or may not choose to adopt; even when applied, he emphasizes, logos/thinking "has to console itself with the unity of its application within the locked walls of the world"(SE 47/ SR 43).

Finally, Rosenzweig makes explicit the revelatory potential of *Gesicht*, which was only implicit in its coupling with לחי ראי, in the opening paragraph of *Star* III:2. As an exposition to the "eternal way" leading to the consummation of his redemptive scheme, Rosenzweig invokes Maimonides' discussion of false and true Messiah in *Mishneh Torah, Hilkhot Melachim*, citing the medieval master's prooftext "proving" the misguidedness of Christianity:

> ... abtrünnige Söhne deines Volks, die sich vermessen, **zu erfüllen die Gesichte**, – und kommen zu Fall". (Daniel 11:14)[13]

"The renegade sons of your people shall venture to fulfil the vision, and shall come to a fall", translates Rosenzweig in line with Maimonides' association of the verse with Jesus' failed messianic prophecy. This unique rendition melds together the Jewish readings by Zunz and Philippson[14] of חזון (*chazon*=vision) as *Gesicht*, with the Christian readings by Luther and Kautzsch of להעמיד (le-ha'amid= to establish, fulfil) as *erfüllen*.

---

[13] SE 373/SR 336. I discuss Rosenzweig's use of this verse in the context of his reception of Maimonides in chapter 3 below.

[14] Rosenzweig refers to Philippson twice in letters to his parents in the years 1915–1916 (19791a, 179; 263; 265), and therefore it is likely that he consulted his Bible translation.

Tab. 1.1: Daniel 11:14

Zunz	Philippson	Luther	Kautzsch
... und die abtrünnigen Söhne deines Volkes werden sich erheben, um festzustellen das Gesicht, aber sie straucheln.	... auch die wildesten Söhne deines Volkes erheben sich, bekräftigend das Gesicht, und werden straucheln.	... auch werden sich Abtrünnige aus deinem Volk erheben und die Weissagung erfüllen, und werden fallen.	... und gewaltthätige Volksgenossen von dir werden sich empören, um die Weissagung zu erfüllen, aber sie werden zu Falle kommen.

But Rosenzweig was not concerned here with literary exercises. To use a beautiful image from his diaries, he plucked the ripe fruit from the tree, driven by the hope of having another golden apple fall into his hands from heaven (Tagebücher I, 12–13). The human encounter with the fullness of the ever-renewing world Rosenzweig describes in the diaries, initially sparked by Hagar's encounter with the God who sees her, was posited over and against the classifying *Denken*; in the *Star*, *die Fülle der Gesichte* became the manifestation of the world's vibrancy, in opposition to God's static infinity and as the object to which the logos applies itself; throughout this evolution, however, *die Fülle der Gesichte* remained independently vibrant. Therefore, Rosenzweig's translation of Daniel 11:14 externalises the hitherto implicit revelatory quality of the concept, by adding layers of meaning on the foundations laid in the diary entry.

As we will see in Chapter 4, Rosenzweig's employment of *Gesicht* anticipates a yet more explicit articulation of the encounter with the divine, through his selective use of *Angesicht*—face—to describe the personal encounter with the divine face as the ultimate redemptive moment in one's life.

1.2.2 The Judeo–Christian Orbit

In an entry dated 29.9.1906 Rosenzweig outlines the different metaphysical groundings of Jewish and Christian ethics. In this passage, we find a very early example for a method of citation that will become central to Rosenzweig's use of Jewish sources, whereby an argument is made by letting the source "speak for itself", through direction quotation:

> A metaphysical grounding of Christian ethics: 'What you have done to one of them, you have done to me'–[Matthew 25:40][15]; of Jewish ethics: 'You shall be holy; for I the Eternal, your God am holy'. [Leviticus 19:2] (often appears in abbreviated form: אני ה' אלהכם).[16]

This "theological sketch" is an abrupt shift from a two-page discussion of completely different matters such as subjectivity, high points in the history of 19th century German culture, and man–woman relationships. It also appears to maintain a certain tension with the entry recorded on the day following, 30th September, in which Rosenzweig conjures an obscure image of the primordial knowledge of God as all-permeating gas, which religion had transformed into a soluble liquid and that Kant, in turn, vaporized back into gas (*Tagebücher* III, 2–3). Is Scripture part of the primordial state, or does it belong to the epoch of religion, as Rosenzweig defines it? The diary does not offer any clues. But the affinity with the New Testament, and viewing it as an equally important source of knowledge within a fluid Judeo–Christian theological framework, which the young Rosenzweig entertained without any scruples, persevered in his thought, as did the specific reading of the verses in the 29th September entry. And so, we come to see that this succinct observation is a nascent version of the distinction that Rosenzweig makes in the *Star* between the "Christian act" and the "Jewish act" in *Star* III:2.

Matthew 25:40 relates the answer of God as King at the End of Days, to the question of the righteous who cared for the needy, whereby through these acts they in fact cared for Jesus himself, and hence were able to join him at the End of Days. The acts that Rosenzweig refers to as "Christian" and "Jewish" in the *Star* are the respective paths for the members of each faith to cross over from temporal existence to eternity. The Christian believer may enter eternity precisely by following the words of Matthew 25:40, which Rosenzweig paraphrases and appropriates without giving away his source: "The church is the communion of all those who see each other. It joins men as coevals" (SE 383/SR 345), he asserts. But seeing one's self and one's other concurrently is an impossibility on the temporal continuum, since, "The moment in which one catches sight of oneself can only precede or follow the moment where one catches sight of another" (SE 383/SR 346). Therefore, the simultaneous perception of one's own and one's fellow's needs, which Matthew 25:40 praises as virtuous, and idolatry does not make possible, is, according to the *Star*, the brotherliness [*Brüderlichkeit*] that transports the Christian into the midpoint "between eternity and eternity" (ibid).

---

15 Luther: *"Was ihr getan habt einem unter diesen meinen geringsten Brüdern, das habt ihr mir getan"*.
16 Rosenzweig, *Tagebücher* III, 2.

The "Jewish act" enables partaking of eternity by acknowledging the holiness of the Jewish people in its manifestation as the chain of transmission, or the ongoing furthering of tradition: "Descendant and ancestor are thus the true incarnation of the eternal people, both of them of each other, and both together for him who stands between them, just as the fellow-man become brother is the Church incarnate for the Christian" (SE 384/SR 346). One could expect that the maxim Love your fellow, *Liebe deinen Nächsten*, which forms the core of the ethics of the mature Rosenzweig as well as the individual's relationship with God, would be the Jewish counterpart of the Christian ethical act. However, both in the diary and the *Star* Rosenzweig pits the care for one's fellow in Christianity against the holiness of the eternal Jewish people with their God. Indeed, in the diary Rosenzweig does not share his reading of the dictum "You shall be holy". In the *Star*, we learn that the "Jewish act", the reciprocity between ancestor and descendant that continues throughout the generations, is the bridge that leads to the God of the Jewish people, to אני ה' אלוהכם:

> It is thus that the bridge of eternity does its spanning for us: from the starry heaven of the promise which arches over the mountain of revelation whence sprang the river of our eternal life, unto the limitless sands of the promise washed by the sea into which that river empties, the sea of which will rise the Star of Redemption when once the earth froths over, like its flood tides, with the knowledge of the Lord.[17]

The metaphysical characterization of the Jewish people as eternal is grounded both in the *Star* and the diary in God's direct address to the People of Israel, asserting that He is their God. In the diary, this is made clear by Rosenzweig's choice of Zunz's translation of Leviticus 20:26,[18] "*Heilig sollt ihr sein, denn heilig bin ich **der Ewige**, euer Gott*", which emphasizes the eternity of the divine name, over that of Luther, "*Ihr sollt heilig sein; denn ich bin heilig, **der HERR**, euer Gott*", which emphasizes His eternal rule. Rosenzweig's parenthetical comment, that the assertion of eternity usually appears in abbreviated form as אני ה' אלוהיכם, quite plausibly refers to the opening declaration of the Ten Commandments given at Mount Sinai,[19] to which the poetic conclusion of the "Jewish act" in the *Star* refers as the "mountain of revelation".

---

17 Rosenzweig, *SE* 385; *SR*, 347. Translation altered.
18 The editors of *BT* erroneously attribute the translation to Mendelssohn, which reads: "*ihr müsst heilig sein; denn ich der Ewige euer Gott, bin heilig*". This is in all likelihood on account of the translation of the divine name as "*der Ewige*". See *BT* I, 57 n.3.
19 Although in Exodus 20:2 the address is to the second person singular (אלהיך), not to the second person plural (אלהיכם) of Exodus 6:7; 16:12; Leviticus 11:44; 18:2, 4, 30; 19:2 (and many other places).

It is important to recall that despite the striking links between the diary entries of 1906 and their correlates in the *Star*, the 19-year-old Rosenzweig was far from formulating a comprehensive philosophical position. He had ahead of him years of trial and error, hope and disappointment, before distilling his original synthesis of revelation and philosophical system. And yet, the above readings make clear that he recognized the importance of translation as a philosophical practice, and the unique inspiration that Scripture offers to speculative investigations. At this point in Rosenzweig's intellectual development, this hermeneutic core was surrounded by the flesh of sour fruit. In search of a role model that would inspire the successful escape from the personal and intellectual perplexities with which he was confronted, Rosenzweig would adopt and abandon Goethe, Kant, Hegel and later Schelling, as well as be simultaneously inspired and appalled by Nietzsche. Loyal to his economy of ideas, Rosenzweig developed his mature system in part by engaging in a dialectic of retention and rejection of the thought of his former role models. Out of this line of intellectual guides, Hegel stands out as the one whose power of influence came second only to the bitterness of disappointment that it generated.

1.3 Failed Messianic Hopes

In following Rosenzweig's earliest recorded readings of Scripture and their contribution to his mature hermeneutics in the *Star*, we must not lose sight of the redemptive orientation that guided them. To do so, it is necessary to discern the hopes that Rosenzweig attached to his respective role models. The towering influence that Goethe exerted on Rosenzweig throughout his life has been amply noted (Sax 2011). In his diaries, Rosenzweig often expressed his reverence for Goethe by using Nietzsche as a counter-example.[20] On the whole, his view of Nietzsche was ambivalent, as he sometimes lauded his work[21] and other times utterly rejected it:[22]

---

[20] E.g., 5.2.1906: "You can't *build* anything on Nietzsche, as you might on Goethe or nature" (emphasis in the original). Rosenzweig, *Tagebücher* I, 8; translated in Glatzer 1953, 5. 19.2. 1906; "Nietzsche's method: distrust and scepticism. Goethe's method: wonder and scrutiny". *Tagebücher* I, 13; translated in Glatzer 1953, 7. As Mendes-Flohr and Reinharz observe, Rosenzweig's reading of Nietzsche only deepened his admiration for Goethe. Idem, 1977, 166.
[21] Comparing Nietzsche with Rousseau and Tolstoy, Rosenzweig hails him as "the last of our greater prophets ... [who] has given us the most effective word for a view of human history ... the *Übermensch* ..." 25.5.1906; *Tagebücher* II, 9.

> Who can possibly be a disciple of Nietzsche, base anything on him? He is neither a foundation, nor all-embracing as nature. He is a scaler of heights [*Gipfelkletterer*] and therefore lonely. Who dares follow him? Who has enough conceit for that?[23]

The image of a fearless mount climber, a salient Nietzschean trope,[24] reappears in the *Star*, in a passage entitled "Goethe and Nietzsche", where the latter is said to have failed in trying to follow Goethe's footsteps on the precipice that leads to faith, which is surrounded by deep abysses on both sides:

> Goethe's life is truly a walk along a ridge (*Kammwanderung*) between two abysses … A votive tablet is erected on the ridge. It illustrates, *through the example of Zoroaster's decline and fall*, how one can become a sinner and a fanatic in one person.[25]

We may read the mount climbing image in the *Star* as a reflection of the mature Rosenzweig on his earlier days, during which he looked up to Goethe and Nietzsche in their ascent on the steep precipice. But in his intellectual youth, not only was he unable to see that he is on the wrong path; he was not yet prepared to frame his personal and intellectual quest in religious terms. Still, in retrospect he describes his philosophical search, like that of Kierkegaard and Nietzsche, as a possible search for salvation.[26]

Rosenzweig's self-conscious development is made manifest in a diary entry dated 25.5.1908, in which he reflects on its course:

> The following has a place in this book: From the autumn of 1900 to autumn 1906, continuous development; from then to autumn 1907, negation of that development. At first I developed 'within Goethe'; then I went beyond him, moving along his boundaries – [a venture] expressed with one word: *Critique of Pure Reason*. Finally, starting in the autumn of 1907, contact [with Goethe] is renewed: the thesis, Goethe, and the antithesis, Kant, have been followed by a synthesis for which as yet I have no name. It therefore must, so I hope, be my own.[27]

---

22 29.2.1908: "Nietzsche was also only for that reason a worse philosopher, because he was a better historian". *Tagebücher* III, 29.
23 *Tagebücher* I, 8; translated in Glatzer 1953, 5. Mendes-Flohr and Reinharz read this statement rather as an expression of admiration, see 1977, 167.
24 On Nietzsche's use of mountain and mountaineering imagery in his work, both positively and negatively, see Ireton 2009.
25 SE 318/SR 286. (translation altered, my emphasis)
26 According to Stéphane Mosès' interpretation of Rosenzweig's comment to Buber in a letter (20.12.1922; *BT* II, 876), that the biographical background of Kiergegaard's paradoxes is what makes them believable, in his eyes. See Mosès 1992, 39.
27 *Tagebücher* IV, 15; translated (without the final sentence) in Mendes-Flohr & Reinharz, 167.

Rosenzweig provides us with a clear line of demarcation, with the hindsight of a mere few months, for his abandonment of Goethe as his primary role model, and his new quest for a yet-unknown replacement. The identity of Rosenzweig's new inspiring figure becomes clear in a footnote added to the same entry, dated 20.7. 1910, in which he comments that he has indeed found a name for the synthesis of Goethe and Kant. Unfortunately, to retrieve that name he refers the reader to an entry dated 12.11.1908, which must have existed in a folio of his diaries that is now lost. In a letter written only one day after the lost diary entry, however, Rosenzweig wrote to his mother how enthralled he is with Meinecke's *Cosmopolitanism and the National State*, and that he would have given "ten years of my life to write such a book" (*BT* I, 88–89). In his memoirs, Meinecke recalls that "it was through the chapter on Hegel in my *Cosmoplitanism* that Franz Rosenzweig was inspired to write his subtle book on Hegel and the State" (Meinecke 1949, 97).[28] According to Meinecke, in his book Rosenzweig explored the development of Hegel's concept of national spirit, which went beyond the scope of *Cosmopolitanism* (Meinecke 1970, 198 n.3). And indeed, Meinecke's brief chapter on Hegel's philosophy of the state ends with the observation that

> [Hegel] much preferred to linger in the world of the transcendent, and he tried to force his contemporaries to judge actual historical life from this point of view ... Whoever surrendered completely to the spirit of Hegel's theory always stood in danger of transforming actual life in this world into a shadow-play [*Schattenspiel*]—stood in danger, too ... of forcefully and prematurely imposing the universal element onto the life of the state and nation.[29]

In deference to his mentor, Rosenzweig considered Hegel's universalism to have yet graver repercussions in relation to God's place in history, rather than the empirical particularities of nations and states.

At Meinecke's encouragement, Rosenzweig organized together with Rudolph Ehrenberg a gathering of young intellectuals in the south-German resort of Baden-Baden, which took place on 9th January, 1910.[30] Rosenzweig was part of a circle of young intellectuals who maintained a critical approach to "'Hegel's 'religious intellectualism,' and the overemphasis on a history in which God supposedly reveals himself" (Glatzer 1953, xiii). But rather than develop his Hegelian affinities, Rosenzweig became doubtful of the absolutist view of history that anticipated the complete revelation of Truth with the final stage of history's unfolding. As those doubts deepened, Rosenzweig's concerns were exacerbated by

---

28 Cited in Mendes-Flohr & Reinharz, 171.
29 Meinecke 1922, 279 / 1970, 202.
30 According to the memoires of Viktor von Weizsäcker, quoted in *BT* I, 96. See also Mendes-Flohr 1988a, 4–5.

the relativism professed by other contemporary schools of thought (ibid). This relativism was one of several reactions to what is sometimes referred to as the "collapse of Idealism", philosophy's inability to defend its absolutist claims in the face of subjectivist, historicist and scientific critiques. The renewed interest in Hegel among young intellectuals in response to this crisis was extensive enough for Wilhelm Windelband to describe it as, "the renewal of Hegelianism" (Schnädelbach, 92–93). This trend was characterised by simultaneous attachment to and protest against Hegel's thought, which served as a catalyst to a return to one form of orthodoxy or another, including Jewish and Christian movements of renewal (Pöggeler 1988a, 840).

Rosenzweig's correspondence with his colleagues before and after the conference makes it clear that he perceived the gathering as a momentous event, personally as much as historically. Ahead of the conference, he explains to Walter Sohm that *Konstruktion*,

> ... is a venomous word for us, historians ... *Konstruktionen* can be either true or false and they can be either profound or superficial. The trip to Baden-Baden lies in the two alternatives. Trueness and falsity [*Ricktigkeit und Falschheit*] will be discussed there; should the *Konstruktion* be false, there will be woe to me, but not woe to us. [31]

To Franz Frank he writes of the horror that seizes him when encountering "Romantics" who still perceive history within a 19th century framework, which he designates symbolically as "1800". Rosenzweig establishes 1900 as the polar opposite of the former historical perception, which, instead of battling against 1800, should adopt the ripe contents of its thought as a natural part of modern historical consciousness, and thus possess them as elements of a new civilization, no less (*BT* I, 100–101). Rosenzweig then frames this dramatic cultural-historical development envisaged for Baden-Baden in theological terms:

> ... The individual who will come to Baden-Baden it shall be assumed [*soll vorausgesetzt wird*], instead of having the urge [*Trieb*] to adopt a private God for his own worship ... will find himself more or less objectively conscious of the time, and herein one will revere something greater, the God who reveals Himself in terms of the here and now.[32]

Rosenzweig's conceptualisation of historical consciousness in terms of divine worship and his dramatic, almost messianic expectations from Baden-Baden, coincided with the ripening of his critique of Hegel. In the wake of the confer-

---

[31] Undated letter to Walter Sohm, *BT* I, 99.
[32] Undated letter to Franz Frank, *BT* I, 101. Partially translated in Altmann 1969, 28.

ence that failed to yield the desired results, Rosenzweig was able to formulate the shortcomings of Hegelian historical consciousness as the failure to account for God's relationship with humans. In his oft-quoted letter to Hans Ehrenberg of 26th September, 1910,[33] Rosenzweig takes Meinecke's judgment of Hegel's problematic universalisation of history.[34] Hegel's predilection for transcendence at the expense of historical particularities, Rosenzweig avers, is not only devastating for the understanding of history, but more so for our understanding of God's place within it. Only once history ceases to be perceived as the unfolding of Being and becomes the discrete acts of men [*Tat der Täter*], he explains in the letter, can God be accounted for in His relation to humans; since human acts become sinful as soon as they enter history, God cannot redeem them through history, but through religion (Mendes-Flohr 1988b, 143). And so "for us, [the historians seeking to establish a 20th century historical consciousness] religion is the only true theodicy; the struggle against history in its 19th century-sense is therefore precisely the struggle for religion in its 20th century-sense" (*BT* I, 113).

As Mendes-Flohr and Reinharz observe, this conclusion was at the time still a rational deduction rather than a statement of faith (Mendes-Flohr & Reinharz, 173). Indeed, he went as far as announcing his disillusionment from German Idealism,[35] triggering the transition from a monochromatic *Weltanschauung* of "an historian", a "philosopher", or a "Hegelian thinker", to the multivalent complex of philosophical and theological ideas.[36] Indeed, the final step in Rosenzweig's intellectual development, in which philosophy and theology were brought together within a single intellectual framework, called for more than academic reflections; it required first-hand experience of religion (Altmann 1969, 29). And yet, by 1910 Rosenzweig was becoming increasingly preoccupied with religion in general, and his Jewish identity in particular.[37]

---

33 Cf. Altmann 1969, 28–29; Mendes-Flohr & Reinharz, 173; Mendes-Flohr, 1988b, 142–143; Pollock 2012b, 189–190.
34 To appreciate the dramatic change in Rosenzweig's historical approach, compare his letter to Hans Ehrenberg of 6.8.1909, where he describes his plan for an extensive historical study of the emergence of modern Germany: *BT* I, 93.
35 "Without B.[aden] B.[aden] I would not have felt this worldly lust [for reconciling philosophy with historical reality] and would have remained forever a *naive* Idealist." (italics in the original), *BT* I, 116.
36 "We might say that following Baden-Baden, Rosenzweig took his first important steps of intellectual 'dissimilation' away from liberal German, and German–Jewish culture". Myers 2003, 80.
37 See for example the diary entries dated 12.8.1910 (*Tagebücher* V, 3); 21.8.1910 (*Tagebücher* V, 9); 1.9.1910 (*Tagebücher* V, 16).

In his most recent monograph, Benjamin Pollock peruses newly-discovered materials from 1910 and 1911, showing that Rosenzweig was immersed in theological speculation with his two cousins, Hans and Rudolph Ehrenberg, at a period that is customarily associated with Rosenzweig's "relativism". Pollock asserts that Rosenzweig had upheld a position of faith already prior to the 1913 *Leipziger Nachtgespräch*, and thus could not have been "converted" to religious faith, as maintained by the standard narrative of Rosenzweig's biography (Pollock 2014, 3; 2012a, 225). Pollock bases his thesis on a substantial body of evidence: Rosenzweig's correspondence with several confidants (the Ehrenberg cousins, Rosenstock and his wife Margit Rosenstock-Huessy); Rudolph Ehrenberg's play *Halbhunderttag* and Rosenzweig's six-sonnet cycle entitled *Die Schechina*; a letter from Rosenzweig to Hans Ehrenberg recording a visionary night-dream in which the young Hegel appeared before Rosenzweig to account for "the very greatness of the Enlightenment God", which is, "wrapped up in His distance from the world, and in His being free from the world's imperfections" (Pollock 2012b, 191); and Rosenzweig's extensive notes from 1916, which he entitled "Paralipomena".

The sum total of evidence leads Pollock to conclude that "Strange bed-fellows that they certainly are, Judaism and Marcionism thus came to be identified in Rosenzweig's mind as the twin doctrines he must turn away from in converting to a Christianity that acts in the world," and that "it is not at all the spiritual side of Judaism that Rosenzweig found lacking, but rather its *worldly* side" (Pollock 2014, 105). By Marcionism, Pollock is invoking Rosenzweig's use of the term to denote a radical theology (inspired by 2nd century gnostic Marcion of Sinope), whereby worldly reality is perceived as an illusion fabricated by an evil demiurge, while redemption may be attained through knowledge of the God of Truth gained laboriously by a select few (Pollock 2014, 17–20). For our purposes, it is particularly important to note Pollock's observation that Rosenzweig's decision to remain a Jew was largely based on an intellectual process, rather than on a dramatic experience (Pollock 2014, 99). In this process, Pollock emphasizes, he came to reject Marcionism by accepting the Old Testament's disclosure of the Godhead's tripartite role as the God of creation, revelation and redemption (Pollock 2014, 110–111; 120–121).

Pollock's observations about the nature of Rosenzweig's personal crisis throughout 1910–1913 as theological, his choice of an intellectual approach (as opposed to an experiential one) to the crisis, and his insistence that Rosenzweig had remained closer to Judaism during this period than previously thought, gains further backing from testimonies of Rosenzweig's close friends (assembled by Hans Tramer) of his mounting interest in Jewish learning, and his shared interest in theology with the "*Ehrenberg Freunde*" (Hans and Rudolph, joined by Rosenstock) and his Jewish friends in Berlin, among whom Bruno Strauss' influence was of particular importance (Tramer, 25).

Tramer's description of Rosenzweig's social circle in Berlin in the crucial years 1909–1911, in addition to his close engagement with the Ehrenberg cousins and Rosenstock, adds a crucial link to the jigsaw puzzle of his biography. The paucity of surviving documents from those years has forced scholars to speculate on the process that led to the *Nachtgespräch*. As we have seen above, the majority of speculations were based on the assumption that Rosenzweig was an a-religious sceptic who came to decide that he should convert to Christianity long after he had already made up his mind to turn his back on Judaism.

In his biographical essay, Tramer asserts that Rosenzweig affiliated himself with two social circles—one of Jewish friends deeply interested in their religious and spiritual heritage; and one of Christian friends immersed in theological questions of their faith. Tramer thus reinforces Pollock's claim that Rosenzweig's interest in theology increased substantially in the years leading up to the *Nachtgespräch*. Tramer, however, contributes several surprising observations, which combined with other neglected testimonies of Rosenzweig's friends, suggest that he continued taking interest in Jewish theology up to a year or so before the *Nachtgespräch*.

Tramer's most dramatic assertion is that upon arriving in Berlin to finish writing his Hegel dissertation, Rosenzweig engaged in intensive study of the Hebrew Bible with a group of friends. Meeting his new acquaintances via his childhood friend Joseph Prager, Tramer contends, Rosenzweig joined a group of friends that included Bruno Strauss, his wife Bertha Badt-Strauss, her brother Hermann Badt and Prager himself (Tramer 1940, 20). This joint Bible study, Tramer asserts, formed Rosenzweig's future engagement with Scripture (Tramer, 21).

Unfortunately, this account must be treated with great caution due to its clash with a testimony of non other than Prager himself. In a commemorative book published several months after Rosenzweig's passing, his childhood friend recounts that at a random encounter in Leipzig in 1912 "after not seeing each other for five years," Franz told him excitedly that he was reading the Book of Isaiah with vigor, describing it as "grand".[38] That is, if the two childhood friends had not seen each other once between 1907 and 1912, then Prager could not have attended the Bible study sessions with the Strausses. Nonetheless, adding to our

---

38 Editorial note, *BT* I, 125. This account also appears in English translation in Glatzer 1953, 23. Both works fail to provide the source: Joseph Prager, "Begegnungen auf dem Wege" in Mayer 1930, 40.

confusion, Prager mentions in the very same commemorative piece that shortly after this encounter (that is, in early 1913) Rosenzweig organized back in Berlin a small course on the Bible's prophets, with very demanding requirements from its participants (Mayer 1930, 40). Hence, although the circumstances remain vague,[39] both accounts concur in relation to Rosenzweig's deep interest in the Hebrew Bible.

Another contributor to the commemorative volume, Margarete Susman, also recalls that in the years 1912–1913 a decision between the two worlds in which he was rooted—German culture and Judaism—forced itself upon Rosenzweig (Mayer 1930, 10).

Rosenzweig's letters offer two additional indications that in the years 1910–1912 he had not completely dissociated himself from all things Jewish: (1) his positive impression from a lecture by Rabbi Emil Cohn (*BT* I, 117); and (2) evidence that he spent Yom Kippur in 1912 fasting and also visited synagogue with his cousin Gertrude Oppenheim and her husband Louis (*BT* I, 123 editorial note).

Toward his essay's conclusion, Tramer agrees with Pollock's evidence, to the extent that Rosenzweig's return to Leipzig after submitting his dissertation was a decisive step that brought him closer to Christianity while pushing Judaism farther back into the background (Tramer, 25). What Tramer adds, however, is the likely presence of a social circle that offered, at least up to a point, counterweight to the dominant presence of the Ehrenberg-Rosenstock circle that drew Rosenzweig into the depths of Christian theological debate.

Put together, Pollock's and Tramer's work agree with the thesis put forth here, whereby Rosenzweig's interest in Judaism's intellectual and spiritual legacy, though indeed inconsistent, and in the months leading up to Yom Kippur of 1913 even erratic, had a constant presence in his intellectual development. And so, the redemptive drive described here as having guided Rosenzweig's in the early stages of his career, was inspired at least to a degree by Rosenzweig's fascination with the Hebrew Bible, which was inextricably bound up with his self-identification as a Jew.

This view does not diverge from the accepted narratives and interpretations of Rosenzweig's biography; it support the argument that despite its mercurial, eclectic and impulsive development, Rosenzweig's thought was underlain by an organic unity, provided by his unremitting interest in the possibility of re-

---

39 Tramer insists that Prager had personally provided him the details of Rosenzweig's time in Berlin when the two of them met in Breslau ca. 1930, and thanks Prager for the information. See Tramer, 20–21, n2.

demption and inspired by the Hebrew Bible. This argument is supported further by Rosenzweig's so-called economy of ideas outlined in this chapter. If it wasn't for this organic unity, the likelihood of Rosenzweig using materials developed in his university years in the *Star* would have been radically diminished. Pollock's "Gnostic thesis" should thus be viewed in the broader context of Rosenzweig's redemptive quest, as the penultimate stage before it acquired the solid Jewish framework of his mature work.

What this redemptive scheme meant for Rosenzweig at this stage can be described as a reconciliation between one's personal need for salvation (a solid foundation for one's self-perception and spiritual orientation), and an ultimate regulating principle (be it God, Spirit, totality, or system). As demonstrated in this chapter in the course of this quest Rosenzweig also searched for a role model to show him the way. Nietzsche, Goethe (and to a lesser degree Kant) were abandoned after Rosenzweig's disillusionment with them. But Hegel was another matter.

Unlike Goethe and Nietzsche, Rosenzweig's disenchantment with Hegel in 1910 did not lead to an abrupt break. By that time, he was engrossed in research for his dissertation on the Owl of Minerva; his letters and diaries from the period do not indicate that Rosenzweig contemplated ditching the project. In certain respects, the book adaptation of his dissertation *Hegel und der Staat* is more revealing of Rosenzweig's redemptive expectations from Hegel than the *Star*, and of the powerful impact of his legacy despite its failure to meet those expectations.[40] The study, which "... portrays the emergence of Hegel's political thought according to the historicist method ... is an unabashedly evolutionist narrative, couched in the language of anticipation" (Gordon 2003, 102). The full extent of the work's anticipation of a cathartic distillation of a "state idea" is revealed in its introduction and afterword, written with the hindsight of Rosenzweig the war veteran and author of the *Star* (whose draft he completed by then). Based on a brilliant reading of the introduction, Shlomo Avinery asserts that

> Rosenzweig's *Weltanschauung* has undergone a transformation not only because of his personal crisis of faith, but also because of what happened to Germany and to the German spirit ... The lesson for Rosenzweig was two-fold: first, Germany could not anymore be the addressee of his philosophy, as the actualization of German idealism, from Ionia to Jena, had ended (twice) in Verdun and Versailles. Hence the turn from conversion to Christianity (and

---

40 For an assessment of interpretations of *Hegel und der Staat* see Gordon 2003, 82–83 and 83, n.4, for references. For a summary of Rosenzweig's argument in the work see ibid, 100–110. Pöggeler and Bienenstock have pointed out that the persistence of Hegel's ideas in Rosenzweig's mature work attests to his inability to either overcome or let go of his legacy: Bienenstock 1992; Pöggeler 1988a and 1988b; see also Honneth 2010.

true integration into the German spirit and reality) to the rediscovery of Judaism represent also a new historical dimension, not only a personal choice. In Judaism, not in German idealism, will the spirit actualize itself for Rosenzweig. (Avineri 1988, 835)

Avineri concludes that Rosenzweig's disillusionment with the redemptive promise of German Idealism for an ideal state also found expression in his full exclusion of the political dimension from the future redemptive scheme of Judaism.[41] As Rosenzweig's Jewish identity emerged from the backstage of his intellectual pursuits to take centre stage, the philosophical tradition incontrovertibly ceded its place as an exclusive path toward personal, intellectual, spiritual, and even political redemption.

* * *

The Baden-Baden conference proved fateful for Rosenzweig in yet another respect, as he first met there Eugen Rosenstock, who became a close friend and an important influence on the development of his original ideas. A converted Jew and prolific scholar of philosophy, religion and law, Rosenstock told Rosenzweig about his concept of *Offenbarungsglaube*, faith based on revelation, in time persuading his Jewish friend that "a votary of culture and reason could with integrity affirm faith in revelation, and that indeed it was the only sensible way of overcoming the philosophical and historical relativism of the day" (Mendes-Flohr 1988a, 5).

Indeed, Rosenzweig later established religiosity as the middle-ground between the individual and the All, proposing a synthesis under which,

> What was for philosophy a demand in the interest of objectivity, will turn out to be a demand in the interests of subjectivity for theology. They are dependent on each other and so generate jointly a new type, be it philosopher or theologian, situated between theology and philosophy. (SE 118/SR 106)

One of Rosenzweig's main challenges in the *Star*, was to present a conception of God that is grounded neither in religious dogma (since Idealism had already refuted it irrevocably), nor in rationalist argumentation (which he rejected in his own critique of Idealism). Uniquely, he retained, rather that dispelled, the tension between these two polar opposites, as "although he was in total agreement with the assumption concerning the atheistic nature of rational thinking, he nev-

---

[41] Avineri 1988, 838. For a thorough analysis of Rosenzweig's painful disavowal of German politics in the wake of the war, see Meineke 1991.

ertheless approached, in a different way the possibility of Jewish philosophy qua system" (Schwarcz 1977, 130).

As we have seen in this chapter, Rosenzweig discovered the immense potential of the interplay between rational and religious thought in the course of a protracted search. In the years that followed, his interests were to continue to shift between ideas and texts, disciplines and traditions; nevertheless, their cohesion was guaranteed by two factors: the yearning for a redemptive resolution of the search, and the astute use of intellectual resources. The ideas that he explored and later dismissed as untenable were to prove just as important as those he came to appreciate as representing ultimate truths.

Chapter 2:
Between Intellectual Homelands (1):
Germanic Revolution

The *Leipziger Nachtgespräch* prompted Rosenzweig to embrace a life of faith. After a tempestuous summer that led to a deep transformation around Yom Kippur 1913, he resolved to accept *Offenbarungsglaube* moored in his religion from birth: Judaism. The practical implications immediately followed: he was to attend the *Lehranstalt für die Wissenschaft des Judentums* in Berlin,[1] while continuing to pursue research on German Idealism. Rosenzweig's diaries from this period, which recommence after a long hiatus, begin on 10.5.1914 and end on 14.1. 1916.[2] The entries, divided between comments on Jewish sources and German Idealism, reflect the fledgling synthesis between philosophy and theology that was to receive systematic formulation in the *Star*. It came, however, under the shadow of the clash between the universalist claims of philosophy and the particularism of Jewish thought. Rosenzweig's decision to remain committed, on some level, to German Idealism, was compounded by his acute awareness of the immanently Christian allegiances of its paragons, Hegel and F.W.J. Schelling. His *Hochkultur* upbringing and relatively late absorption of the intellectual heritage of his ancestors made him feel equally at home in both realms. Unlike his Jewish predecessors, from Philo of Alexandria to Hermann Cohen, Rosenzweig's engagement with non-Jewish ideas was not a foray into foreign lands; it was a tour of his motherland. At the same time, his passionate immersion in Jewish learning emerged to be an act of settlement in a territory that he turned into a new home.

As we have seen in the previous chapter, Rosenzweig's painful realisation that Hegel's thought was not to lead him to a redemptive resolution came as early as 1910, in the aftermath of the Baden-Baden conference. And yet, unlike the two pervious heroes that had guided Rosenzweig's quest, Goethe and

---

[1] Founded by Abraham Geiger and Moritz Lazarus in 1870 and opened to students in 1872, the *Lehranstalt* (originally *Hochschule*) was a progressive institution for training rabbis and Judaica scholars. It closed in 1922 and reopened in 1934 until finally closing down in 1942. See Lowenstein 1977. Hermann Cohen's *Religion der Vernunft* was crafted from his lectures at the *Lehranstalt*. See Elbogen 1922, 130–135.
[2] An additional diary entry "out of some notebook" dated on 1916 is included in *BT* I, 184. The diary typescripts of 1914, *Tagebücher* VI, end on 9.7.1914, and their cover notes "Original lost!". All entries past this date are from the *BT* edition. *Tagebücher* V begins 31.7.1910 and ends 12.9. 1910.

Nietzsche, Hegel's influence persisted and seeped deeper into the work of the young thinker. In the years that remained until the outbreak of the First World War, Rosenzweig's research concentrated on his Hegel dissertation, and after its submission in 1912 on its adaptation into a book. In the *Star*, the colossus of German Idealism became the primary target for Rosenzweig's relentless attack on the Western philosophical tradition. Nonetheless, this critique did not lead Rosenzweig to a wholesale rejection of his previous inspiration. Scholars have made note of the hostile interpretation and convoluted reception of Hegel's thought in the book, rightly focusing on Rosenzweig's insistence to retain system as the superstructure of philosophical argumentation.[3]

Quite understandably, the *Star*'s balanced interest in philosophical and theological speculation left its readers arguing over the nature of the book: is it a study in general philosophy or a work of theology? Perhaps it is a sophisticated exercise in Jewish thought? Sensing that his book is grossly misunderstood, Rosenzweig published in 1925 a clarificatory essay, whose title announces the name of his original system: New Thinking.[4] Yet, its intentional universalist ring, and Rosenzweig's statement at the essay's outset that the *Star* is not a Jewish book,[5] only intensified the controversy, rather than quelled it. Since then, too many studies of Rosenzweig's thought have addressed important issues in one dimension, either philosophical or theological, at the expense of its counterparts. Within such a discourse, it became difficult to develop adequate sensitivity to the synthetic mode underlying Rosenzweig's ideas, and to explore their full riches.

In the current chapter and the one that follows it I propose to understand the *Star* as a work in which Rosenzweig bridged between his Germanic and Hebraic intellectual homelands. I will argue that the system of the *Star* is the product of a dialogue between philosophical discourse and revelatory texts, in which the exchange of ideas is both constructive and critical. Despite its manifest inadequacies, German Idealism proved an indispensable framework for the development of Rosenzweig's new ideas. The Hegelian notion of system, the Kantian tools of critical analysis, and Schelling's fusion of myth and philosophical speculation were to serve as his systematic infrastructure. The Hebrew Bible and the philosophical, exegetical and devotional discourses it gave rise to, is where Rosenzweig found the firm intellectual and spiritual ground he had been seeking for

---

3 For a literature survey see Scharf 2014, 53–56.
4 *Zweistromland*, 139–161. Translations cited from *Theological Writings*, 109–139. Also translated in Galli 1999, 67–102.
5 *Zweistromland* 140/*Theological Writings*, 110. I discuss the implications of this statement on the reception of Rosenzweig's work in chapter 3.

so long. The aspect of this dialogue that has been most obscured by single-dimensional readings of the *Star* is its grounding in the interaction between Rosenzweig's biblical interpretation and systematic thought. While various aspects of this synthesis have been noted in previous studies, the place of two specific figures that inspired Rosenzweig's daring innovation seems to have been overlooked, and in the case of the latter figure of the two, completely unnoticed: Georg Wilhelm Friedrich Hegel, and Rabbi Moses son of Maimon, known as Maimonides. As a mark of his intellectual coming of age, Rosenzweig's engagement with the two thinkers' ideas broke away with his characteristic pattern of idolization followed by disappointment, yielding an original position that is simultaneously informed by and critical of his sources of inspiration.

Rosenzweig's own contribution to the single-dimensional readings of the *Star* owed mostly to the rhetoric of his prose. Imbued with Goethe's poetics and pervaded by the terminologies of Kant, Hegel and Schelling, the text was carefully devised to make cultured German readers feel in familiar territory as they followed its author's journey toward the Star of Redemption. As a result, the sweeping majority of the biblical and rabbinical sources Rosenzweig cited and rephrased were lost on most readers. Conceding this to be a problem, Rosenzweig instructed Glatzer to draw up an index of citations from Jewish sources, added to the book's second edition that came out a mere few months after Rosenzweig's passing (Rosenzweig 1954).

In order to penetrate the book's rhetorical veneer, our discussion in the current chapter and the one that follows will begin with an exposition of Rosenzweig's argument against German Idealism and his proposed solution, moving on to assess suitable methodological approaches to interpret his proposed synthesis between philosophy and theology. The heart of the discussion will present the pivotal role that both Hegel and Maimonides played in the development of Rosenzweig's system as emblems of his Germanic and Hebraic homelands. As their decisive contributions were either obscured (in Hegel's case) or quietly noted (in Maimonides' case), the inspiring role both thinkers played in the development of a system that fuses together philosophy with theology was submerged. The following discussion will attempt to bring this unusual dialogue between the medieval religious thinker and the Enlightenment philosopher into full view.

2.1 Critique of Pure Idealism

2.1.1 Metaphysical Monism

According to Rosenzweig, Idealist metaphysics had failed because its proponents cleaved to a reductionist approach, whereby the entire system of thought must derive from a single ground principle:

> This [Idealist] philosophy takes reduction in general to be something so self-evident that if she takes the trouble to burn such a heretic, she accuses him only of a prohibited method of reduction ... That someone would not at all want to say: everything "is" ..., does not enter her mind. But, in the "what-is"? question directed at everything, lies the entire error of the answers"(*Zweistromland*, 143/*Theological Writings*, 116).

According to Rosenzweig, the fundamental error of traditional philosophy—from the ancients of Iona to the moderns of Jena—lies in an inherent structural collision between three disciplines. Logic, ethics and metaphysics, designated to explain nature, humans and God, respectively, defy philosophy's insistence to cleave to a monistic worldview. In the *Star*, these sciences are granted "meta" status, as Rosenzweig releases them from the strictures of the reductive system upon which monism rests. Therefore, they are designated as metalogic, metaethics, and metaphysics, respectively (SE, 14–21/SR, 9–19). Any attempt to establish a reductive relation between two of these elements, leaves the third unaccounted for: "It is not demonstrated that none of the concepts can be reduced to the two others, but rather, conversely, that each is to be reduced only to itself"(*Zweistromland*, 144/*Theological Writings*, 117). Significantly, Rosenzweig finds the path out of this impasse in Kant's formulation of the limits of reason, the "Naught of knowledge" as Rosenzweig puts it, "as no longer uniform but triform" (SE 24/SR 21): the *Ding an sich*—the Thing in Itself—is the impregnable boundary of knowledge of objects in their true essence, the "naught of metalogic"; the "intelligible character" of moral precepts that lacks concrete manifestations in practical reality, is the "naught of metaethics"; and the mysterious "root" of practical philosophies of nature and morals is what Kant designates in the *Critique of Judgment* as the faculty of a-priori intuition (SE 24/SR 21).[6]

Rosenzweig's proclamation that the *Star* is "nothing other than the reduction *ad absurdum* of the old philosophy and, simultaneously, its salvation" (*Zweistromland*, 142–143/*Theological Writings*, 114–115), may be understood in

---

[6] My exposition of Rosenzweig's idiosyncratic interpretation of Kant follows Schwarcz's commentary in *Kokhav*, 63 n.15. See also Pollock 2009, 27.

light of Kant's discussion of the separate realms of reason in the *Critique of Judgment*. Kant concedes that philosophy divides into two purportedly unbridgeable parts—theoretical reason that applies to the laws of nature, and practical reason that applies to the laws of freedom and morality—and that his task is to establish pure reason as the realm that brings the two together to form the unity of reason (Kant 2000, 13–14). As shown above, under Rosenzweig's analysis, the monist conclusion of Kant's reduction cannot be substantiated; and yet he retains Kant's division to shape the contours of his own system.

2.1.2 Reason and Reality, One and All

While Kant laboured to prove the unity of reason, Hegel expanded reason's claim to unity not only with itself, but with the whole of being.[7] Perhaps the most fundamental concept in Hegel's *Phenomenology of Spirit*—the claim to the unity of reason and being—is the foundation for a system of philosophy of the Absolute. If reason encompasses both itself and the real world, it captures the totality of being. Following in Schelling's footsteps (Schwarcz 1978, 214), Rosenzweig seeks to break the spell of Hegel's absolutist conclusion by pointing out its inherent contradiction:

> ... the identity of reasoning and being presupposes an inner nonidentity. Though reasoning refers throughout to being, it is at the same time a diversity in itself because it also, at the same time, refers to itself. Thus reasoning, itself the unity of its own inner multiplicity, in addition establishes the unity of being [*die Einheit des Seins*], not as unity but insofar as it is multiplicity (SE, 14/SR, 13; trans. altered).

Faced with reason's absolutist claim, the subject discovers that after reason "has taken up everything within itself and has proclaimed its exclusive existence ... he, who has long been philosophically digested, is still there" (*Zweistromland*, 126–127/*Theological Writings*, 52–53). Rosenzweig is referring here to the Hegelian subject who, subsumed into the All, maintains a discrete identity only insofar as he contributes to the actualization of Spirit. A glaring example to this conception of the subject is Hegel's assertion that

> ... the particular individual is an incomplete spirit, a concrete shape whose entire existence falls into one determinateness... In any spirit that stands higher than another, the lower

---

[7] "Thus the Hegelian dialectic as the necessary substructure of the Kantian critique" (*Zweistromland*, 127/*Theological Writings*, 55.)

> concrete existence has descended to the status of an insignificant moment ... (Hegel 2018, 18).

According to Hegel, the individual is a moment in Spirit's progression in history (and hence incomplete), whose entire existence is determined externally by the system. What is more, as a moment, it is discarded of like an empty shell once a more highly developed moment appears. Set against this quote from Hegel, Rosenzweig's counterclaim is all the more poignant: despite the system's indifference to his uniqueness, in real life the subject remains a singular individual, an "I, the quite ordinary private subject, I first and last name, I dust and ashes" (*Zweistromland*, 127/*Theological Writings*, 53).

2.1.3 Staking out New Territory

The internal conflict that had confounded Rosenzweig in the Baden-Baden conference, between Hegelian affinities and Rosenstock's *Offerbarungsglaube*, seems to have ripened in the *Star*. Rosenzweig lays at the heart of his system the "path" (*Bahn*) of three divine acts – creation, revelation and redemption – on which the three elements – God, man and world – travel together:

> By undertaking to equalize and adapt [*Ausgleichung und Angleichung*], to rhyme the unrhymable [*die Reimung des Ungereimten*], Idealism only destroys the pure factuality in which the three [elements] primordially [*ursprünglich*] stand each to itself [*jedes für sich*] ... If, however, the elements are simply accepted, then they can walk together [*zusammentreten*], not in order to be "rhymed" [*nicht um sich zu "reimen"*], but, by virtue of their reciprocity, break a path [*eine Bahn zu erzeugen*] ... What becomes immediately visible in revelation is neither God nor man nor world ... What does become visible is their reciprocal interaction. That which is here immediately experienced is not God, man and world but rather creation, revelation, and redemption (SE, 435/SR, 391; trans. altered).

Earlier on in the *Star*, these three divine acts are explicitly grounded in corresponding passages from the Bible: Genesis chapter 1—creation; Song of Songs —revelation; and Psalm 115—redemption. From the above passage we learn that the complete release from Idealism's mistakes leads to the knowledge of being in its truthfulness, i.e., to knowledge of God, man and world as framed by the three divine acts experienced by the individual's encounter with revelation. Once more, Rosenzweig emphasizes that philosophy is not discarded of in favour of theology; it remains essential to the exploration of being:

As practiced by the theologian, philosophy becomes a prognostication of revelation, in a manner of speaking the "Old Testament" of theology. But thereby revelation regains before our amazed eyes the character of authentic miracle—authentic because it becomes wholly and solely the fulfilment of the promise made in creation. And philosophy is the Sybilline Oracle which, by predicting the miracle, turns it into a "sign", the sign of divine providence (SE ,120/SR, 108).

The uncanny role reversal between philosophy and theology, whereby the former is "Old Testament" to the latter, exemplifies the organic connection between the two. By drawing an analogy between philosophy and the Old Testament, the primordial testimony of revelation and providence, Rosenzweig implies that the systematic task that he has undertaken is possible only through acknowledgement of philosophy's and theology's shared metaphysical burden of proof. The philosophical endeavour of pure reason has failed; theology's dogmatic interpretation of Scripture, and its sibling, the philosophical dogmatism against which German Idealism did battle, collapsed long ago. But a reading of Scripture through reason's critical lens will lead to the right path: one that eliminates the breach over which reason had to leap in order to embrace revelation. Now they are intertwined.

"*Stark wie der Tod ist Liebe*"—Love is strong as death (SE, 174/SE, 156). With these opening words of his chapter on revelation placed at the *Star*'s epicentre, Rosenzweig demonstrates how the verses of Scripture bear testimony to the truth of his philosophical investigation. In Song of Songs 8:6, the introductory declaration[8] and concluding statement[9] of the *Star* are fused together. The dialectic between the quest for universal knowledge driven by the fear of death on the one hand, and the desire to defy death by living as a singular human being with a first and last name on the other hand, is attained through God's love for each and every person, "first and last name", among us, and is reflected in earthly love between humans (Mendes-Flohr 2009, 313–316).

2.1.4 Philosophus vel Theologus

The mottos of the introductions to *Star* I and II, *in philosophos* [against philosophers] and *in theologos* [against theologians], respectively announce the demise of the two as self-standing disciplines. Rosenzweig believed that only by pursu-

---

[8] "*Vom Tode, von der Furcht des Todes, hebt alles Erkennen des All an*" (From death, from the fear of death, originates all cognition of the All.) (SE, 3/SR, 3). My translation.
[9] "*Wohinaus aber öffnen sich die Flügel des Tors? Du weißt es nicht? INS LEBEN*". (Whither, then, do the wings of the gate open? You know it not? INTO LIFE) (SE, 472/SR, 424; trans. altered).

ing philosophy's interest in objectivity and theology's interest in subjectivity as equally vital, the disciplines may be saved from a state of advanced atrophy. Quite remarkably, despite Rosenzweig's straightforward call for a "new type" of thinker "situated between theology and philosophy", in the main his masterpiece continues to be interpreted *either* philosophically *or* theologically, without taking seriously enough the option of synthetic interpretation.

Rosenzweig's writing in the *Star* draws heavily on the German Idealist tradition in terminology, methodology and content, while its highly original religious imagination is deeply inspired by the Hebrew Bible and other Jewish sources. Critics' tendency to focus on one of these dimensions, which they consider to dominate his thought, usually leads to either belittle its counterparts or apply unsuitable interpretive tools. While a division of Rosenzweig studies into two categories—"philosophical" and "theological"—is somewhat crude and even simplistic, it gives a sense of the tendency to decline the opportunity to fully celebrate its richness and originality.

In an aptly-titled review essay, Paul Franks suggests that philosophical studies of Rosenzweig should be set in a context encompassing his own intellectual preoccupations, as well as the German Idealist philosophers with whom he engaged in dialogue (Franks, 391). Based on this assertion, he both rejects the decontextualization of Rosenzweig in Levinasian readings of his work, and emphasizes that unlike other disciplines, "the history of philosophy can be a contribution to contemporary philosophy" (Franks 393–394). A richer assessment of Rosenzweig's work should therefore address the German Idealist and Jewish traditions as coeval objects of inquiry, alongside his textual strategies and rhetoric. Such an approach to the study of Rosenzweig's synthesis between system and Scripture in the *Star* may be found in the work of two Israeli scholars, Moshe Schwarcz and Eliezer Schweid.[10]

Schwarcz places Rosenzweig on the trajectory of Jewish non-rational responses to the rationalism of Enlightenment and post-Enlightenment philosophy. According to Schwarcz, Rosenzweig's predecessor on this trajectory is Salomon Ludwig Steinheim (1789–1866), whose *Die Offenbarung nach dem Lehrbegriffe der Synagoge* (1835) is an edifice founded on a Torah-based concept of revelation that is set apart from and in perfect opposition to philosophical rea-

---

[10] The work of Yehoyada Amir, a disciple of Schweid's and son of the *Star*'s translator into Hebrew, Yehoshua Amir, develops some of the possibilities of his teacher's and Schwarcz's models for a fuller appreciation of Rosenzweig's synthesis. See Amir 2004. His discussion of Rosenzweig's biblical interpretation in the *Star*, however, focuses on the grammatical analyses in Part Two of the *Star*, and does not address the more hidden presence of exegesis in Rosenzweig's argumentation.

soning (Schwarcz 1966, 26–36; 123–140). Steinheim's view of Jewish theology as anchored in a unique conception of revelation, Schwarcz observes, equally resistant to mystical and rational interpretations, was very similar to Rosenzweig's (Schwarcz 1977, 129).

Schwarcz applies a two-pronged approach that aims to trace the relevant historical sources and their interrelationships, while critically assessing the ideas formed from those sources (Scwarcz 1977, 129–130). In his broader historical assessment of the confluence of Jewish thought with Western philosophy, Schwarcz observes that the non-systematic, non-rational structure of the Jewish tradition necessitated reliance on extraneous sources for the formulation of theoretical categories, "because from the beginning of its existence [Judaism] was 'life teachings'—*torat hayim*—and not speculative and reflective teachings, as the Bible proclaims: 'Ask you father and he will declare to you; ask your elders and they will tell you'" (Deuteronomy 32:7) (Schwarcz 1966, 5). With the advent of the Enlightenment, new philosophical approaches offered particularly efficient tools for a systematic critique of Jewish ideas (Schwarcz 1966, 6–7). One consequence of these developments was the emergence of rational enquiries into religion, myth and art, which clashed with the inherently non-rational nature of these objects of reflection. Non-rational responses to this development soon followed, taking language as a central manifestation of religious experience, downplaying the instrumental function of language and emphasising its fundamentally hermeneutical function, by which Schwarcz means that language is understood as formative of reality, as it underlies any unifying and specific interpretation of reality, that is, of scientific enquiry, aesthetic interpretation and practical judgment (Schwarcz 1966, 8–9). In defying the philosophies that confined religious discourse to the limits of reason, non-rational Jewish thinkers did not dismiss reasoning altogether; rather, they employed this self-limiting principle of philosophy to attain a threefold purpose: (1) establishing religious faith (revelatory knowledge) and philosophical speculation (rational knowledge) as mutually exclusive; (2) applying philosophical critique as a positive and constructive practice aimed to secure the epistemologically privileged status of religious faith (Schwarcz 1966, 18); (3) and juxtaposing revelatory discourse on rational discourse in order to gain insights on the nature of one discourse by examining it in light of its counterpart:

> ... by the very performance of reflection, reason's self-critical activity becomes ecstatic (ekstasis), i.e., it negates contents that lie beyond the scope of its discourse. This ec-static activity, which is identical with reason's self-negation, is conditioned upon the recognition that rational knowledge is neither absolute nor the exclusive critical organon for the sum of human *knowledge* ... [the non-rational approach therefore] needs *revelation* as a mode of understanding as distinct from rational understanding. It establishes the episte-

mological validity of revelation and therefore it is called upon to inquire into the nature of revelatory knowledge by comparing it with rational knowledge (Schwarcz 1966, 18; italics in the original).

Within this broad historical development, Schwarcz sees Rosenzweig as the foremost successor of Schelling in the early 20th century, and the *Star* as the completion of Schelling's unfinished work, *Die Weltalter*, which adds to the eon of creation two counterparts missing from the original work—revelation and redemption (Schwarcz 1966, 185).[11] This observation is by no means a strictly philosophical one, as Schwarcz emphatically opposes the interpretations portraying Rosenzweig as either an anti-Hegelian or an advocate of Jewish particularism. In his view, Rosenzweig complements a critique of Idealism, founded on the non-identity of reason and reality, with Jewish tradition as the necessary existential (or perhaps phenomenological) demonstration of the system derived from this critique (Schwarcz 1978, 294). Emphasizing the status of Judaism as *torat hayim*, Rosenzweig draws on liturgy, Jewish customs and the Jewish year-cycle, to address problems that lie beyond the reach of pure speculation (Schwarcz 1978, 298).

Unfortunately, Schwarcz's premature death at 53 robbed us of the possibility of a detailed critical assessment by him of Rosenzweig's reliance on and interpretation of Jewish sources in the *Star*.[12] Moreover, as indicated above, Schwarcz was less inclined to view the Hebrew Bible as the source that Rosenzweig privileged over the "life teachings" that evolved from its study, and gave shape to practice, liturgy and worship. This is why Schweid's focus on Rosenzweig's turn to the Bible is a crucial supplement to Schwarcz's historical-critical framework.

Schweid grasps Rosenzweig's move as a reaction to the collapse of Idealist philosophy in an attempt to remedy it. He reads the *Star* as embodying Rosenzweig's biography of intellectual and spiritual reorientation, through its literary

---

11 Schelling SW I/8 194–344. Described by a twentieth century critic as "his greatest masterpiece, the peak of his philosophy", Schelling commenced work on *Die Weltalter* circa 1810 and produced two drafts, in 1811 and 1813, but never completed the project. For the evolution of the work see Fuhrmans 1954, here at 192, 196–198. Rosenzweig read the 1912 Reclam edition of the latest (1814/1815) version, and could not have had access to the 1811 and 1813 drafts (Bienenstock 2004, 282 n.24). His acquaintance with Schelling's later philosophy probably took place only in 1916 (Bienenstock 2003, 234). For a concise account of Rosenzweig's encounter with Schelling's thought see Schwarcz 1978, 211–216.

12 Schwarcz 1971, 9–42, offers a sketchy historical assessment and does not address the question; but his annotations to the Hebrew translation of the *Star* are a clear indication that he was fully cognizant of the centrality of Jewish sources to Rosenzweig's thought.

structure, style and most of all, philosophical methodology (Schweid 1981, 232). By reorientation Schweid means a dialectical engagement with Idealist philosophy, which is critical of its methodological errors and constructive in its use of fundamental truths that the system retains; but Idealism's greatest mistake, its vain attempt to have reason alone usurp religion, may be overcome only by moving beyond the limits of philosophical discourse into religion, that is, to the reality of spiritual life (Schweid 1981, 234–235). Like Schwarcz, Schweid considers Rosenzweig's theory of language as the bridge on which he crosses over from philosophy to New Thinking. Having demolished the Idealist equation of reason with reality, Rosenzweig found an alternative unifying framework in language, where speech has a vital function. Abstract concepts, the multiple forms for describing reality that are formative of both our perception and engagement with it, interpersonal communication, and the possibility of acquiring knowledge of God and of experiencing Him through revelation, have their shared ground in language as speech, a theory Rosenzweig called Speech Thinking (*Sprachdenken*).[13] But while Schwarcz's discussion tends to be more theoretical, as he focuses on Rosenzweig's relation to other revelatory conceptions of language in modern Jewish thought, Schweid is interested in *Sprachdenken* as a philosophical practice. As such, he understands Rosenzweig's project as the application of philosophical reasoning as a hermeneutic device employed to unearth the revelatory truths found in Scripture (Schweid 1985, 299). This application, says Schweid, is what gave shape to the entire architectonic of the *Star:* "When viewed as a whole architectonic creation, *The Star of Redemption* is, as said, a philosophical midrash in essence. Its literary framework, reflecting the methodology of linguistic existentialism [i.e., *Sprachdenken*], makes calculated use of elements carved out of the verses of the Bible, rabbinical sayings and the Jewish prayer book" (Schweid 1985, 311). Whereas from a structural point of view, "… Rosenzweig develops the tools for his midrashic interpretation in Part I [of the *Star*], in Part II he applies his midrash specifically to the Bible, and in Part III he reaches the liturgical cycle by passing through the Bible and rabbinical exegesis" (Schweid 1985, 312).

To be sure, Schweid's interpretation is not without its weaknesses.[14] Still, his and Schwarcz's studies offer an especially compelling dialogue with Rosenzweig

---

13 Schweid 1981, 247–248; Schwarcz 1978, 263–291, esp. 270 ff.
14 In the first half of his essay, Schweid formulates Rosenzweig's explanation of the Bible's canonical status and its philosophical implications by moving back and forth between the *Star* and later essays. The result is a pastiche that is useful for understanding the main tenets of his perception, which nonetheless obscures the intricacies of his biblical interpretations in

on his own terms; that is, their readings his of work in light of both their philosophical and theological sources point out Rosenzweig's innovative integration of the two disciplines.[15]

2.2 Hegel Revisited

Even among the most astute commentators of the *Star*, Rosenzweig's interpretations and critique of German Idealism are neigh irresistible to identify with. The book's presentation of a triform system as a counter-reaction to philosophers' infatuation with the prospect of attaining absolute knowledge by means of reason appears to have a seamless internal logic. As part of this argument, Hegel becomes an effigy that stands for everything Rosenzweig considers problematic in the Western philosophical tradition. Although Hegel's numerous contributions to the system of the *Star* have been duly noted, analyses of the *Star* appear to have left intact Hegel's figure as Rosenzweig paints him in the book: the last and hence most misguided adherent of a tradition that has led human thought to the brink of implosion.

Throughout the *Star*, Rosenzweig's references to Hegel construct the image of a philosopher who is single-handedly responsible for leading German Idealism to a *cul de sac*. Rosenzweig charges Hegel with the subsumption of divine revelation and its promise under the regulating function of reason:

> [In Hegelian Philosophy] The knowable world becomes known through the same law of reasoning [*Denkgesetz*] that recurs in the system's apex in the form of the supreme law of being [*Seinsgesetz*]. And this law of reasoning and being was first formulated as world-historical in revelation. Hence philosophy in a sense does nothing more than actualise that which is promised by revelation (SE, 7/SR, 6–7; trans. altered).

---

the *Star*. Despite the coherence and consistency of Rosenzweig's mature thought, such juxtapositions should be made with extreme caution.

[15] Recently two comprehensive studies of Rosenzweig's theology through distinctively Jewish prisms appeared in print. Leon Dow Wiener (Wiener 2017) presents the first systematic attempt to read Rosenzweig as a halakhic thinker, whereas Benjamin Sommer (Sommer 2015) presents Rosenzweig (along with Abraham Joshua Heschel) as casting the Hebrew Bible as both the grounding of faith in divine revelation and the object of destabilising critiques of divine authority. Wiener's and Sommer's important contributions notwithstanding, in my view Schwarcz and Schweid continue to offer the most compelling models for interpreting Rosenzweig's synthesis between German philosophy and Jewish thought.

He also charges Hegel with precluding the religious believer ("lover of God") from enjoying the fruit of science, i.e. knowledge, which is the exclusive propriety of the philosopher ("lover of knowledge"):

> For the lover of God [*Liebhaber Gottes*] is often not the lover of knowledge [*Liebhaber des Wissens*] and vice versa. No such contrast exists between the lover of world and that of knowledge; on the contrary, like the concepts of world and knowelge they more or less depend on one another. Hence "the conclusion of science" that man can know nothing about God was more palatable than the same conclusion with respect to the world (SE, 44/SR, 41; trans. altered).

The majority of references to Hegel in the *Star* are passages where he does not appear by name, but rather as the unnamed emblematic representative of German Idealism as a whole. As such, the year 1800 which for Rosenzweig marks the ripening of modern philosophy, is also cast as marking the descent of the complacency of Hegel's philosophy with its declaration of attaining knowledge of the All; the moment of Being at the Destination (*am Ziel Sein*) which eclipses the content of religious faith (*Glaube*). At the same time, Rosenzweig identifies the indelible fingerprints of Christian theology in Hegel's complete spiritualization of religious faith, which had led to forgetting the body:

> The Petrine Church had disclosed the weak point in its all-too corporeal nature through the evil idea of the dualistic [*zweifachen*] truth. Just so the German Idealistic Movement which followed those three centuries made known the weakness of the all too, or rather: merely spiritual nature of relgious faith. Spirit deemed itself so completely "alone" so as to be able to generate everything out of itself alone, and out of itself alone everything. Preoccupied with the spirit, Faith had simply forgotten the body (SE, 313/SR, 281–282; trans. altered).

Once more, Rosenzweig constructs a Hegel figure that blurs the distinction between the individual person and the representative of a philosophical movement—German Idealism. At the hands of the author of the *Star*, then, Hegel becomes synonymous with philosophy's hubris and triumphalism over theology. I would like to argue that this de-personalization is essential for Rosenzweig's move, precisely because of his lasting admiration for Hegel to the point of self-identification.

2.2.1 Revolution as Resolution

Rosenzweig hints at this self-identification in the lead-up to a section entitled "Institution and Revolution" at the conclusion of Part II of the *Star*, which uncoincidentally discloses the resolution of Rosenzweig's system: redemption.

> The act of love thus appears to take effect only on the chaos of an "Anything at all" [*eines Irgend*]. In reality, without knowing it, it presupposes that the world, all the world it has to do with, is growing life. It is by no means enough for the act of love that the world have creaturely existence. It demands more of it: duration as a matter of law, interconnection, formation [*Gliederung*], growth—in short, everything that it itself appears to deny in the anarchic freedom, immediacy, ephemerality of its act. Just because it consciously denies it, it unconsciously presupposes it. The soul demands, as object animated with soul by it, a well-formed life [*ein gegliedertes Leben*]. It then exercises its freedom on this life, animating it in all its individual members, and everywhere inseminating this ground of the living formation with the seeds of name, animated individuality, immortality (SE, 268/SR, 240–241; trans. altered).

This description of the worldly function of love, of brotherly love as partaking of the redemptive process immediately, precedes "Institution and Revolution". Rosenzweig's choice of this title is peculiar, as its content lacks any direct reference to either institution or revolution. Instead, it outlines the worldly operation of brotherly love in bridging between creation, revelation and redemption. The designation of chaos and anarchy as manifestations of its quintessence—freedom—constitute the revolutionary element expected to lead to institution (i. e. – stability), once love directs itself at a well-defined area of life when it fulfills its redemptive function.

This brief reference to revolution resonates with Rosenzweig's description in *Hegel and the State* of Hegel's philosophical interpretation of the French Revolution in the *Phenomenology of Spirit*. This passage lucidly demonstrates the inspiration Rosenzweig found in Hegel, as well as the shortcomings he identified in his system. For the author of *Hegel and the State*, the French Revolution is the world-historical event that in Hegel's eyes *was* the redemptive moment, the full actualisation of Spirit. Rosenzweig's account of this moment is intriguing especially in light of his insistence on its dominant religious dimension; as the hour of reckoning in the clash between faith and reality approached,

> Faith is the deified reality that holds sway against fleeing from the world [*Weltflucht*] and with pure consciousness encounters and ultimately struggles with the other inhabitans of the other-worldly region. In this state, its loftiest ideas, the ideal of the complete lack of ideals, as it were, is finally in its possession, which in the old life [pre-1789] was visible from [the vantage points of] an ever-ruptured centre of the Godless world of reality of *Bildung* and brought reality-less, pure thinking together with faith. 'Both worlds', the section concludes, 'are reconciled, and the heavens become transplanted in the earth below.[16] And with this bright trumpet call the representation of the year of this "majestic sunset" [1789] is

---

[16] Compare SE, 7: 'So scheint der alte Streit [zwischen Offenbarung und Philosophie] geschlichtet, Himmel und Erde versöhnt.' Translation of Hegel citation from Hegel 2018, 339.

arrived at. Here begins the conclusion of part of the 'self-alientated spirit,' rewritten as 'the absolute freedom and the Terror' (Rosenzweig 2010, 258–259).

The emergence of Jean Jacque Rousseau's notion of collective will provided Hegel with the historical subject that concretised the absolute positing of the end of time in the present (... *die absolute Verdiesseitigung des Jenseits*; Rosenzweig 2010, 259). Rosenzweig identifies the concept of collective will as the addition to Hegel's system that dealt individual will its final deathblow (Rosenzweig 2010, 260).

The absolute freedom that the Revolution introduced into the course of history dissolved the barrier between individual will (which is internal) and collective will (which is external): "In the French Revolution, this world of *Bildung* (*ancien regime*) ran into the ground as either external or yet inner-worldly forces became closer to recognizing the collective will, at which point it became the cornerstone of the Third Republic" (Rosenzweig 2010, 261).

This next stage in the course of history, when the Revolution was to march into Germany, according to Hegel, was to arrive initially as the moral spirit of the Revolution, which was to prepare for the final stage in its unfolding: that spirit become "absolute Religion, absolute knowledge" (Rosenzweig 2010, 263).

The redemptive role of Freedom as embodied by love in the *Star* therefore emerges as a meta-commentary on Rosenzweig's own analysis of the French Revolution in the *Phenomenology of Spirit*. The destructive impact that the young Hegel scholar identified with absolute freedom is transformed by the author of the *Star* into the constructive role of brotherly love. This constructive act, in turn, asserts anew the indissolubility and indispensability of the individual will, which faced annihilation in Hegel's system (Rosenzweig reiterates this point in the account of Hegel's interpretation of the French Revolution). These gestures are consistent with the critique of Hegel earlier on in the *Star*, premised on the synthesis between philosophy and theology that Rosenzweig establishes in *Star* II:1. As shown above, a similar synthesis is presented in Rosenzweig's reading of Hegel's analysis of the French Revolution: gone are the hubris and triumphalism of a monistic system that defies revelation and denigrates theology, which the *Star* ascribes to the paragon of German Idealism. Expressing an entirely different mindset, Rosenzweig concludes the passage on the French Revolution by citing Hegel's end-of-year speech at the *Frankfurt Kolleg*, as its director, in 1806:

> We are living in an important epoch of fermentation, whereby Spirit turns back, shedding its previous form [*Gestalt*] , and assumes a new one [...] It prepares a new arrival of Spirit. Previously philosophy had welcomed its appearance and recognition or otwerise power-

lessly resisted it, and all this time, the clueless masses accounted for its appearance [*Ercheinens*]. Philosophy, however, recognized it [Spirit] as the Eternal, wishing to pay it its due respect" (Rosenzweig 2010, 264).

Rosenzweig adduces the following observation:

> The thinker's self-perception is so highstrung nowadays. He faces time eye-to-eye. Moreover: he calls at Time and she speaks back at him [...] He has crossed the Dantesque "middle of our lives". The milestones of his life transform him as he passes through the epochs of world history. The stream of thought breaks through the barriers of its bank and irrigates the thirsty pastureland of time" (Rosenzweig 2010, 264).

Who is the "we" in the reference to Dante's famous opening of Canto I of the *Inferno*? Humanity in its transition from the old world to modernity? The German Republic of Letters' coming of age? Or perhaps just the two thinkers—Hegel and Rosenzweig—whom the 20th century philosopher sought to present as sharing the one and the same fate? The sensitive poetic cadence leaves this question open. But a substantial body of evidence gives reasons to believe that Rosenzweig was alluding to the latter possibility. Nonetheless, as the question remains unanswered it orients our discussion once more to revolution, this time as the site of trauma.

2.2.2 Revolution as Trauma

The collision between intellectual crisis and political upheaval is an experience common to both Hegel and Rosenzweig. Though the circumstances vary considerably, and are more than a century apart, the spectre of Hegel (to borrow Louis Althusser's phrase) remained firm in Rosenzweig's mind long after his departure from academic research. As Roberto Navarette Alonso demonstrates, despite Rosenzweig's wish to shed the author image of *Hegel and the State* and to be associated only with the *Star*, he continued to identify with the Idealist philosopher on a personal level (Navarette Alonso 2016, 278–280).[17] Benjamin Pollock has shown that Hegel's obsession with the 27th life year as a crucial signpost in one's development was embraced by Rosenzweig, reflected in the chapter entitled "Frankfurt" (where Hegel spent his 27th year) in his Hegel tome (Pollock 2014, 51–58).

---

17 Navarette Alonso cites at 259 Rosenzweig's letter to his parents of 6.2.1917: "I am living Hegel's fate with his yearly political writings" (*BT* I, 346).

Echoing Rosenzweig's above comment to his mother, Peter Eli Gordon underscores the impact of Hegel's early theological writings on Rosenzweig's two published books, the *Hegel* and the *Star* (Gordon 2003, 100–117). Navarette Alonso, however, places particular emphasis on the dissonance between Rosenzweig's admiring interpretation of Hegel's biography in his monograph and the ambivalence he expressed toward both the monograph and its subject matter after the First World War (Navarette Alonso 2016, 283–293). Avineri convincingly argues that Rosenzweig's departure from Hegel owed at least in part to the painful awakening from the dream of an ideal German state that the First World War had forced upon him.[18] As Avineri points out further, the Foreword and Closing Remarks in *Hegel and the State* lament the waste that the war had laid to Germany to the point of rendering Hegel's idea of the state obsolete: "The hard and limited Hegelian idea of the state [...] will disintegrate, so to speak, before the reader's very eyes in its evolution throughout the thinker's life, opening a vista on a spacious German future, both internally and externally. Things turned out otherwise" (Rosenzweig 2010, 18). The fate of Hegel's philosophy, Rosenzweig concludes, is the direct result of the fall of the second Reich: "A field of ruins marks the place where the Reich used to stand". (Rosenzweig 2010, 18). He goes on to assert that the War had brought about a rupture to the effect that, "[...] in origin and also in intention [*Hegel and the State* is] testimony to the Spirit of the prewar years, not the 'Spirit' of 1919" (Rosenzweig 2010, 18).

In *Mourning Sickness: Hegel and the French Revolution*, Rebecca Comay unpacks Hegel's historico-metaphysical analysis of the French Revolution to expose the profound traumatic impact it had had on him. The process she describes, whereby the political upheaval in France was perceived on the German side of the border with aloofness bolstered by the belief that the nation had already completed its own revolutionary transformation into modernity in the Reformation, was forced later on to accommodate (philosophically) and come to terms with (historically and personally) the devastating violence that spilled over national borders and over the city of Jena with Napoleon's troops, precisely as Hegel was completing his *Phenomenology of Spirit* (Comay 2011, 55–56).

Insisting that the trauma Hegel inscribes into his analysis of the Revolution was individual rather than personal, Comay shows how the historical event becomes in the *Phenomenology* into the scourge of modernity (Comay 2011, 76).[19] The transformation from enthusiastic spectator into helpless victim of the col-

---

18 See the quotations from Avineri on p.23 above.
19 For a critique of the *ad hominem* argument of Comay's interpretation see de Boer 2018.

lapse of the French monarchy, says Comay, had a painful sobering effect on the young Hegel: "The task of modernity will be to explore this fissure. The rubble of *Sittlichkeit* [morality] had revealed what all ruins do, namely that the world is constructed (Comay 2011, 59)". This insight, she contends, was translated in the *Phenomenology* into the intractability of destruction from modernity:

> Modernity takes ruination (*Verwüstung*) as its foundation (*PhG* § 472).[20] The world in which we find ourselves is a manufactured one, beauty is a masquerade [...] and we must henceforth invent we what discover. This is why the modern world defines itself explicitly as "culture" (*Bildung*): it is our way of registering that we place ourselves in a world of our own making (*PhG* § 484). The task of Spirit will be to reconstruct an existence amid the debris of empire. (Comay 2011, 59, my italics).

Resonating Rosenzweig, Comay points out that as part of the sobering effect of the French Revolution, Hegel attempts in the *Phenomenology* to lead faith and reality to their ultimate reconciliation by having philosophy internalise Christianity to the point of identity (Comay 2011, 64). Identifying trauma as the underlying motivation of this move on Hegel's part, she articulates in Freudian terms the shock that Rosenzweig discloses in his Foreword to *Hegel and the State:*

> 'Enlightenment is not very enlightened about itself' (§556). Its contempt expresses its own hidden fundamentalism—an empty ritual of disenchantment that must turn eventually against itself. Hegel repeatedly anticipates Freud's terminology as he investigates Enlightenment's inquisitorial agenda: disavowal (*Verleugnung*), perversion (*Verkehrung*), splitting (*Trennung, Entzweiung*), isolation (*Isolierung*), the stubborn forgetting (*Vergessen*) of the lost object—the catalogue details the defensive apparatus of a subject bent on sustaining itself on what it gives up. The melancholia afflicting Enlightenment condemns it to disown the violence it perpetrates on a faith whose grief is matched only by insight's own manic jubilation: Enlightenment fails to register faith's losses as its own. (Comay 2011, 64–65).

The experience of revolution in Germany of 1806 and 1918 by two thinkers grappling with the dual trauma of political rupture and the ruin of philosophical equilibrium thus emerges as a plausible source of personal and intellectual affinity that Rosenzweig retained for Hegel even in the war's aftermath. It also provides further support for my argument for a Hegelian subtext of Rosenzweig's assignation of a redemptive function to revolution in the *Star*. The furnace of

---

[20] Comay is referring to the following passage: "However, the polity will honor the one it found to be on its side; in contrast, the government, the re-established simplicity of the self of the polity, will punish the one who had already proclaimed on the walls of the city the devastation he would wreak, and this punishment will be that of denying him final honors." (Hegel 2018, 274).

revolutionary trauma also forged the thinkers' respective systems of philosophy that shed the naiveté of their pre-revolutionary incarnations.

The dissonance between the sober affiliation of the mature Rosenzweig with Hegel's life and thought on the one hand, and the caricature of Hegel's philosophy in the *Star* on the other hand, must not obscure the inspiration that the author of the *Phenomenology* continued to exert on the author of the *Star*. This observation is far beyond anecdotal: it is vital for our charting of Rosenzweig's Germanic fatherland and for outlining its contiguous border with his Hebraic homeland. As I have argued here, the equilibrium between faith and reality that Hegel attains in his *Phenomenology* marked for Rosenzweig the farthest outreach of philosophical discourse, to the point where argumentation can no longer rely on terminologies and reasoning, and must be joined with the words of Scripture.

Chapter 3:
Between Intellectual Homelands (2): Hebraic Redemption

Rosenzweig's concurrent preoccupation with the history of German Idealism and the study of Jewish sources in the year following Yom Kippur, 1913, was certainly noted by scholars. Benjamin Sax's focus on Rosenzweig's encounter with Ismar Elbogen at the *Lehranstalt* (Sax, 2011; 2018), and Benjamin's Pollock investigation of his 1914 essay, *Die Älteste Systemprogramm der deutsche Idealismus* (Pollock, 2009, 14–16), contribute to our understanding of the theological and philosophical dimensions of Rosenzweig's work. They also underscore the formative impact of his activities in the academic year 1913–1914 on his mature thought. But as far as the available literature is concerned, a lynchpin that fastened these two realms within the system of the *Star*, does not appear to readily present itself.

A notion permeating Rosenzweig's thought, both in its early and late stages, is the importance he ascribed to constitutive moments in the historical development of his objects of study.[1] His 1914 diary entries indicate that he had identified a preparatory stage in philosophy's progress toward 1800, in an attempt to shed the pagan elements it had imbibed in antiquity. The renewed ascendancy of Aristotelian thought, he reflects, collided with unprecedented vigilance in the theological discourses of Judaism, Christianity and Islam against expressions of idolatry. In this state of disarray, Maimonides stood out as a beacon of lucidity, which Hegel and Schelling refined some six centuries later.

Although those insights are mentioned in the *Star*, Maimonides remains one of the thinkers that are least associated with Rosenzweig.[2] His relation to the medieval thinker has been studied in only a handful of articles, sometimes viewed as an expression of Hermann Cohen's influence.[3] But if one were to line up all of Rosen-

---

[1] E.g., 1800 for philosophy, 313 CE for Christian theology and 70 CE for Jewish history. See for example *BT* I, 302–306/Rosenzweig & Rostestock, 156–161.

[2] "… Buber and Rosenzweig were sheer outsiders to Maimonideanism". Harvey 1980, 260. Rosenzweig's translation of Yehudah Halevy's poems, accompanied by expressions of reverence later in his life, contributed to the commonly held view that the medieval poet-thinker had inspired his earlier work. Other than one reference in the *Star*, however, there is no evidence indicating substantial familiarity with Halevy's work prior to the commencement of the translation project. See Amir 2011, 15–16, n.56.

[3] Gordon 1995,1–6; Batnitzky 2000, 17–31, esp. 21–24; Seeskin, 154–157, 161–162; Kavka 2004, 103–113; Samuelson 2006, 155–165; Fisher, 187–188, briefly points out Rosenzweig's invocation of Maimonides in constructing his argument of creation as the negation of nothingness.

zweig's references to Maimonides, one were to find that he not only studied his two masterpieces seriously,[4] but developed a profound and under-recognised affinity with the legacy of the medieval thinker. By making this claim, I not implying that Rosenzweig was by any means a "closet Maimonidean"; the differences between their respective approaches are fundamental and irreconcilable. Rather, I contend that Rosenzweig's study of Maimonides, which he undertook as he was formulating a systematic response to Rosenstock's assault, had inspired the development of a synthetic methodology, or to use Schwarcz's term, an organon, for his emerging system. To be sure, Rosenzweig expresses in the *Star* his indebtedness to Maimonides only modestly, and does not present his influence as related to the dialogue between philosophy and revelation within his system. Yet, as the following investigation will show, this fact may be attributed in part to rhetorical considerations, as well as to his later critique of Maimonides' position on anthropomorphism. Still, Rosenzweig's disclosure of his ideas in raw form in his diaries documents an evolutionary moment in his intellectual biography, which, like Wittgenstein's ladder, was discarded of once it elevated him to the level of "seeing the world rightly" (Wittgenstein 1966, 150–151). From this higher vantage point, the dialogue between system and Scripture became for Rosenzweig an almost logical conclusion.

* * *

Between November 1913 and fall 1914,[5] Rosenzweig attended Hermann Cohen's class on Maimonides' *Guide of the Perplexed* at the *Lehranstalt für die Wissenschaft des Judentums* in Berlin. As one of his friends described it, Rosenzweig's study at the *Lehranstalt* was, "like a thunderstorm on a dry field" (E. Mayer 1930, 53). His letters and diaries are the evidence offering the least-filtered access to his pursuits, ideas and plans. Recommencing in May 1914 after a gap of nearly four years, the diaries reflect Rosenzweig's intense, two-pronged effort: (1) research on the history of German Idealism, particularly in relation to Hegel and Schelling; (2) commentary on Jewish sources: biblical verses, Talmudic passages and contemporary research, which Rosenzweig perused at the *Lehranstalt*.

Contrary to the impression that Franks and Morgan's summary of the 1914 diaries creates (*Theological Writings*, 5), Rosenzweig's readings of Jewish sources there-

---

[4] Rosenzweig's assiduous study of Maimonides is attested to by his cousin Gertrud Oppenheim, who told the editors of *Gesammelte Schriften* that he had begun studying Arabic after Hermann Cohen chided him for not being able to read Maimonides in the original. See *BT I*, 151.
[5] *Zweistromland*, 239. Rosenzweig joined a Red Cross paramedic course in early September, for which he travelled to Belgium (*BT* II, 1333).

in are not the musings of a novice (although in terms of formal training he certainly was one). Some of the notes indeed remained concise comments; but others, such as the reference to the piyyut *Lecha Dodi* (*Tagebücher* IV, 7) and the uniqueness of the Jewish people as the only "blood community" in world history (*Tagebücher* VI, 5) record the birth of ideas developed in the *Star* (SE III:332/SR, 299). Moreover, testimonies from Rosenzweig's circle of close friends indicate that his engagement in intense study of the Bible had begun in 1911, and continued throughout his study at the University of Leipzig in the spring and summer semesters 1913.[6]

3.1 Absolute Difference

Before examining Rosenzweig's reception of Maimonides, let us backtrack to consider the context in which it took shape. The dramatic turn of events of summer and autumn 1913 had left two indelible marks on Rosenzweig: he embraced Rosenstock's *Offenbarungsglaube* and rejected his claim that Christianity is the only faith through which it can be practiced (Mendes-Flohr 1988b, 5, 7). Consequently, Rosenzweig took it upon himself to assert the role of Judaism as the ultimate affirmation of faith based on revelation. A mere two months after Rosenzweig's transformation, we find him formulating these ideas with cool clarity in two letters to Hans Ehrenberg. In the first letter, of 6.12.1913, Rosenzweig points out to his cousin that his portrayal of history as a struggle between reason and faith is misguided, and that "one must and may portray [history] as the struggle between man and God" (*BT* I, 144–145). His disenchantment in the wake of Baden-Baden, Rosenzweig says, had made it impossible to think of history as biography, because it would fail to comprehend the historical totality [*geschichtliche Totalität*]. To this end, history is to be construed as framed by absolute beginning and absolute end [*absoluten Anfang und absolutes Ende*] (*BT* I, 144). Five days later, Rosenzweig makes the oft-cited declaration that Hegel was "The last of the philosophers (the way in which he perceived himself) and the first of the new Church Fathers (the way in which he did not perceive himself)" (*BT* II, 146). According to Rosenzweig, Hegel marks a crucial moment in the history of philosophy: he stands at the conclusion of a long and winding history of the rivalry between *Wissenschaft*[7] (the form of

---

6 See pp.24–25 above.
7 Glatzer 1953, xv, translates *Wissenschaft* here as "philosophy". Rosenzweig's use of this term, rather than *Philosophie*, follows Hans Ehrenberg's designation as "simply God as the Absolute", together with the simultaneous use of philosophy and science as the names of disciplines driven by the world ("*Welt betriebenen Beschäftigung*"). Rosenzweig says in the current letter that he now also holds this to be correct.

pagan thinking) and revelation (represented by the Church), throughout which they existed as coeval yet distinct activities. But the history of *Wissenschaft* and *Offenbarung* is not self-contained: it stretches between the pole of absolute beginning and absolute end, the "I am the first, and I am the last", of Isaiah 44:6 (*BT* I, 145), and its unfolding between these two poles anticipated by the "I am the alpha and the omega" of the Book of Revelation 1:8; 21:7; 22:13 (*BT* I, 145–146).

The Scholastics, Ronsenzweig avers in the letter, were the last thinkers in Church history to set themselves apart from reason, before the Church wed itself to *Wissenschaft* during the Reformation:

> Descartes, Spinoza, Leibniz did not see themselves anymore as pagans outside of the Church ... but as living, more or less vocal, heretics [*Ketzer*] in its midst. It then followed, that these heretics returned to the bosom of the Church: Kant, Fichte, Schelling, Hegel. From then on the fate of "science" is bound up with the Church ... The philosopher is no longer the *discipulus Graeciae*, whom Tertullian distinguished from the *discipulus coeli*, but simply, without reservations, a Christian.[8]

Hegel's inadequate account of God's revelation to man within his philosophical system, which Rosenzweig had already identified in the aftermath of the Baden-Baden conference, now assumes a theological dimension. The inadequacy is not only systematic: it defines the fateful bond between Church and *Wissenschaft*. The biographical approach against which Rosenzweig warned Hans Ehrenberg, turned out to be directed at "... the attempts of Lessing, Herder, Kant, and other less significant thinkers around them to present the human life of Jesus as the life of the great Teacher ... Instead of believing in the God-man, what counted was allowing oneself to be taught by the Teacher" (*Zweistromland*, 687–688/ *Theological Writings*, 11–12).

Rather than blunt Rosenzweig's interest in philosophy, his new concerns served as a whetstone for his fast-developing critique of German Idealism. And so, his work on the adaptation of his dissertation into a book, and his discovery in March 1914 of the fragment that he entitled "The Oldest System Program of German Idealism" (Glatzer 1953, 31; 364),[9] was framed by his perception of them as Christian, in the particular historical function that he outlines in his letters to Hans Ehrenberg.

---

8 *BT* I, 146–147. Translation adapted from Glatzer 1953, xv–xvi. Glatzer's presentation of these ideas is somewhat misleading, since he concludes with it his account of Rosenzweig's encounter with Rosenstock, *before* describing the events of Yom Kippur 1913. As I have emphasized in chapter 1, the fact that Rosenzweig wrote this letter *after* his decision to remain a Jew changes entirely the context in which the role of Christianity is to be understood.

9 For the circumstances of the article's composition and publication see chapter 1.

Notably, Rosenzweig expressed his concerns regarding the inadequacy of Idealism as a Christianised brand of philosophy selectively, leaving them out of his "System Program" essay. Based on careful philological analysis of the text, Rosenzweig established that the fragment was written by Hegel's hand (*Zweistromland*, 7–10), but his reading of the text led him to conclude that, "only one man in the philosophical Germany of the year 1796 possessed this youthful, victorious tone": Schelling (*Zweistromland*, 10).[10] Consequently, Rosenzweig interpreted the fragment as documenting Schelling's designation of system as the task of philosophy, and this task as the leitmotiv of his life's work (*Zweistromland*, 44).[11]

Read in light of Rosenzweig's critique of pagan and Christian philosophies, it becomes clear that the task of system and the legacy of German Idealism did not encompass the full scope of Rosenzweig's project, even at this early stage in its formation. Clearly, he would have to find elsewhere the transition from the absolute beginning into philosophy, and from philosophy into the absolute end, which he outlined in the letter of 11.12.1913.

The fragment ends with a call for

> A new mythology ... [which] must be in the service of ideas, it must be in the service of reason ... mythology must become philosophical in order to make the people rational, and philosophy must become mythological in order to make the philosophers sensible.[12]

It is hard to ignore the similarities between this passage and Rosenzweig's announcement of the need for a new type of thinker, serving the needs of both philosophy and theology (SE, 118/SR, 106).[13] Yet the resemblance does not hide the differences: in the fragment, the synthesis does not erode the primacy of reason within the system[14]; and according to Rosenzweig's interpretation, the system program sought to make "the religion of reason" [*Vernunftreligion*], originally identical with Christianity, into positive religion (*Zweistromland*, 37–38). But as the letters to Hans Ehrenberg indicate, even when conjoined with myth, reason remains for him a necessary though insufficient condition for the project's

---

10 Translation cited from Farrell Krell, Oldest Program, 3. The provenance of the fragment, however, remains controversial to this day, cf. Pollock 2009, 15 n.5.
11 This conclusion goes against the more common view in Schelling scholarship of the 1910s of his oeuvre as comprising distinct and radically different period. See Schwarcz 1978, 17–21.
12 Hegel 2002, 111. The anthology's editor neglects to attribute the fragment's discovery to Rosenzweig.
13 See chapter 1 above.
14 "... a new religion was revealed [to Schelling], whereby idealist philosophy was clad with the attire of a new mythology". *Zweistromland*, 34.

fulfillment. By now it was clear to Rosenzweig that the sufficient condition for the system's completion is revelation as documented by Scripture:

> The difference between revelation and reason is absolute. Over and against it, is the difference between Scripture and interpretation, as well as the internal different within revelation, which is entirely relative; both Scripture and interpretation are not revelation, they engage [*handeln*] exclusively with it (*Tagebücher* VI, 24).[15]

Crucially, Rosenzweig says nothing here about a need to either abolish or transcend this absolute difference between revelation and reason. In other words, they maintain a relationship characterised by radical tension ("absolute difference"). Several questions immediately come to mind: If they are not mutually exclusive, what is the nature of the relationship that reason and revelation maintain? Could the tension between them be bridged, and if so, how? To recall, Rosenzweig records this observation as he is working on his Hegel book and processing the philosophical implications of his discovery of the "System Program" fragment;[16] his practical conclusion is not to abandon his preoccupation with philosophy and dedicate his efforts to the study of revelation through the interpretation of Scripture. He does something completely different.

3.2 In Search of Bridges

This is the juncture at which Rosenzweig appears to have taken a special interest in Maimonides. In several entries written in the course of July 1914 he examines the place of the medieval thinker in the historical development of pagan and revelatory philosophies, within the same framework sketched in his letters to Hans Ehrenberg.[17] Maimonides does not emerge from the diaries as merely an historical figure, but as a thinker who interests Rosenzweig in relation to a variety of topics. His reception of the author of the *Guide of the Perplexed* emphasises his philosophical justification of God's metaphysical priority with the doctrine

---

[15] For a discussion of the implications of this diary entry on Rosenzweig's approach to Bible interpretation see chapter 4 below.
[16] As noted above, according to Glatzer (1953, 31), Rosenzweig discovered the manuscript in March 1914 and worked on the essay through May. The handwritten draft in the archive of Leo Baeck Institute New York is dated 1914, without specifying the month. AR 3001, 2/29, title page. Available at http://www.archive.org/stream/franzrosenzweig_03_reel03#page/n661/mode/1up.
[17] Indeed, the first reference to Maimonides in the diaries pretains to David Kaufmann's article "Der 'Führer' des Maimonides in der Weltliteratur", *Archiv für Geschichte der Philosophie* 9.2 (1898): 335–373. *Tagebücher* VI, 5.

known as "negative theology", a title Rosenzweig uses for the opening section of *Star* I:1, and mentions along with Maimonides three other times in the work.[18] More surprising is Rosenzweig's reference in *Star* III:2 to the messianic doctrine appearing in Hilkhot Melachim u-Milhamot (Laws of Kings and Wars), the tractate closing Maimonides' monumental halakhic codex, the Mishneh Torah. As I purport to show, the sum total of textual evidence, historical circumstances and ideational similitudes suggests that Maimonides may be cast as the emblem of Rosenzweig's Hebraic homeland, as he inspired the author of the *Star* to attempt bridging over the unbridgeable: philosophy and revelation.

3.2.1 From Parable to Myth

In an entry dated 1.7.1914, Rosenzweig reflects:

> The mythological perception [Fassung] of the notion of trial [Versuchungsbegriffes] (God tries [man] in order to know) lies, according to Maimonides, within the sphere of revelation [in den Kreis der Offenbarung], to which He draws humanity (as in Exodus 31:13[19]): God tries in order for *man* to know [Gott versucht, damit man erfahre]. This is certainly correct (Tagebücher VI, 37).

In *Moreh* III:24,[20] Maimonides designates trial in the Bible as "one of the greatest difficulties of the Law" (*Guide*, 497).[21] God's infliction of calamities on persons who have not sinned in order to increase their reward goes against the biblical principle according to which He is, "A God of faithfulness and without iniquity" (Deuteronomy 32:4), and the rabbinic dictum "no death without sin and no suffering without iniquity" (Bavli, Shabbat 55a). That is why, says Maimonides, a clarification of divine trial is in order:

> Know that the aim and meaning of all the trials mentioned in the Torah is to let people know that they ought to do or what they must believe. Accordingly the notion of a trial consists as it were in a certain act being done, the purpose being not the accomplishment of that particular act, but the latter's being a model to be imitated and followed (*Moreh* III:24; *Guide* 498).

---

18 SE, 26–26/SR, 23–24. On Maimonides' influence of Rosenzweig's discussion ad loc. see Samuelson 2006, 156–159.
19 *BT* I, 168, mistakenly refers to 31:3.
20 Reference taken from Horwitz 1987, 53 n.1.
21 Hereinafter, citations will refer to the Ibn Tibbon translation as *Moreh* and to Pines' English translation as *Guide*.

Rosenzweig designation of the משל (*mashal*)²² as mythological is indicative of his unorthodox reading of Maimonides here.²³ The elucidation of the *meshalim* of the books of the prophets is the second goal that Maimonides sets for the *Guide* in his introduction to the work.²⁴ Among these *meshalim* he emphasizes the Bible's teachings of the two sciences comprising human knowledge: physics and metaphysics.²⁵ Maimonides' use of the term *mashal* has been traditionally understood as denoting parable or allegory (J. Stern 2009, 212). However, Rosenzweig's concept of myth, which is an offshoot of Schelling's philosophy of myth, is utterly different from either parable or allegory, i.e., a text whose literal meaning is a door to hidden meanings that may be accessed if the right key is used for its interpretation. The chasm between Rosenzweig's myth and Maimonides' *mashal* is best illustrated by their reading of Song of Songs: for Rosenzweig it is a direct representation of the amorous dialogue between God and the human soul (SE, 221/*Star*, 199); for Maimonides, it is an allegory for the believer's ideal love of God.²⁶ How, then, does Rosenzweig circumvent this clash, and why?

---

22 Pines' translation as "dictum" obscures the context relevant to our discussion (*Guide*, 498). Michael Schwarz translates it as "example": Maimonides 2002, 504.
23 As it emerges from Gertrude Oppenheim's recollection (see n.4 above), Rosenzweig studied the *Guide* in Shmuel Ibn Tibbon's translation.
24 "This Treatise also has a second purpose: namely, the explanation of very obscure parables [*meshalim*] occurring in the books of the prophets, but not explicitly identified there as such. Hence an ignorant or heedless individual might think that they possess only an external sense, but no internal one. However, even when one who truly possesses knowledge considers these parables and interprets them according to their external meaning, he too is overtaken by great perplexity. But if we explain these parables to him or if we draw his attention to their being parables, he will take the right road and be delivered from this perplexity. That is why I have called this Treatise 'The Guide of the Perplexed'" (*Guide*, 6).
25 "We have already explained in our legal compilations some general propositions concerning this subject and have drawn attention to many themes. Thus we have mentioned there that מעשה בראשית [*ma'aseh beresheet*] is identical with natural science, and מעשה מרכבה [*ma'aseh merkavah*] with divine science; and have explained the rabbinic saying: *ma'aseh merkavah* ought not to be taught even to one man, except if he be wise and able to understand by himself ... only the chapter heading may be transmitted to him ... Know that with regard to natural matters as well, it is impossible to give a clear exposition when teaching some of their principles as they are ... Hence these matters too occur in parables in the books of prophecy. The sages of blessed memory ... likewise have spoken of them in riddles and parables ..." *Guide*, Introduction, 6–7. Translation altered.
26 Maimonides, *Mishneh Torah*, *Hilkhot Teshuva* 10:3; *Moreh* II: 43, 45, 47; III: 33, 51, 54. For a discussion of Maimonides' philosophical interpretation of Song of Songs and its impact on later medieval readings see Rosenberg 1990, 138–141. On medieval, post-Maimonidean allegorical readings of the scroll see Talmage 1986.

Schelling identified symbolism as the form of representation (*Darstellung*) in which the general and the particular become an absolute unity (*wo beide absolut eins sind*) (Schelling, SW I/5, 407), and mythology as the only discourse in which symbolism may attain its full realization (Schelling, SW I/6, 67). He juxtaposes this theoretical framework upon two mythological traditions, which his new mythology would aim to integrate: Greek, pagan mythology, whose material (*Stoff*) is nature, and hence provides an outlook on the universe as nature; and Christian mythology, whose material the general outlook on the universe is manifested in history, i.e., as a world of providence (*als einer Welt der Vorsehung*) (Schelling, SW I/5, 407).[27]

Up to this point Rosenzweig's Maimonides appears to anticipate the vision of the "System Program": the myth of divine trial serves the dual purpose of making the masses more rational, and the philosophers more sensible.[28] What is more, its purpose is didactic: "The purpose ... [to offer] a model [*mashal*] to be imitated and followed" (*Moreh* III:24, *Guide*, 498).

Aware of the insufficient grounding that his philosophical interpretation provides, however, Maimonides supplements it with biblical prooftexts (Genesis 22:12; Deuteronomy 13:4; 8:2; 13:4). Out of these, Rosenzweig singles out Exodus 31:13 as expressing Maimonides' grounding of myth within "the sphere of revelation": "That you may know that I, the LORD, sanctify you". The foundation of Jewish myth, Rosenzweig implies, runs deeper than either reason, nature, or history; it is the sanctification of the People of Israel enunciated by the God of the Bible: He who is First and Last, Who was before pagan philosophy came into being and will prevail after Christian philosophy reaches its consummation. Therefore, Rosenzweig could not possibly consider Schelling's philosophy of myth as the fulfillment of the "System Program's" call for a new mythology. As my reading of the diary entry suggests, Rosenzweig found in Maimonides a third, more enduring, mythological tradition: revelation in the Hebrew Bible.

---

27 Schwarcz 1978, 45–46. Schwarcz's account is based on the section entitled "*Ableitung der Mythologie als Stoffs der Kunst*", from Schelling's *Philosophie der Kunst*, lectures he gave in Jena on winter 1802–1803, and in Würzburg in 1804 and 1805. Cf. Schelling, *SW* I/5, 388–407.
28 Menachem Lorberbaum proposes to describe Maimonides' epistemology of the divine as "rationalistic mysticism". It would be intriguing to compare this concept with the "philosophical mythology" of the "System Program", but such an inquiry exceeds the scope of the current work. See Lorberbaum 2011, 33–36, esp. 33 n.74 for a bibliography.

3.2.2 From Creation to Revelation

In entries recorded on July 11th and 18th, 1914, Rosenzweig elaborates on Maimonides' contribution to philosophy's outgrowing its pagan elements:

> "Plato" and "Aristotle" maintain [*erhalten*] the (negated or affirmed) *concept of God* through the presupposition [*Voraussetzung*] of the world, always with the *World*; Maimonides and later Hegel in opposition to the (negated) presupposition of the *negated* world, do so through the presupposition of *God*. It is in Hegel, that Maimonides is addressed successfully for the first time in the history of philosophy; for Thomas [Aquinas] and medieval thinkers, [Maimonides'] addressing of the concept of creation was merely a truer [*Meister*] Eckhart, a scarf, a buffer against the perishable influence of pre-Christian philosophy. Therefore, it is what Schelling says in [the concept of] the I, the "original [*ursprüngliche*] form of all possible synthesis" is "the affirmation of non-being through being" [*Bestimmung des Nichtseins durch das Sein*] (*BT* I, 170).[29]

A week later, on July 18th he observes:

> Is the unity of reason and will in God, the way Maimonides establishes it (God wills only the rational – His will is not arbitrary – God does not "rectify" [*richtung*] His will in accordance with the (rational) Aristotelian? [This is] impossible. This question is completely irrelevant, because for Aristotle, as for pagan thought as a whole, being the willing subject goes against God's essence, (God is loved, He does not love). This is well until an attempt is made to bring together God as reason (Greek philosophy) with God as will (revelation) …
>
> The [Aristotelian-Averroesian] task of rationalising reality … remains, however, unresolved, as long as God's rationality is grounded in the simple negation of the world's reality. *It first became possible with the scheme of double negation.* Thus Maimonides perhaps intervened further, not indeed with his later metaphysical synthesis, but with the idea in which he conceived God's creative powers (not as His essence – this is his later synthesis–) (but) as an attribute of His essence.
>
> Schelling, on the true concept of the philosophy of nature and the correct way, resolved this problem (*BT* I, 171–172. My italics).

Rosenzweig's Maimonides is a medieval precursor of Hegel and Schelling, the post-pagan philosophers, who countered the world-negating philosophy of Plato, Aristotle, and their medieval followers, among whom Rosenzweig includes Shlomo Ibn Gabirol (*BT* I, 171). In this historical process, sketched already in the letter of 11.12.1913, Rosenzweig identifies Maimonides' three major contributions to the development of philosophy, as all derived from his theory of cre-

---

[29] The current and the following entries are missing from *Tagebücher* and hence their references pertain to *BT*.

ation: God's premordiality; "the scheme of double negation"; and the assertion of God's free will. According to this overtly Hegelian analysis of Rosenzweig's, Maimonides' place in the history of philosophy meant that he would not lead reason to its ultimate consummation. Rosenzweig sees the scholastics (Jewish as well as Christian) as the thinkers who established a theory of revelation grounded in reason-compatible, knowable truths (*vernunftgemäß erkennbaren Wahrheiten*; *Tagebücher* VI, 6–7).

Reason-compatible theories of the origin of the world ("*jeder 'vernunftgemäßen' Theorie des Ursprungs der Welt*") are also at the focus of the section entitled "The Logic of Creation vs. The Logic of the Idea", in *Star* II:1 (SE, 153–155/SR, 138–140).[30] Their inadequacy, says Rosenzweig, derives from two mistakes:
1. Intrinsically, they posit the world as antecedent to God. Expressed algebraically as A=B, reason-compatible theories of creation reverse the logic of grammar by applying the particular (*das Besondere*)—World—as a predicate of the universal (*das Allgemeine*) subject—God—and hence they are the theories that Rosenzweig had identified with pagan *Wissenschaft* in the letters and diary entries discussed above, which are based on a presupposition of the world: "Thus the particular becomes the pre-supposition [*Voraus-setzung*] of universal being [*das allgemeinen Daseins*]" (SE, 153/SR, 138).
2. Extrinsically, these theories are self-defeating because they incorporate only two of the elements, world and God. Remaining within the limits of a purely ontological discourse, they are inevitably confronted with the formidable problem of creation *ex nihilo*. The system of the *Star* avoids these problems by constructing "the concept of creation out of the [three] elements as they emerged from themselves ... To put it less formulaically, *we developed the idea of creation in the light of revelation*" (SE, 154/SR, 139. My italics).

The idea of creation in the light of revelation is indeed developed some twenty pages earlier, where Rosenzweig openly expresses his indebtedness to Maimonides, whom he crowns as "the great Jewish theoretician of revelation":

> And so in the genuine [*echte*] idea of revelation, the three "actual" elements of the All—God world man—emerge from themselves, belong to one another in opposing the assertion of the Creator's arbitrariness [*Willkür*]. And so it was precisely in this point that Maimonides, the great Jewish theoretician of revelation, diverged from Arabic Scholasticism and, with utmost decisiveness, asserted God's creativity [*Schöpfertum*] as his essential attribute and

---

[30] Hallo's translation of *vernunftgemäß* as "reasonable" connotes commonsense, whereas both in the diary and in the *Star* Rosenzweig wishes to emphasise the inadequacy of Reason, *Vernunft*, as the ground of a theory of creation.

even developed the entire doctrine of the attributes of divine essence in clear methodological alignment [*Angleichung*] with this attribute of creative power [*schöpferische Macht*] (SE, 126/SR, 115).³¹

Finally, we come across direct evidence that Rosenzweig's interest in Maimonides was not merely historical; it made a decisive contribution to his move *past* the Idealist concept of creation by asserting that it is simultaneously creative and revelatory. Granted, Rosenzweig's reading of Maimonides' theory of creation is nothing less than iconoclastic. As he himself observed in a diary entry cited below, revelation was for the medieval thinker the point where his rationalism ended.³² And yet, in following up the references to the *Guide* in the condensed summary of *Star* II:1 it becomes evident that Rosenzweig found Maimonides' work highly instructive in working out the reciprocal relations of critique and supplementation between philosophy and Scripture, which enabled him to build his own bridge across the absolute difference between reason and revelation. I would like to emphasise once more that I am making this claim in spite of the limited interest Rosenzweig showed in Maimonides, and most importantly, while acknowledging the fundamental differences between the two thinkers. However, the sum total of direct references, correlations, the timing of the diary entries, and not least Rosenzweig's uncharacteristic expressions of admiration for Maimonides in the *Star*, all imply that his encounter with the legacy of the Great Eagle in all likelihood had profound impact on him.

Maimonides' assertion of divine will, in opposition to the arbitrary deity conjured up by "Arabic Scholasticism", and its transformation into "attributes of action", occur in a liminal zone between the words of Scripture and the limits of reason, where philosophy is unable to provide an argument anchored in sound proof (Maimonides' example for such an argument is God's incorporeality). The negation of attributes exposed Maimonides to the risk of ending up with an arbitrary and passive unmoved mover, which stands in stark contradiction with the active and involved God that the Bible describes. Maimonides addresses this problem in *Moreh* I:50–55, where he makes a distinction between attributes of action denoting contingency, and attributes of action denoting essence.³³ The latter category of attributes serves to explain how the Bible's de-

---

31 Translation altered.
32 For a radical anti-anthropomorphic theology such as that of Maimonides, explicit accounts of revelation posed one of the greatest threats to his position. See for example Klein-Braslavi 2011, 202–205.
33 "... the diverse actions proceed from one simple essence in which no multiplicity is posited and to which no notion is superadded. Every attribute that is found in the books of the deity,

scription of different divine acts is consistent with God's perfection, unity and incorporeality.

Yet, the very reason why Maimonides enters this discussion is philosophy's failure to produce demonstrable proof for the nature of creation: had there been one, Maimonides would have been able to arrive at the nature of the deity by making a logical inference: creation *ex-nihilo* would mean that God was moved to action and His essence is therefore arbitrary; whereas the eternality of the world means that Genesis 1 describes creation out of free will. This problem is addressed in *Moreh* II:25–27: the Arisotetlian theory is simply antithetical to the biblical account of creation, and therefore must be rejected[34]; the Platonic theory of the eternality of the world is compelling in light of its congruence with Scripture, but lacks demonstrable proof, and therefore cannot be accepted.[35] Maimonides' conclusion is that we are forced to read Genesis 1 literally, and to refrain from interpreting it according to known philosophical theories.[36] And so, contrary to philosophers' claims to having successfully deduced God's essence from a theory of creation, the Bible's description of God's creative powers has no privileged epistemological status over any other biblical account of divine actions.

Finally, Rosenzweig's praise for Maimonides as the great theoretician of revelation begins to appear less odd. God's creative power may have driven the medieval thinker to develop the theory of attributes of action, but under this theory creation sheds the privileged position accorded by philosophers, and becomes coeval with God's other actions. In other words, creation is no longer considered on its own; it is considered in the light of revelation.

---

may He be exalted, is therefore an attribute of His action and not an attribute of His essence, or it is indicative of absolute perfection" (*Moreh*, I:53; Guide, 121).

34 "... the belief in eternity the way Aristotle sees it ... destroys the Law in its principle ... and reduces to inanity all the hopes and threats that the Law has held out "... (*Moreh* II:25; Guide, 328).

35 "... the opinion of Plato ... would not destroy the foundation of the Torah ... However, no necessity could impel us to do this unless this opinion were demonstrated" (*Moreh* II:25; Guide, 328–329). Translation altered.

36 "In view of the fact that it has not been demonstrated, we shall not favour this opinion, nor shall we at all heed that other opinion, but rather shall take the texts according to their external sense and shall say: the Torah has given us knowledge of a matter the grasp of which is not within our power, and the miracle attests to the correctness of our claims" (*Moreh* II.25; Guide, 329). Translation altered.

Tab. 3.1: The *Guide of the Perplexed* in the *Star of Redemption*

Star of Redemption	*Guide of the Perplexed*
1. SE, 154 /SR, 139: Idealism ... possesses the sense that it must solve the riddle of the world here ... For it cannot grant validity to anything outside of the world and of knowledge. It must at all costs place these elements ... into a rational relationship.	II: 25: In view of the fact that it has not been demonstrated, we shall not favour this opinion, nor shall we at all heed that other opinion, but rather shall take the texts according to their external sense and shall say: The *Torah* has given us knowledge of a matter the grasp of which is not within our power, and the miracle attests to the correctness of our claims. (p.329)
Postulate: In the beginning God created	
2. SE, 155/SR, 139: We can freely allow the concept of creation to count as a beginning of knowledge, without bringing everything to a conclusion in it. We put it in the larger context of revelation	I:53: Most of these attributes are attributes pertaining to His diverse actions. Now there need not be a diversity in the notions subsisting in an agent because of the diversity of his various actions [...] (p.120) We shall mention that as to which all of them agree and consider to be cognized by the intellect and in which case there is no need to follow the text of the word of a prophet. There are four attributes: living, possessing power, possessing knowledge, possessing will [...] (pp.121–122). Rather have these attributes been thought of in reference to the diverse relations that may obtain between God, may He be exalted, and the things created by him. For He possesses the power to create what He created, and possesses the power to bring into being that which exists in the manner in which He has brought it into being [...](p.122)
3. SE, 155/SR, 140: Creation cannot therefore be simply placed alongside of the concept of generation ... Creation is at home in the land of revelation ...	II:30: [...] the four words that occur with reference to the relation between the heaven and God. These words are אל, קנה, עשה, ברא [*el, kanah, assa, bara*]. It says, 'God created the heaven and the earth' ... As for the word יצירה [*yetzirah*], it does not occur in this sense; for it seems to me that *yetzirah* is only applied to shaping and forming a configuration or to one of the other accidents (p.358).

3.2.3 From Rationalism to Revelation

In early July 1914, Rosenzweig comments on Maimonides' methodology of biblical interpretation:

> Maimonides' rationalism is so far-reaching, that he is aware that he may follow the old Amora: reading into the Torah any and all ideas. In contrast, he does not think about the concept of revelation any further, and this is also where his rationalism ends (*BT* I, 169).

Maimonides' method of biblical interpretation has been the subject of innumerable studies and commentaries, from his lifetime to this very day.[37] Unfortunately the brevity of Rosenzweig's comment makes it impossible to identify the sources (if any) on which he drew, making comparative discussions with other receptions of Maimonides as biblical interpreter highly speculative. Nonetheless, this fact does not detract from the premise regarding its pithy impact on Rosenzweig's approach to biblical interpretation. Indeed, read alongside the diary entry of 23.6. 1914 discussed above it becomes immediately clear that Rosenzweig reads Maimonides within the framework of the absolute difference between revelation and reason outlined therein.

In spite of Maimonides' far-reaching rationalism ("*geht so weit*"), which he applies to all ideas ("*jeden beliebigen Gedanken*") in the Torah by following the precedent set by Talmudic exegesis, he places revelation outside the limits of rationalism. And so, even though Rosenzweig's Maimonides "does not think of the concept of revelation [*über den Begriff der Offenbarung*] any further", revelation is not placed outside the limits of discussion.

As a student of Hermann Cohen, Rosenzweig's encounter with Maimonides was framed by his image as "the wise and clear guide of our rationalism" (H Cohen 1924, 173).[38] In his comment on Maimonides' biblical interpretation, however, Rosenzweig disagrees with Cohen. In addition, Rosenzweig acquired from his celebrated teacher at the *Lehranstalt* guidance through the chapters in the *Guide* presenting its authors' negative theology (I:50–59), central to Cohen's reading of Maimonides later in the *Religion der Reinen Vernunft* (Kohler 2012, 183–184).

The concluding sentence of the above diary entry, asserting that revelation is where Maimonides' rationalism ends, indicates that Rosenzweig finds a strong tension in Maimonides between radical rationalism, which dominates his inter-

---

[37] For a few examples relevant to the current context see Rosenberg 1981; Harvey 1980; Ravitzky 1991; Robinson 2009; Fraenkel 2009; Kohler.
[38] Cited in: Hyman 2005, 358.

pretation of Scripture, and a non-rational discourse, which he is forced to adopt with regards to revelation. This observation is probably made in reference to Maimonides' distinction in *Moreh* I:59 between the attainability of knowledge of God's existence, and the unattainability of God's essence (Davidson 2011, 189):

> ... all men, those of the past and those of the future, affirm clearly that God, may He be exalted, cannot be apprehended by the intellects, and that none but He Himself can apprehend what He is, and that apprehension of Him consists in the inability to attain the ultimate term in apprehending Him. Thus all the philosophers say: *We are dazzled by His beauty, and He is hidden from us* because of the intensity with which He becomes manifest, just as the sun is hidden to eyes that are too weak to apprehend it ... The most apt phrase concerning this subject is the dictum occurring in the Psalms, 'Silence is praise to thee...' (*Moreh* I:59; Guide 139).

Unlike Kant's *Ding an sich*, or Wittgenstein's silence, and even in spite of Maimonides' own advice to exercise silence as the highest form of praise, Rosenzweig does not place God behind an impregnable veil. The sun analogy in *Moreh* I:59 could have been taken merely as a didactic device, if it was not for the utterance placed in the mouths of the philosophers: "*We are dazzled by his beauty*".[39] Beyond the boundary Maimonides circumscribes for philosophy, God's sublimity as the ultimate being emanates as blinding, dazzling beauty. This somewhat mystical, Plotinian description suggests that the impermeable barrier separating God from the grasp of the human intellect is in some ambiguous sense permeable.[40]

Evidence in the *Star* suggests that Rosenzweig's reception of these ideas percolated into his work. Maimonides' equivocation of the attainable knowledge in relation to God, albeit in the attenuated version of *Moreh* I:59, is uncharacteristically cited with attribution to its author and source: "No man has the power to grasp the thought of the Creator for 'his ways are not our ways and his thoughts are not our thoughts'".[41] Maimonides' derivative conclusion in *Moreh* I:59 that the best form of praise for God is to practice silence, appears to find an echo in Rosenzweig's equating the silence of liturgy with consummated understanding (*vollendeten Verstehen*s; SE, 328/SR 295). In the introduction to *Star* III, Ro-

---

[39] For literature on parallels and influences see Maimonides 2002, 148–149, n.13; Altmann 1987, 122, n.99.
[40] For a discussion of the ambiguities in Maimonides' definition of the limits of knowledge, see Pines 1979, 82–109; esp. 89–100.
[41] The attribution appears later in the sentence: "This description of God's ways concludes the great survey of the entire contents of oral and written law which Maimonides has presented to us as the 'Repetition of the Law'" (SE, 373/SR, 336). The citation is from Maimonides *Mishneh Torah, Hilkhot Melachim u-Milkhamot* 11:4. Compare the reference to Yehudah Halevy's allegory of the seed and tree from *Kuzari* IV:24, in SE, 422 /SR, 379.

senzweig explains that the progression from mathematical symbols in Part One, which "represented something past, the a priori heirlooms of a prior creation", over to the forms of grammar in Part Two, which "express miracle directly ... manifest signs of a manifest world", directed the reader to the forms of liturgy (*die Gestalten der Liturgik*) of Part Three, which "... are the light, by which we see light. They are the silent anticipation of a world gleaming in the silence of the future" (SE, 327–328/SR, 294–295). The Maimonidean context becomes clear soon thereafter. The future in which the silence of consummated understanding will prevail, is of course the *redemptive* future. Since "Nothing shows so clearly that the world is unredeemed as the diversity of languages" (SE, 328/SR, 295),[42] the foremost manifestation of that future shall be the "'purified lip' which is promised for 'that day' to the peoples divided by language [*sprachgeschiedenen Völkern*]" (SE, 329/SR, 296).[43] This quote from Zephaniah 3:9 reappears in the above-mentioned reference to the *Mishneh Torah*, in a passage in which Rosenzweig endorses Maimonides' account of the messianic future according to which the Zephaniah prooftext and Daniel 11:14 articulate the preparatory stages that will lead to the worship of God by "the whole world" at the End of Days.

3.2.4 From Christ Back to the Prophets

In addition to the "System Program" and *The Ages of the World*, another work of Schelling's contributed to the long gestation of the *Star*. More precisely, it is the closing sentence of the work, the *Stuttgart Private Lectures* (Schelling SW I/7, 417–484), which Rosenzweig turns into a watchword: "[Then God will be in reality] all in all [and pantheism will be true]".[44] Originally from I Corinthians 15:28,[45] the phrase "all in all" (*Alles in Allem*) is cited only twice in Rosenzweig's writings with a reference, both times to the New Testament rather than Schelling.[46] What is more, studies that attribute the citation to Schelling,[47] rely on Alexander Altmann's association of Rosenzweig's use of the phrase with the phi-

---

42 Compare diary entry dated 27.15.1915 (*BT* I, 183) where Rosenzweig leaves the phrase untranslated.
43 Translation altered.
44 "[*Dann ist Gott wirklich*] *Alles in Allem*, [*der Pantheismus wahr*]". Schelling SW I/7, 484.
45 "And when all things shall be subdued unto him, then shall the Son also himself be subject unto him that put all things under him, *that God may be all in all*".
46 *Zweistromland*, 91; *BT* II, 775.
47 Schwarcz, 1978, 306–307; Horwitz, 1987, 236, n.2; Pollock, 2009, 228–229, n.24.

losopher, which in itself is based on circumstantial evidence.⁴⁸ In light of this rather shaky connection, it would seem advisable to heed Bienenstock's cautioning against reading into the *Star* the influence of Schelling works that Rosenzweig had probably never read.⁴⁹ Yet, in this particular instance, even if was not directly derived from the *Private Lectures*, Rosenzweig's use of the phrase in the *Star* is overtly Schellingian. It demarcates the final limit of reason as the organon of both philosophy and Christian theology, and points at the path that lies beyond this boundary, with Maimonides as his guide. Thus, in a sense, Rosenzweig's repeated reference to the New Testament's vision of "all in all" may be seen as the ultimate example for his synthesis between philosophical system and scriptural exegesis.

From its first mention in his writings (*BT* I, 134–135), "all in all" appears to epitomise for Rosenzweig the consummation of Christian eschatology. No doubt still overwhelmed by the tantalising experience of Yom Kippur 1913, Rosenzweig wrote to Rudolph Ehrenberg a short time thereafter:

> Christianity acknowledges the God of the Jews, not as God but as the "Father of Jesus Christ". Christianity itself cleaves to the "Lord" because it knows that the Father can only be reached through him. With his church, he remains "the Lord" for all time until the end of the world, but then he will cease to be the Lord, and he too will be subject to the Father who will, on this day, be all in all [I Corinthians 15:28]. We are wholly agreed as to what Christ and his church mean to the world: no one can reach the Father save through him [John 1:46]. No one can reach the Father! But the situation is quite different for one who does not have to reach the Father because he is already with him. And this is now the case of the People of Israel (not of individual Jews) (*BT* I, 134–135).⁵⁰

For the Church, he tells Ehrenberg, the God of Israel is a means to the end of final unification of Christ with God, which will conclude with God "being all in all". Notably, the context in which this is argued is strictly theological. The passage was written only a day after Rosenzweig wrote to Ehrenberg of his decision to remain a Jew, and was included in that same letter. The reply, penned immediately thereafter (*BT* I, 138–140),⁵¹ makes it clear that the cousins were pre-

---

48 Altmann 1988, 136–137 n.87, provides the reference to the *Private Lectures* and cites Paul Tillich's positing of Schelling's claim as the consummation of his system in Tillich 1912, 121.
49 Bienenstock 2004, 275 and n.8 ibid. Bienenstock notes this in relation to *Philosophie der Offenbarung*, which is enthusiastically compared with the *Star* in Betz 2003.
50 Translated in Glatzer 1953, 341. Translation altered.
51 By 1913, Ehrenberg, who had converted in 1909, was a practicing pastor. Therefore the citation without reference, like several others in the letter, referred to I Corinthians 15:28.

occupied with Rosenzweig's religious identity and its impact on his view on Christian theology.

Two semesters at the *Lehranstalt* later, Rosenzweig was able to reflect on his schematic argument in the context of Jewish interpretations of the redemptive future. Unlike the Christian who must wait for the End of Days to witness the actualisation of "all in all", says Rosenzweig, the Jew, according to Maimonides' and Cohen's interpretations of the New Year's prayer, grounds the idea of the redemptive future as pure and moral [*so rein und moralisch gefaßt sein*]. This is possible in virtue of the perception that the redemptive future is present in Jewish life here and now:[52]

> What covers the all-year-round presence of [God's] judgment of the world for us? That we are "already at the destination" [*schon am Ziel*].[53] This is why we may ground the concept of future in the present so pure and moral (Maimonides! Cohen!), because the End of Days is perceived religiously as already part of the present [*gegenwärtig*]. The אחד [*ehad*] on the closing prayer[54] contains what for the Christian may lie in *Alles in Allem* for the first time at the earth's end ... (*Tagebücher* VI, 30).

Alles in Allem will serve Rosenzweig's system as a corollary to the Jewish concept of redemption rather than as the encapsulation of its redemptive consummation, was made clear in his letter to Rudolph Ehrenberg of 18.11.1917. Outlining the system of the *Star* in, Rosenzweig chooses the phrase "*Eins und Alles*" (One and All) (*Zweistromland*, 136/*Theological Writings*, 66) to describe God's permeating the relations between the three elements—God, humans, world—in the redemptive future. Rosenzweig uses the phrase to express his allegiance to the Idealist vision of the communion between Spirit and reality as the consummation of the philosophical system (*Theological Writings*, 66–67 n.44.) This allegiance is not without reservations: the letter's reference to *Eins und Alles* is an invocation of the Greek *Hen kai pan* (lit. "one and all"), a phrase that as students at the *Tübingen Stift* Hegel, Schelling and Friedrich Hölderlin adopted to express their

---

[52] H. Cohen, 1988 (First edition published 1919), 360–361. Maimonides, *Mishneh Torah, Hilkhot Teshuvah* 8:8. In the *Star*, Rosenzweig developed a more elaborate variation on this idea, whereby the individual's standing before God to receive judgment on Yom Kippur is the moment in the yearly cycle when redemption is brought into the present, dropping, however, the allusions to Maimonides and Cohen (SE, 359–364/SR, 323–327).
[53] Cf. SE, 365: "Seine Welt ist am Ziel".
[54] The prayer concluding worship on Yom Kippur, the *Ne'ilah*.

shared subversive belief in pantheism (Baeumer 1967, 131–133)[55]; yet Rosenzweig does not interpret the systems of either Hegel or Schelling as founded on a purely pantheistic vision. For him, the Idealists' motto retains God's integrity and distinctness as the One, which the All joins as the system reaches its full consummation; hence, even as the All is subsumed under Him, God remains distinct from nature and their unity is not a complete fusion of elements. This may be gleaned from the fact that *Eins und Alles* does not reappear in the *Star*, whereas *Alles in Allem* is employed to mark the farthest outpost on the Christian road to redemption. Indeed, Rosenzweig concedes the temptation to embrace it as the final destination of his path:

> Only at the end of history there looms the prospect of a kingdom free of struggle and contradiction in which God will be all-in-all … To comprehend this wealth fully within itself, Christianity had to walk the two separate but parallel ways, the way of the state and the way of the church, and these meet there at the end of all history (SE, 446/SR 401).

This description is reminiscent of Schelling's account of the meeting of state and church at the end of history upon God's attainment of unity in the Stuttgart Lectures:

> The state stands as an attempt to bring about a completely different unity [to the unity of nature and God], grounded in revelation, against another institution, which proceeds to bring about [God's unity] internally or the unity of feeling [*Gemüthseinheit*]: the Church (Schelling, SW I/7, 464).[56]

But instead of unity, Rosenzweig warns, Christianity's yearning for God being all in all leads to three inevitable dangers: (1) making either the world divine [*Weltvergötterung*] or God worldly [*Gottverweltlichung*]; (2) forgetting the One above all in favour of all-in-all; (3) forfeiting the free, self-renewing soul in order to unite the worldly division between particular and universal.[57] This "threefold parting

---

55 In all likelihood, they adopted *Hen kai pan* from Friedrich Heinrich Jacobi's indictment against Spinoza's pantheism (and Gotthold Ephraim Lessing's avid support thereof) in *Über die Lehre des Spinoza, in Briefen an Moses Mendelssohn*. (Baeumer 1967, 131–132).
56 The plausibility that Rosenzweig is referring to Schelling's work increases, when considered alongside Rosenzweig's earlier description of state and church as defined by a relation of rivalry, which does not lead to any form of unity. See SE, 390–392/SR, 352–353.
57 Rosenzweig, SE, 446/SR, 401. In the next section, "The Christian Dangers", Rosenzweig defines them as follows: that Spirit, and not God, will lead all of the ways; that the Son of God will be the truth and not God; that God will be All-in-All and not one above all. SE, 447/ SR, 402.

of ways", as Rosenzweig designates it, also marks his parting of ways with Schelling.

The abstract facade of Rosenzweig's prose covers over (mostly) Jewish sources whose interpretation produced the argument put forth in the text. The return from Christ back to the prophets as a systematic conclusion is no exception. In this case as well, it was inspired by Maimonides.

3.2.5 The End of Days

The reference to the *Mishneh Torah* in *Star* III:2 is an oddity. As we have seen, although the *Guide of the Perplexed* served the construction of Rosenzweig's system more than the *Mishneh Torah*, he did not mention the philosophical treatise by name in the *Star*. The Halakhic compendium's listing and classification of the whole of Jewish law is worlds apart from Rosenzweig's mode of thought. And yet, Maimonides' compendium not only receives open recognition, rare in the *Star*; Rosenzweig's citation of *Hilkhot Melachim* 11:4 indicates that he did not rely on the standard print editions available at the time, Warsaw or Vilna (Maimonides 1900).[58] The passage cited in the *Star* is famous for its polemic against the messianic visions of Christianity and Islam. The volatile potential of its dismissal of Christ and Mohammed as false messiahs led to varying censorships and emendations that eliminated the references to "Christ" and "the Ishmaelite" (Mohammed the Prophet) (Maimonides 1955, 13), or expunged altogether the closing paragraph of the tractate's chapter. Rosenzweig paraphrases the version we know from the modern print edition (Maimonides 1962).[59] Most likely, he had access to one of the more mildly censored editions, such as Rome or Constantinople (Maimonides 1972), from which the references to ישוע (*Yeshu'a*) were omitted but those to Mohammed the Prophet were retained. Even with Jesus *in absentio*, the polemical tenor of Maimonides' messianic theory was not lost on Rosenzweig, who heightened tensions by placing it as the introduction to his account of the Christian liturgical year. Read alongside his sweeping rejection of all-in-all later on in the *Star*, *Hilkhot Melachim* appears to have provided Rosenzweig with the biblical prooftexts necessary to refute the three dangers he identifies in Christianity:

---

58 Schwarcz notes this in *Kokhav*, 327.
59 Beginning in *Hilchot Melachim* 10:3, the editor notes numerous discrepancies between manuscripts, stating that he added the censured passages by relying on the Yemen manuscript. See 515, nn.31, 33.

1. Maimonides' paraphrasing of Isaiah 55:8, "His ways are not our ways and His thoughts are not our thoughts",[60] explains why God cannot be all-in-all and can only be One above All.
2. Daniel's (11:4) castigation of the false vision of the "renegade sons" [abtrünnige Sohne] that fail to apprehend the fullness of the vision [zu erfüllen die Gesichte] warns against seeing truth in Christ and not in God.
3. Zephaniah's (3:9) call for worshipping God with "purified lips" [geläuterte Lippen] prevents the possibility of following the lead of Spirit, instead of God (SE, 373/SR, 336).

Above all else, this passage provides a rare example of Rosenzweig directly borrowing a long passage from another source, almost verbatim: Maimonides' methodology of basing a philosophical argument on biblical prooftext, or in other words, creating the synthesis between system and Scripture. We have already seen in chapter 1, Rosenzweig linking his original readings of Genesis 16:13 and Leviticus 20:6 with broader philosophical concerns, which also found their way into the *Star*. In the current passage, the *Mishneh Torah*'s intertwining of Isaiah 55:8, Daniel 11:4 and Zephaniah 3:9 functions as a litmus test for the truthfulness or falsity of statements regarding the End of Days. Thus, the distinctions made in the passage prepare the ground for the parting of ways between Judaism and Christianity, which Rosenzweig will describe later on in the same part of the *Star*.

By placing his trust in Maimonides in this context, Rosenzweig makes two uncharacteristic gestures: 1) He adds a laudation hailing the medieval thinker as "the great teacher", and the *Mishneh Torah* as "the great survey of the teachings of oral and written Torah" (SE, 373/SR, 336)[61]; 2) he adopts Maimonides' contrasting of the false redemptive promises of Jesus and Mohammed with the figure of the "King Messiah" destined to stand and restore the kingship of the House of David of old" (*Hilkhot Melachim* 11:1). While the former gesture is anecdotal, the latter gesture introduces a substantive argument, which does not quite fit Rosenzweig's own conception of redemption. In the *Star* redemption is a state of almost total abstraction, as differences dissolve during the near-convergence of the three elements—humans, world and God—at the conclusion of the system's actualization. According to Maimonides, redemption will be brought about by a messianic figure, "King Messiah", who will trigger a series of dramatic transformations: "[he will] reinstate the House of David's first government of old,

---

[60] Cf. "For my thoughts are not your thoughts: nor your ways my ways, says the Lord".
[61] Translation altered.

build the temple, and bring back the exiles of Israel. And the Law will be put back in place in his day. Making sacrifices, and practicing *shmitah*[62] and jubilees as commanded in the Torah". Moreoever, Maimonides stresses that this vision is the only true scenario, to the point of casting objectors and sceptics as "not only misbelievers in the other prophets, but in the Torah and Moses our Teacher". Although Rosenzweig does acknowledge the place of Messiah son of David in Jewish eschatology elsewhere (SE, 253, 341; SR, 227, 307), he can hardly be said to do so within the framework of an elaborate reiteration of the Maimonidean dictum.

The importance of this passage cannot be overstated: it discloses a key methodology Rosenzweig employs in melding together the concerns of philosophy and theology within his system, which distinctively belongs to his Hebraic homeland. His indebtedness to Maimonides illustrated in this chapter may serve to explain this messianic excursus. Practically all of the examples analysed in this book reflect the literary elegance and philosophical precision with which the verses from Isaiah, Daniel and Zephaniah are intertwined to form a forceful argument. Rosenzweig's innovation was to practice this tradtional technique within the context of a modern philosophical discourse, with interlocutors such as Hegel, Schelling and Kant. In view of the aggregate evidence presented above, Maimonides appears to have provided the inspiration and practical guidance for Rosenzweig's application of this technique, pointing at the trail that would lead him to his Hebraic intellectual homeland.

3.3 On the Threshold

The *Schwelle*, the Threshold between parts II and III of the *Star*, is a short interlude in which Rosenzweig embosses into the text the figure of the Star of Redemption that has lain sunken in the background until that point. Highly abstract, devoid of allusions to Jewish sources, and bedecked with citations from Goethe and Schiller (SE, 283–291/SR, 254–261), this section offers a summary of the progression from the critique of philosophy and the division of the All into the three elements, via the introduction of the three divine acts, to eternity, which is about to be explored in Part III. Rosenzweig analogises the Hegelian system to a sphere that abides by the laws of mathematics and thus is constructed in relation to a single point of reference, which dictates its debilitating self-contained and self-absorbed nature (SE, 283/SR, 255).

---

[62] *Shmitah:* the commandment of ceasing from agricultural cultivation of farmland in the Land of Israel every seven years (Leviticus 25:2–8).

The shape of the Star, made up of two superimposed triangles, is geometrical in an aesthetic, rather than mathematical sense. Rosenzweig employs this symbolic function in order to assert that the Star is not a figure (*Figur*), but a configuration, or form (*Gestalt*) (SE, 284/SR, 256). The extraction of these figures from the relativity of mathematics and their transformation into absolute configurations became possible by the conclusion of Part Two, as we recognised (*erkannten*), "God as Creator and Revealer, the world ... as Created [*Geschöpf*][63] and man ... as beloved" (SE, 286/SR, 257). The final destination of the system's path is the ultimate unity: "... only God becomes the unity that fully consummates the all [*die alles voll-endet*]" (SE, 287/SR, 258. Translation altered).

Absent from Rosenzweig's overview is an explanation, or rather a justification, of this transfiguration: how did God's creation and revelation, and their impact on man and world become known and their knowledge superior to philosophical knowledge? How can the circular, self-contained infinity of Hegel's system be replaced by a system of an utterly different nature: a shape that is not a figure, but a configuration; a concept borrowed from geometry that is not mathematical, which supersedes mathematics? And what, then, is the stuff of which the Star is made in actual truth?

To answer these questions, we must follow the clues that Rosenzweig left in the text:

1. The absolute beginning and absolute end, of which Rosenzweig had told Hans Ehrenberg in December 1913, lie outside of the scope of the philosophical, self-contained infinity, "*im Anfang*" and "*am 'Ende der Tage'*"—that is, in the Bible's adumbration of the "I am First and I am Last".
2. Rosenzweig states that, "Man's eternity is planted in the ground of creation". This is verified by man's having been created by God (*Gottgeschöpflichkeit*) and in God's image (*Gottebenbildlichkeit*), as attested by Genesis 1:27.[64]
3. The closing words of the *Schwelle*, which connect the opening of Part Two, declaring miracle to be the beloved child of faith (*des Glaubens liebstes Kind ist*), with the *Tor*, or Gate, which opens "into life" at the *Star*'s very end:

Wir schreiten hinan über die Schwelle
der Übertwelt, die Schwelle
vom Wunder zur
Erleuchtung (SE, 291).

---

[63] Hallo translates it as "creature".
[64] Both the Hebrew and English translations of these qualifications make this evident by using the wording of the Genesis verse, instead of translating Rosenzweig's word constructions more literally. See SR, 259; *Kochav*, 287.

As chapter four will illustrate, the *Erleuchtung* that Rosenzweig places beyond the threshold is not Hallo's "enlightenment" (SR, 261) or Galli's "illumination" (Galli, 280), or even Amir's "הארה" (*he'arah*; *Kokhav*, 289). It is God's shining face directed at the believer, of Numbers 6:25. As Rosenzweig's translation of יָאֵר יְהוָה פָּנָיו אֵלֶיךָ—"*er lasse dir leuchten sein Antlitz*"—makes clear.

The question of justification, then, returns with yet greater acuteness: how is this orientation, which is wholly derived from Scripture, compatible with the philosophical construction of the Star-shaped system; how can it antecede both logically and ontologically, the consummation of philosophy in Hegelian Idealism? As I have tried to show in this chapter, it is through the transformation of philosophy into the hermeneutic methodology he employs in interpreting the Bible, and the designation of Scripture as the "other soil" in which the "eternal life" is planted. It is through the philosophical interpretation of creation as double negation, the positing of reason as a border-concept that need be approached from both sides—redemption and revelation—and the de-Christianisation of Idealism's eschatological fulfillment through God's becoming All-in-All, that Rosenzweig discovered is the manner in which system and Scripture are to be synthesized.

While the evidence available indicate's that Maimonides' influence on Rosenzweig was moderate, my discussion showed that it far exceeded the impact that most scholars have detected. The biographical inquiry offered a new and useful approach to the *Star* as a work in which its author practices ek-stasis—critical reflection from an external viewpoint—on the philosophical and Jewish theological discourses that shaped his work.

Chapter 4:
"Eternal Life in Our Midst": Bible, Translation and the Bridge between Transcendence and Immanence

On the 23rd of June, 1914, 28-year-old Franz Rosenzweig wrote in his diary:

> The existence of the Jewish people is the ground of my faith, not the giving of the Torah. The one can have but a single relation to the other:
>
> אשר נתן לנו תורת אמת וחיי עולם נטע בתוכנו.
>
> (*Tagebücher* IV, 24)

"Blessed be the Lord, our God, master of the universe, who has given us a Torah of truth, and has planted life of eternity in our midst", is the benediction recited every time after a portion of Torah is read at synagogue. If one were to take the pulse of Rosenzweig's mind, this benediction would be its regular heartbeat, as it captures the spiritual, poetic and philosophical inspiration that he found in the Hebrew Bible.

Indeed, in the *Star of Redemption* Rosenzweig translated and transmuted this benediction into the duct through which eternal life is planted in the midst of the present, whereby the giving of the Torah becomes the endowment of the Jewish people with the exclusive potential of drawing eternity into the present. Pre-eminently, this literal reading is a reflection of Rosenzweig's perception of the Hebrew Bible as both and at the same time the repository of eternal truths and the ground of religious experience.

This perception has far- and wide-reaching implications that, I believe, resulted in Rosenzweig's unique view of the governing ethos of Judaism. To be sure, Rosenzweig had no interest in distilling from the Bible an ethos that draws on historical reality. Moreover, he emphasised that his own interpretation of Judaism (to which Scripture is pivotal), resists any notion of religious or cultural particularism.[1] Indeed, he went to great lengths to fuse the philosophical

---

[1] Cf. his oft-quoted statement that the *Star of Redemption* is a work of philosophy, and not a Jewish book (*Zweistromland* 140/*Theological Writings*, 110). Norbert Samuelson cautions against literal readings of this statement: "What Rosenzweig meant [by making this statement] is that this book is a serious work in a tradition of serious academic theology and philosophy that is not to be confused with the kinds of popular books for religious and Jewish masses current both then and now" (Samuelson 2010, 575).

conclusions of his interpretation of key verses and the redemptive scheme he derived from the Jewish liturgical calendar, with the universal yearning for redemption he identified in the German Idealist tradition. As such, Rosenzweig not only offers a theology for the followers of the Jewish faith; his theology entails a bridging of thought with action through careful excavation of the bond that the Hebrew Bible establishes between transcendence and immanence.[2]

In this and the following chapter I will seek to show that this ambitious project was shaped to a large extent by Rosenzweig's subtle and sophisticated use of translation of the Hebrew Bible in the *Star*. The current chapter will address the function of Bible translation within the discursive part of the system, and the next chapter will explore its constitutive role in the final stage of the system's unfolding, extending beyond discursive reflection into pure religious experience. Scholars have been aware that Rosenzweig translated himself the Jewish sources he cites in the work, but very few studies have attach any importance to this fact.[3] This partly owes to the tendency to date Rosenzweig's earliest experimentation with translation to 1920 with the translation of the Food Benediction, or *Tischdank* (literally: thanksgiving at table).[4] In this chapter, I will show that the Bible and its translation open up important trajectories for our understanding of Rosenzweig's achievement in the *Star*, by examining his inscription of exegetical insights into the philosophical system through the citation and translation of biblical verses. This will be done, however, not by discussing technique and craft as much as by following in the footsteps of inspiration.

My main argument is that the Bible permeates Rosenzweig's thought in many, and varied ways; and that his inspiration is induced by the cross-fertilisa-

---

[2] I employ these terms broadly: by transcendence I mean the quality of concepts or entities that are not subjected to the limits of mundane reality (e. g., God, eternity); by immanence I mean the quality of concepts or entities that are subject to the limits of mundane reality (e.g., humans, death).

[3] Mara Benjamin's nuanced exposure of Rosenzweig's literary techniques of incorporating biblical allusions in the *Star*'s prose does not mention, let alone address, the reliance on his own translation, see M. Benjamin 2009, 38–52. Anna Elisabeth Bauer's studious exposition of Rosenzweig's development of *Sprachdenken* in the *Star* and its bearings on *Die Schrift* also lacks any reference to his extensive use of translation in his systematic work. This is poignantly evident in the conclusion of the first part of her book, *Fragen an eine Übersetzungsarbeit*, which approaches translation in the *Star* as a purely theoretical question. See Bauer 1992, 321–324.

[4] Rosenzweig 1920. See for example Mach 1988, 251; Batnitzky 2000, 105; Askani 1997, 5. The only exception I have found is Everett Fox's article on "Franz Rosenzweig as Translator", who notes that "there are indications in his intellectual development that issues of translation had concerned him for a long time," referring to his brief stint at the Lehranstalt as decisive in his development as a translator (Fox 1989, 380).

tion between his reading of the source as interpreter and his re-reading as translator. To illustrate my argument, I will describe how this dynamic shaped two central themes in the *Star:* the image of God and the system's temporal dimension. If the *Star* could be read as a novel, God would certainly be the main protagonist. His presence in the work is relentless. Sometimes He is described through obsessive repetition of appellations; other times His infinity is made manifest through a succession of daring observations. Yet, despite the many things Rosenzweig says about God, he is very careful *not* to articulate it with the philosophical formula "God is ..." and he is equally careful not to ground the things that he does say about God in an authoritative source that is extraneous to his system. Part I of this chapter will follow Rosenzweig's reliance on the Bible for developing the image of God as the antithesis to the mythical gods of idolatrous cultures in *Star* I:1; and as *der Ewige*—the Eternal—in part III. Time, both as the cycle regulating human lives and as eternity, which transcends the temporal continuum, is the subject the chapter's second part. Here the biblical prescription of religious festivals will emerge as Rosenzweig's blueprint for re-imagining the Jewish liturgical calendar.

Both parts will expose in different ways Rosenzweig's reliance on the Bible as a bridge between transcendence and immanence. Through concrete citations and translations, as well as through more diffuse forms of textual assimilation, Rosenzweig shows how the derivative pairs of polar opposites that philosophy traditionally fails to accommodate—concept and subject, universal and particular, ephemeral and eternal—are in fact mutually *in*clusive.

The constructive dialectic that he develops from this notion will be explored in a reflection on Rosenzweig's use of the benediction after Torah readings as a leitmotif in Part III of the *Star.* Ending the chapter, the discussion will point out the function of this statement as both a culmination of the *Star*'s conclusions, and as a cipher for ideas that exceed the limits of linguistic expression. As such, "eternal life in our midst" may be understood as Rosenzweig's presaging of his involvement in the translation of the Hebrew Bible—*Die Schrift*. Indeed, throughout the chapter, his work on *Die Schrift* will emerge as the refinement of ideas addressed in the *Star*, which offer yet another demonstration of the mutually-complementing dynamic between translation and philosophical reflection in his work.

4.1 Divinity

In Part I of the *Star* Rosenzweig is most engaged with philosophical debates and least concerned with the interpretation of Jewish sources, as the sparseness of

Nahum Glatzer's index for this part indicates (Rosenzweig 1954).⁵ Outlining the tripartite division of the All into the elements of God, world and man, Part I is framed as a critique of the regnant philosophical tradition in Western thought and of the pagan culture from which, Rosenzweig asserts, it had emerged. The God element of the system that Rosenzweig advances is articulated with algebraic equations and the opaque designations *der Gott der Offenbarung*, "the God of revelation", and *der lebendige Gott*, "the living God".

The paucity of biblical allusions in Part I is of course contrasted with the centrality of the Bible in part II, which offers an extensive interpretation (or as Rosenzweig calls it, "grammatical analysis"), of three textual units representing the path of divine actions: Genesis 1, Song of Songs, and Psalms 115, representing creation, revelation and redemption, respectively. As the occurrence of references to Jewish sources increases in part II and becomes ubiquitous in Part III, the symmetry of the system of the *Star* requires that the sources apply with equal weight to Part I.⁶ Therefore, Rosenzweig's long goodbye from the philosophical legacy of ancient Greece in the opening part of his tome, is in fact underlain by the same biblical ethos that will become more pronounced in Parts II and III of the *Star*.

The deconstruction of mythical models of divinity in *Star* I:1 as part of the construction of the God element in Rosenzweig's system is of particular importance for our understanding of its underlying synthesis. Concluding the part, the discussion brings into focus the deities of Asian and ancient Greek religions as the mythical counterparts of Idealist philosophy: both are based on the same untenable ontology of a misguided approach to the problem of nothingness. Critics have tended to address Rosenzweig's original presentation of the concept of nothingness, *Nichts*, in *Star* I:1 primarily as a philosophical problem.⁷ Between

---

⁵ The 1930 edition of the *Star* has separate pagination for each part. Threefore, Glatzer's "Nachweis der jüdischen Quellen" appears at the book's conclusion but paginated 1–18 in "Nachweise und Register".

⁶ As Paul Mendes-Flohr demonstrated, "Philosophy, as pursued in Part I of *The Star* ... anticipates 'the contents of faith,' or more precisely, it establishes the 'foundation' bearing the 'preconditions' of the life of faith". Mendes-Flohr 1989, 364.

⁷ See for example Casper 1967, 84–116, who considers the problem of *Nichts* as framing the entire system of the *Star*; Bertolino 2006a and 2006b. Unfortunately, Bertolino's well-crafted philosophical analysis is complemented by an unconvincing attempt to link Rosenzweig's concept of *Nichts* with the Lurianic notion of צמצום (*tzimtzum*); Gordon 2003, 165–174; Kavka 2004, 135–145; Pollock 2009, 120–180. Gordon and Pollock offer important summaries of Hermann Cohen's analysis of *Nichts* and its impact on Rosenzweig. Kavka 2004, 66–128 offers a comprehensive comparative analysis of Cohen's and Maimonides' notion of nothingness.

Else Freund's pioneering study[8] and Wayne Cristuado's recent work,[9] however, few scholars seem to have paid any attention to the contribution of the idols of the East and West to his critique.[10] This lacuna misses a subtle yet important function of Rosenzweig's critique of the pagan underpinnings of Idealist philosophy as a gateway into the biblical ethos of his revelatory system.

4.1.1 The Death-Swallowing God

As he turns to analyse the mythologies of pagan religions, Rosenzweig quickly flashes over the seeds of biblical thinking that he has planted in the soil of the preceding metaphysical discussion: "It is not by coincidence that revelation, once it started on its way into the world, took the road to the West, not to the East. The living 'gods of Greece' were worthier opponents of the living God than the phantoms of the Asiatic orient" (SE, 38/SR, 35). Ignoring at this point the gross historical inaccuracy of this observation,[11] we may focus on the first instance of explicit, if oblique, equivocation of the God of the system with the God of the Bible: it draws a line connecting the affirming God who overcame nothingness with not-nothingness—*Nichtnichts* (SE, 29/SR, 26–27)— who is the creating God of Yea (SE, 28/SR, 26), with the God who overcame rivalling deities (SE, 38/SR, 35). Rosenzweig bases all three characterizations upon the translation and adaptation of Genesis 1:1, Isaiah 25:8, and possibly a host of other verses.[12]

---

8 Freund 1959, 102–107.
9 Cristuado 2012, 146–157.
10 An exception is Amir 2004, 203–205.
11 As the student of Elbogen and the reader of Zunz and Graetz, Rosenzweig would have certainly been aware of the identity of Near Eastern idolatrous worship against which the Bible battled, and that Greek religion was of concern only to post-biblical Judaism. See, for example, his framing of the clash between the exilic prophets and Babylonian divination (*Weissagung*) as a struggle over the claim to universality (*Tagebücher* IV, 25–26).
12 Michael Fishbane pointed out that in the opening sentence of the *Star* Rosenzweig is inspired by Paul's melding of Hosea 13:14 and Isaiah 25:8 in I Corinthians 15:55. He argues further that while this New Testament interweaving of biblical verses provided Rosenzweig his "base text," the *Star* transforms Christ's triumph over death in I Corinthians into death's triumph over philosophy (Fishbane 1992, 143–44). Ben Sax (2008, 113–118) and Benjamin Pollock (2014, 137–142) emphasise the role of Rosenzweig's allusion to Friedrich Schiller's *Das Ideal und Das Leben* in the same line to link the words of Scripture with the philosophical ambiene of the *Star*. The repetitions and reworkings of Isaiah 25:8 in the *Star* which I analyse below indicate that it bore greater weight than the other texts he drew on for the composition of the opening sentence of his tome.

The positing of the God of revelation as the corrective to the faulty ontology of philosophy and pagan mythology, however, occurs very early on. The first out of seven citations of Isaiah 25:8 in the *Star* appears in the section *Vom Tode*, the very first in the work. It is inserted as a sophisticated articulation of the self-defeating position of philosophy that equates death with nothingness:

> If once all were woven into this mist, death would indeed be *swallowed up*, if not into *the eternal victory*, at least into the one and universal night of the Nought. And it is the ultimate conclusion of this doctrine that death is—Nought. But in truth this is no ultimate conclusion, but a first beginning and truthfully death is not what it seems, not Nought, but an inexorable, inextinguishable something (SE, 4–5 /SR, 4).[13]

The "eternal victory" in which death would be "swallowed up" marks the philosophers' relative and partial success in their attempt to "overcome" death, as opposed to the absolute success of the God of the Bible. The recapitulation of Isaiah 25:8 throughout the *Star* therefore emerges as an important source and rhetorical device for asserting the necessity of the God of revelation for the dissolution of the philosophical equation death=nothingness.

The verse reads:

בִּלַּע הַמָּוֶת לָנֶצַח וּמָחָה אֲדֹנָי יְהוִה דִּמְעָה מֵעַל כָּל־פָּנִים וְחֶרְפַּת עַמּוֹ יָסִיר מֵעַל כָּל־הָאָרֶץ כִּי יְהוָה דִּבֵּר

> [God] will swallow up death forever/in victory; and the Lord GOD will wipe away tears from off all faces; and the rebuke of his people shall he take away from off all the earth: for the LORD has spoken it

In Rosenzweig's adapted translation,[14] the verse articulates with concise precision God's function in the system of the *Star:* (1) <u>ontologically</u>, God triumphs over nothingness both metaphysically, in order for creation to be possible, and existentially, as death must be overcome in order for life to be possible; (2) <u>theo-</u>

---

13 Translation altered; italics added.
14 Compare with the following translations:

Zunz	Philippson	Luther	Kautzsch
Er macht verschwinden den Tod für immer, und es löscht Gott, der Herr, die Thräne von jeglichem Angesichte ...	er tilgt den Tod auf ewig, er nimmt, der Herr, der Ewige, die Zähre von jeglichem Angesichte ...	Er wird den Tod verschlingen ewiglich; und der HERR HERR wird die Tränen von allen Angesichtern abwischen ...	Vernichten wird er den Tod für immer und der Herr Jahwe wird die Thränen von allen Angesichtern abwischen ...

logically, as the God of revelation who shows His love through compassion and consolation. Rosenzweig emphasises the self-contained importance of each of these aspects by breaking up the verse into three discrete units as follows:

Tab. 4.1: Isaiah 25:8 in the *Star of Redemption*

Unit	Function	Citation
1. He will swallow up death forever/in victory	Ontological/ existential	I: Einleitung – "… wäre freilich **der Tod verschlungen,** wenn auch nicht **in den ewigen Sieg,** so doch in die eine und allgemeine Nacht des Nichts. (SE, 4) II:2 – "**diese Liebe ist der ewige Sieg über den tod**". (SE, 183) III:3 – "**Im Ewigen wird der Triumph über den Tod, der darin verschlungen ist,** gefreiert". (SE, 437)
2. And the Lord GOD will wipe away tears from off all faces	Revelatory/ existential	II:2 – "**diese Liebe ist der ewige Sieg über den tod**". (SE, 183) II:3 – "Noch ist **die Träne** nicht **weggewischt von jeglichem Angesicht**". (SE, 244) III:2 – "**Die Träne** des Trauernden **wird weggewischt** von seinem wie **von jeglichem Angesicht**". (SE, 419)
3. And the rebuke of his people shall he take away from off all the earth: for the LORD has spoken it	Redemptive	---

In Rosenzweig's hands, the verb בִּלַּע (*billa'*) – which means in the context of the verse to annihilate or destroy, but with different vowels reads בָּלַע (*balla'*) –swallowed–becomes victory (*Sieg*) and triumph (*Triumph*) by swallowing (*Tod verschlungen*—death was swallowed up). Hence, in Rosenzweig's hands the verse becomes an ontological-existential statement with mythical overtones: both nothingness and death, jointly and severally, are overcome by the God of the Bible, in His dual capacity as creator and revealed God. This duality (which is, of course, complemented by the third function of redeemer), hinges on Rosenzweig's argument for philosophy's equation of nothingness with death. Rosenzweig will present his argument for the positive, discrete ontology of death in *Star* II:1, based on a famous midrash (Genesis Raba (Vilna) 9:5). [15]

If there is a biblical influence on *Star* II:1 that Rosenzweig does *not* try to veil it is that of Genesis 1. Couched in a paraphrase on the famous opening words of the Bible —"*Das Ja ist der Anfang ... Im Anfang ist das Ja*" (SE, 28/SR, 26)—Rosenzweig's account of divine nature and divine freedom is a dense philosophical analysis of the concept of nothingness. Quite understandably, scholars have tended to focus on the ingenious synthesis between Hermann Cohen's theory of infinitesimal calculus and Schelling's philosophies of freedom and myth in Rosenzweig's theory of double negation: God frees Himself from nothingness through its negation, or the affirmation (*Bejahung*) of the not-nothingness: *Nichtnichts*. Rosenzweig's emphasis that the Hebrew Bible's account of creation is the origin of the affirming *Ja*, the overcoming of nothingness, in all likelihood took into account, among other things, the famous opening of John 1:1 and the philosophies inspired by it, most notably, perhaps, Hegel's. Rosenzweig's *Im Anfang ist das Ja* overturning of John's *Im Anfang war das Wort* is threefold: (1) God's *Ja* unites thought with action, as opposed to the New Testament's (and Idealist philosophy's) purging of God's act from corporeality into a strictly verbal-conceptual one (*Wort* is Luther's translation of λογοσ (*logos*) from the original Greek); (2) the assignation of creation to primordial times with the past tense is replaced with the present tense, which asserts the miraculous, constant renewal of creation (SE, 173/SR, 155); (3) *Im Anfang* changes from an adverb into a noun. As the subject of the sentence, *Im Anfang* may also stand for Genesis chapters 1 and 2, positing the biblical account as *the* affirmation that overcomes nothingness.[16] This latter gesture also implies the ontological-phenomenological nexus embodied in the benediction for the eternal life planted in our midst, which Rosenzweig will foreground in *Star* III:1.

---

[15] "The created death of created beings is the preliminary sign of revelation of life beyond createdness [*übergeschöpflichen Lebens*]. Death, which is a fitting agent of fulfilment [*Vollender*] of its thingness as such [*ganzen Dinglichkeit*], returns creation to the past unnoticed, thus turning it into the tacit, constant prediction of the miracle of its renewal. That is why on the sixth day of creation it is not said that it was 'good', but rather, '[God] saw [...] it is very good!' 'Very good', so teach us our sages, very good – that is death" (SE, 173/SR, 155).

[16] Cf. "Philosophy says: actually [*eigentlich*] everything is earth-matter [*Erdenstoff*] or ... heavenly spirit [*Himmelsgeist*] ... or God ... or a-priori. But the truth discloses itself only in the simplest of all denied 'actually' statement, which brings together all of these "possibilities" while never turning them into any 'actually': In the beginning God created the heaven and the earth" (*Zweistromland*, 598).

Nonetheless, Rosenzweig's use of Genesis 1 as a biblical substratum for his ontological discussion is shaped not only by the philosophical subject matter, but also, and perhaps to an even greater extent by biblical and rabbinical myths on the story of creation.[17] These myths portray the God of the Bible as a hero who turned to the work of creation after subduing titanic sea monsters in the time before creation. Rosenzweig's setting of Isaiah 25:8 within the presentation of creation as the overcoming of nothingness-death links the verse to this mythical tradition, in spite, however, of the lack of any such implication in its original context. Rosenzweig invokes this tradition most explicitly as a mythical offset to the algebraic abstraction of God's *physis* into the mathematical symbol A "... whether in this still sea of God's inner *physis* a storm will approach, making its tide surge; whether out of its depths whirlpools and waves will form, stirring the still face of the water, we do not yet know" (SE, 30/SR, 28).[18] A careful consideration of Rosenzweig's choice of words in the above passage shows that despite the silence of Glatzer's index, it was inspired by German translations of biblical images of sea storms and mythical battles with its monsters. The most likely prooftext was Jonah 2:3–4, as the following table illustrates:

Tab. 4.2: Jonah 2:3–4 and the "sea of God's inner *physis*"

Jonah 2:3–4
I called to the LORD, out of my distress, and he answered me; out of the belly of Sheol I cried, and you did hear my voice. For you did cast me into the deep, into the heart of the seas, and a river was round about me; all your waves and your billows passed over me.

Star	**German source**	**English/Hebrew**
der seine **Fluten** aufbrausen läßt	daß die **Fluten** mich umgaben (Luther)	and a flood was round about me וְנָהָר יְסֹבְבֵנִי
aus seinem eigenen **Schoß sich**	aus dem **Schooß** der Hölle hab' ich geschrieen (Zunz) Aus der Unterwelt Schooße schrie ich (Philippson) Aus des Schoß des Scheol schrie ich (Elberfelder) aus dem Schoß des Totenreiches schrie ich (Schlachter)	out of the belly of Sheol I cried מִבֶּטֶן שְׁאוֹל שִׁוַּעְתִּי

---

17 For an account of the evolution of this mythical tradition from the Bible through to the Babylonian Talmud see Fishbane 1998, 41–55.
18 My translation.

Tab. 4.2: Jonah 2:3 – 4 and the "sea of God's inner *physis*" *(Continued)*

Jonah 2:3 – 4
I called to the LORD, out of my distress, and he answered me; out of the belly of Sheol I cried, and you did hear my voice. For you did cast me into the deep, into the heart of the seas, and a river was round about me; all your waves and your billows passed over me.

Star	German source	English/Hebrew
Wirbel und Wellen bilden	und alle diene **Wirbel und Wellen** überfielen mich (Weibel) [*compare:* alle deine **Wogen und Wellen** gingen über mich (Luther)]	all your billows and your waves passed over me כָּל־מִשְׁבָּרֶיךָ וְגַלֶּיךָ עָלַי עָבָרוּ
die in die **stille Fläche strömende** Bewegung bringen	und **Ströme** umgeben mich (Zunz)	and a river was round about me וְנָהָר יְסֹבְבֵנִי
	Und der Geist Gottes schwebend über der **Fläche der Wasser** (Zunz)	(Genesis 1:2) And the spirit of God hovered over the face of the water וְרוּחַ אֱלֹהִים מְרַחֶפֶת עַל־פְּנֵי הַמָּיִם

The unique agglomeration of four expressions that all appear in a single parallel biblical source, make it highly likely that Rosenzweig painted this mythical-poetic image under the inspiration of Jonah's prayer from the fish's bowls. The table above illustrates that Rosenzweig would have consulted a variety of German translations of the verse: the canonical Luther, and Zunz's Jewish Bible (a personal favourite), are his main references: he draws on both translations of נָהָר (*nahar*), as flood/tide (Luther) and river (Zunz) in his depiction of the surging tide (*seine* **Fluten** *aufbrausen*) and the streaming movement on the still face of the water (*in die* **stille Fläche strömende** *Bewegung bringen*).[19]

The pairing *Wirbel und Wellen* is an interesting peculiarity, as the only translation of Jonah 2:4 in which it appears seems to be the popular Catholic *Volks Bilder Bibel*,[20] which Rosenzweig would not have had a particular reason to consult or even have access to. A more likely influence (which could have prompted Rosenzweig to search for a correlate Bible translation) is Goethe's *Legende:*

---

[19] This latter reference to Zunz's translation of Genesis 1:2 is significant, because Luther's "spirit of God" (*Geist Gottes*), as well as that in all other major translations that Rosenzweig would have known or consulted (Mendelssohn and Philippson on the Jewish side; Kautzsch on the Christian side), hovered over the *water*, rather than on the *face* of the water.

[20] "*Die Fluth umgab mich, und alle deine Wirbel und Wellen überfielen mich*". Weibel, 342.

> *Denn des Wassers heilige **Welle***
> *Scheint zu fliehn' sich zu entfernen,*
> *Sie erblickt nur hohler **Wirbel***
> *Grause Tiefen unter sich.*[21]

The subject of Goethe's poem, the Brahman's wife, is watching the holy waves of the Ganges River, in an ominous vision of the hollow of a whirlpool threatening to throw her into the horrific deep. Given his admiration for Goethe, it is likely that Roenzweig's deconstruction of the Brahman's faith in nothingness a few pages later is uncoincidental.

In addition to Goethe's Ganges, the still waters of God's *physis* expecting a storm in the *Star* echo Luther's translation of Psalms 89:9–10, in which the Psalmist describes the aftermath of God's struggle in the high seas.[22] Rosenzweig definitely knew this Psalm,[23] and quite likely at least some of the midrashic versions of the dragon myth[24]; his decision to keep the stormy clash implicit may have been in order to strike a fine balance between myth and philosophical discourse, which his translation and adaptation of Isaiah 25:8 exemplifies. After all, divine triumph over the ailments of philosophy is one thing; the slaying of sea monsters with a mighty arm is an entirely different matter. And yet, the unbearable tension that the imminent storm projects on the divine sea must find resolution outside of the realm of myth. Rosenzweig found this resolution in an ontological deconstruction of images of pagan deities.

The gods of Asia collapse, both ontologically and theologically, due to their negative essence. The Indian Brahman bears an unfulfilled promise of affirmation, as it begins with the negation of nothingness but instead of leading to infinite affirmation, strives for the state of Nirvana – renewed, pure nothingness (SE, 38–39 /SR, 35–36). The Chinese god of the heavens is all-encompassing and all-permeating, but this is either as the transcendent heavens or as a non-act-Tao (SE, 39–40/SR, 36–37). As worshipped deities, then, they are weak due to their enclosedness (*Geschlossenheit*), and resignation from the world (*abschlußhaften*), and the resulting non-productiveness which is camouflaged by feigned productiveness (*erzeugnishaften*) (SE, 38/SR, 35).

---

[21] Goethe 1882–1884, lines 33–36, 152.
[22] "*Du herrschest über das ungestüme Meer; du stillest seine Wellen, wenn sie sich erheben. Du schlägst Rahab zu Tod; du zerstreust deine Feinde mit deinem starken Arm*" (Verses 10–11 in the Hebrew Bible).
[23] He cites verse 16 twice in SE, 174, 471/SR, 157, 424.
[24] Genesis Raba (Vilna) 12:15, in SE 130/SR, 117. Genesis Raba is the most cited midrashic work in the *Star*.

The historical fiction of God's "turn to the West" to contend with the gods of Greece rather than the deities of the Orient, may be seen as another aspect of the selective picture that Rosenzweig paints. Within the context of the biblical tradition that he imagines, he places the God of revelation on the stage of the history of philosophy, brushing aside the "particularist" residue that a more conventional account of the Bible's struggle against idolatry would have created.

Pagan mythology and its corresponding philosophies had also sought to build bridges between the earthly man and world – and the divine. Yet the lacking essence of their deities inevitably lead to the subsumption of the earthly elements in the divine, or in Rosenzweig's formulation, to apotheosis. Divine love became the object of a closed elite whose members aspired to imitate God by attaining perfection in their own existence, thus radically limiting the scope of divine love, and turning it into an act that depends on human initiative: God may only love in return those who love him to begin with. The God of the Bible, however, "is not merely 'amiable' [*liebenswürdig*] and loves regardless of man's relation to him, moreover, He first awakens [*erweckend*] the love of man" (SE, 43/SR, 39). Rosenzweig drives this point home in the only time he combines unit 1 and 2 in Isaiah 25:8, in *Star* II:2: "*Liebe ist der ewige Sieg über den tod*". As we have seen, death in Part I has an existential as well as an ontological function. Hence, according to Rosenzweig's own reinterpretation of the verse, we may also read it here as "*Liebe ist der ewige Sieg über den Nichts*", i.e., as a direct counter-response to the limiting and limited love of the gods of mythology.

4.1.2 From *Der Ewige* to *DASEIN*

In his presentation of pagan models of divinity, Rosenzweig reshapes the Bible's deep anxiety from idolatry to the measures of entirely different concerns. He presents the deities of pagan Asia and Greece as ontologically deficient, incapable of offering their believers genuine providential support. At the conclusion of a critical (and debilitating) analysis of the shortcomings of Western philosophical discourse, the pagan gods are posited as mythological representations of philosophy's failure to overcome the problem of nothingness. Central themes in the Bible's relation to polytheism and idolatrous worship,[25] as well as rabbin-

---

[25] Yehezkel Kaufmann's monolithic account of idolatry in the Bible as fetishist worship of pantheistic deities was groundbreaking, but lacked nuance, see Kaufmann 1956, 255–303, esp. 259, 267, 298. For a critique of his identification of idolatry with fetishism see Faur 1978, esp. 3–5; for an example of the conflicting views of idolatry in the Bible see Knohl 1995; for expansions of the Deuteronomistic view of idolatry in Ezekiel see Ganzel 2010.

ical developments of the category עבודה זרה (*avodah zara*),[26] are nowhere to be found in this discussion. And yet, his employment of mythical motifs to portray the God of the Bible as the antidote to nothingness and death (both as homonyms and as separate ontological categories) identifies the Bible's fundamental function as a bridge between transcendence and immanence. The final step on that bridge, the encounter between man and the loving God of the Bible takes place face-to-face, proper name to proper name, more than "any sense of sensible men, any wisdom of wise men could ever admit" (SE, 43/SR, 39). The insight that the disclosure of God's proper name is the ultimate expression of the Bible's reconciliation of transcendence and immanence was articulated in the *Star*. Yet, Rosenzweig needed years of additional reflection in order to further extend his foray into the mystery of God's essence. It therefore provides an important example for the continuity and evolution of Rosenzweig's ideas in the *Star* in the projects he undertook in the years following its publication.

Based on *Star* I:1 we have already inferred that the living God, the God of affirmation, is the God of the Bible. Rosenzweig substantiates these oblique allusions in *Star* II:2:

> Revelation commences with the "I the Lord" as the great Nay of the concealed God which negates his own concealment. This "I" accompanies revelation through all the individual commandments (SE, 198/SR, 178).

God's self-pronouncement of presence and name in the first commandment in Exodus 20:2,[27] is the abolition of His former hidden-ness as the God of creation; had God chosen *not* to reveal himself in such a way, Rosenzweig maintains, He would have been no different from the idols of other mythologies. The imperative "You shall have no other gods beside Me", which was the hidden thread that ran through the discussion of idolatry in part I, is now disclosed. Just how the second commandment is central to the *Star of Redemption* as a whole becomes clear

---

26 On the discrepancy between biblical zealousness and mishnaic tolerance in relation to idolatry see Furstenberg, 2010; for a discussion of rabbinical retention and attenuation of the biblical injunction to destroy idolatrous worship see Rosen-Zvi, 2009. The scholarly literature on the topic is vast, and the references in this and the previous note offer but a few examples to the richness and problems in reconstructing a coherent position on idolatry from the ancient sources of Judaism. For a philosophical-historical exposition of the topic, see the by now classic Halbertal & Margalit 1992. Batnitzky's reading of their work in the context of Rosenzweig's position on idolatry is interesting, but lacks any references to his presentation of the mythical gods of paganism in *Star* I:1, see Batnitzky 2000, 5–13.

27 On the rivalling traditions regarding the number and division of the commandments in Exodus 20 see *Bavli* Makkot 24a and Ibn Ezra ad loc.

in a letter that Rosenzweig wrote to Martin Buber in 1922, in which he said that the moment he discovered the difference between idolatry and revelation "... was the moment my book was conceived" (*BT* II, 816).[28]

Rosenzweig takes one more step in the *Star* in order to aver what is the precise function of revelation, and how it comes to form a single whole with the beginning and end of the divine path, creation and redemption: "The ground of revelation is mid-point and beginning in one; it is the revelation of the divine name" (SE 208/SR, 188). While YHWH is God's proper name, the single instance in which the full divine name is revealed in the Bible is in Exodus 3:14—אהיה אשר אהיה (*Eheyeh Asher Eheyeh*).[29] For Rosenzweig, the disclosure of the divine name is a performative demonstration of the systematic function of revelation. God is the redeemer of world and man; the anticipation entailed by the notion of redemption is a human construct, as God's eternality does not differentiate between past, present and future: "[God] is eternal, he alone is eternal, he is the Eternal per se. In his mouth, 'I am' is like 'I shall be' and finds explanation in it" (SE, 303/SR, 272).[30] Rosenzweig's designation of God as *der Ewige*,[31] The Eternal, establishes an image of God that is more sublime than present. While *der Ewige* is a powerful contrast to the mythical gods of *Nichts* of *Star* I:1, it corresponds with the first part of Isaiah 25:8, as eternally triumphant over death and nothingness; but it is harder to reconcile with the second part of the verse that Rosenzweig translates twice in II:3 and III:2, "And the Lord GOD will wipe away tears from off all faces". Indeed, in both instances, Rosenzweig omits God's role as an active agent in the verse, changing the active form of the Hebrew verse to the passive.[32] Most interestingly, God's participation in the amorous dialogue that Rosenzweig weaves from Song of Songs in II:2 is in the first person; and although the I–You dialogue between man and God removes the linguistic distinction between transcendence and immanence (SE, 221/SR, 199), Rosenzweig emphasises that love qua love cannot be eternal when it is not ongoing

---

28 After grappling for three and a half years ("from spring 1914 to autumn 1917) with the question of what is the difference between idolatry and revelation, "stumbling over a horrible prickly plant" on the Macedonian front, "there I knew everything (*da wußte ich "alles"*). See also letter to Eugen Rosenstock, *BT* I, 481–483.
29 Customarily translated in English as "I am that I am / I am who I am".
30 My translation.
31 As the editors of the *BT* note (*BT* I, 57 n.3), Rosenzweig was familiar with Mendelssohn's translation of the divine name as *der Ewige* as early as 1906. For a discussion of this diary entry (29.9.1906) see chapter 1 above.
32 See Table 4.1 above.

(SE, 225/SR, 201). Hence, it is not God as The Eternal who loves man with the words of the Bible's worldly-divine love poem.

As Anna Elisabeth Bauer has shown, Rosenzweig considered God's name as the core and orientation of the *Star* (Bauer 1992, 423–425). The evidence she compiled from his correspondence and work with Buber documents the continued preoccupation with God's proper name, both in the Tetragrammaton and in *Eheyeh Asher Eheyeh*, which resulted in an ingenious in *Die Schrift*.[33] In his essay on Mendelssohn's translation of the divine name, Rosenzweig reflected:

> Only through this fusion [of the distant God with the near, the 'whole' with 'one's own'] do we have the 'essence of Judaism' ... Now this union is the kernel of biblical revelation ... Through this union is accomplished at every point an equivalence between the God of creation and the God who is present to me, to you, to everyone ... (*Zweistromland*, 819/*Scripture and Translation*, 108).

The challenge Rosenzweig and Buber faced was how to encapsulate the fusion of the transcendent and immanent dimensions of God's being in the Bible's single, unique, unrepeated statement:

Tab. 4.3: Exodus 3:14

B–R	Luther	Mendelssohn	Zunz	Hirsch
Ich werde dasein, als der dasein werde ... ICH BIN DA schickt mir zu euch	ICH WERDE SEIN, DER ICH SEIN WERDE	Ich bin das Wesen welches ewig ist: ... das ewige Wesen welches sich nennt, Ich bin ewig, hat mich zu euch gesendet	Ich werde seyn der Ich bin ... Ehejeh sendet mich zu euch	אהי' אשר אהי'! (*Eheyeh Asher Eheyeh*) אהי' (*Eheyeh*) hat mich an euch gesandt

אֶהְיֶה אֲשֶׁר אֶהְיֶה וַיֹּאמֶר כֹּה תֹאמַר לִבְנֵי יִשְׂרָאֵל אֶהְיֶה שְׁלָחַנִי אֲלֵיכֶם

---

33 Bauer 1992, 423–438. Casper emphasises Rosenzweig's decisive part in the work on the translation of Exodus 3:14 in Casper 1967, 180–181. For the contribution of the Yehuda Halevy translation to Rosenzweig's reflective process see Galli 1994, 67–68. For a detailed account of Buber's and Rosenzweig's search for a translation that would reflect their perception of the God of the Bible see Losch 2015.

Rosenzweig rejects Luther's Platonic "ICH WERDE SEIN", which equates God with eternal Being. Instead, he opts for Rashi's interpretation (*Arbeitspapiere*, 93),[34] which emphasizes God's *providential* aspect, of *being there* (=*Da-Sein*) for the People of Israel. He utilizes the repetition of God's name אהיה שלחני אליכם (*Eheyeh shelahani aleichem*) to emphasize its providential aspect – "ICH BIN DA" – literally read "I am there", and to be understood as, "I am there for you".

This original interpretation corresponds with two important rabbinical traditions concerning God's image and name. An early and persistent tradition regarding *Eheyeh Asher Eheyeh* lists it among other appellations used to describe God in Scripture, which, when inscribed, become sacrosanct and may not be deleted. This tradition first appears in the minor Talmudic tractates *Sofrim*, *Torah* and *Avot de-Rabbi Nathan*.[35] It recurs in both Talmuds[36] and perhaps most significantly, in Midrash Rabba on Exodus,[37] where Rabbi Abba bar Memel asserts that the appellation *Eheyeh Asher Eheyeh* represents God's actions.[38] Rashi's commentary, which Rosenzweig adopts, relies on two versions of the same tradition. The earlier one, from *Bavli* Berachot 9b, reads: "*Eheyeh Asher Eheyeh:* the blessed holy One told Moses—go and tell Israel: 'I was with you in this subjugation and I shall be with you in subjugation under other kingdoms'". The second version (for which Rashi only cites the reference) appears in the abovementioned paragraph in Exodus Rabba, 3:6, as one of several midrashim on the meaning of *Eheyeh Asher Eheyeh*. Strikingly, Mendelssohn's translation *das Wesen welches ewig ist* (the essence that is eternal) relies on the very same paragraph in Exodus Rabba. The *Be'ur*, Mendelssohn's self-commentary on his translation of the Pentateuch, indeed cites God's pledge to care for Israel in current and future subjugation,[39] albeit as second in importance to God's self-assertion

---

[34] Rosenzweig was familiar with this interpretation as early as 1917; see *BT* I, 426, cited in Casper 1967, 180.

[35] *Avot de Rabi Natan* Version B 38:5, "Ten Names"; *Masekhet Sofrim* 4:1; *Masekhet Sefer Torah* 4:1:

אלו שמות שאין נמחקין (*Elu shemot she-ein nimhakin*)

[36] *Bavli*, Bava Batra 73a, Shvu'ot 35a; *Yerushalmi*, Megilla 71d/9.

[37] Exodus Rabba (Vilna) 3:6.

[38] "אהיה אשר אהיה אני נקרא לפי מעשי"*Eheyeh Asher Eheyeh* – I am called [this way] according to my actions".

[39] רבי יעקב ב"ר אבינא בשם רבי הונא דציפורן אמר, אמר הקב"ה למשה אמור להם בשעבוד זה אהיה עמם, ובשעבוד הן הולכין, ואהיה עמם. ("Rabbi Ya'akov son of Rabbi Avina in the name of Rabbi Huna De-Tziporen said, The Blessed Holy One told Moses: Tell them that I shall be with them in this subjugation, and in [any] subjugation they will go to, I shall be with them.")

of His eternal essence.⁴⁰ While in the *Star* Rosenzweig gave clear precedence to God's eternality over His providential commitment by adopting Mendelssohn's translation of Exodus 20:1, *Ich bin der Ewige* (SE, 198/SR, 178),⁴¹ he changed his priorities in *Die Schrift*. *Ich werde dasein als dasein werde*, which translates rather awkwardly into English.⁴² In German, however, this rendition elegantly converges God's revelatory presence with His eternality, better reflecting *both* conclusions of the critique of pagan divinities in *Star* I:1. It remains moot whether Rosenzweig was familiar with the commentaries in Exodus Raba 3:6 when he wrote the *Star*; assuming he was not, the analysis of the faulty ontology of pagan deities was likely guided by his intuitions, which remained consistent with his later, better-informed, work on *Die Schrift*.⁴³

4.2 Time

For Rosenzweig, Exodus 3:14 was emblematic of the inherent tension between God's transcendence and immanence, which had led him to adopt Mendelssohn's solution in the *Star*, and replace it later on with an original translation of his own. Nevertheless, this evolution in Rosenzweig's understanding of *Eheyeh* marks a shift of emphasis rather than a radical transformation.

As we have seen, Rosenzweig insisted that the translation of Exodus 3:14 must convey both the eternal and revelatory aspects of the God of the Bible, which his translation and adaptations of Isaiah 25:8 throughout the *Star* reflect. The interpretation of Exodus 3:14 in Part III, however, still emphasised rather traditionally the verse's expression of God's eternality and singularity.

Thus, *Eheyeh* underscores a fundamental ontological problem that the system of the *Star* endeavours, but does not fully succeed, to resolve: the simultaneous independence and interconnectedness of the three elements—God, man and world. The path of creation–revelation–redemption entails that God's eternality be concurrently *ex*clusive and *in*clusive of the other two elements; a challenge that philosophy failed to overcome because it insisted on searching for,

---

40 ר' יצחק אומר א"ל הקב"ה למשה אמור להם אני שהייתי ואני הוא עכשיו ואני הוא לעתיד לבא, לכך כתיב אהיה שלשה פעמים. (R. Itzhak says, said the Blessed Holy One to Moshe: Tell them that I am the one who was, and I am now, and I am yet to come, hence its written *Eheyeh* three times.").
41 Appearing with a slight adaptation: "Ich der Ewige".
42 Galli translates it as "I will be there as I who will be there" in 1994, 72. "I will be there as being there will be" is a more literal translation.
43 For a comprehensive but rather technical survey of Rosenzweig's sources and parallels see Weintraub 1967, 107–110.

while presupposing, the unity of Being as a self-contained sphere, or circle (SE, 283/SR, 254). In contradistinction, Rosenzweig does not presuppose this unity but posits it as the ultimate goal of a long process of a "becoming toward unity" (*Werden zur Einheit*), which is exclusive to God: "Only God becomes the Unity, that which consummates everything [*die alles voll-endet*]" (SE, 287/SR, 258).[44] This becoming, Rosenzweig emphasises, "is not a change, growth, increase … [it is only] because of the simultaneity of His being – of yore, always and in eternity [*während-, Allzeit- und Ewigseins*] – we must term the Whole [*das Ganze*] as becoming" (SE, 287–288/SR, 258).[45] He concludes:

> 'God is eternal' thus means that, for Him, eternity is His consummation [*Voll-endung*]. But to repeat: is that so for the world, and for man?
>
> Not at all. Indeed, to attain eternal life they must merge into the world-day of the Lord (SE, 288/SR, 258).[46]

Eternity is uniquely divine, and yet man and world can be included in it by merging "into the world-day of the Lord", i.e., by somehow partaking in it. The challenge remained to explain how this possibility may be actualized.

4.2.1 Time Reckoning–Calendar–Worship

Not without justification, scholars consider Rosenzweig's emphasis on the importance of prayer as a redemption-promoting activity as the definitive actualisation of the human potential to partake in eternity. A progression from the systematic interrelationships between the two triads—God–man–world and creation–revelation–redemption—to devotional life as manifested in the liturgy of synagogue and church, however, is exposed to the risk of leaping irresponsibly from the transcendence of eternity to the immanence of present. To be sure, Rosenzweig makes every effort to avoid such a leap. From a systematic viewpoint, the melding of the transcendent and the immanent relies upon seamless continuity that it purports to establish between the cosmological, calendrical and cultic dimensions of time. This continuity is supported by biblical descriptions (of cosmology) and prescription (of calendar and worship), and further developments in post-biblical traditions. As the exposition of this continuum pro-

---

44 Translation altered.
45 My translation.
46 Translation altered. For a discussion of the interrelationships between the three temporal dimensions see Ehrlich 1988, 732–735.

gresses, the Bible itself transforms from a repository of eternal truths into an artifact of worship.

Rosenzweig insisted that his interpretation of Jewish and Christian calendars is strictly sociological.[47] On closer inspection, however, the description of the Jewish calendar emerges as an audacious imagining of a history of time reckoning, calendar and worship through the embedment of citations and allusions that conjures a uniform Jewish conception of temporality perfectly in tune with the structure and dynamics of the system of the *Star*.[48] When one suspends expectations for historical or scientific accuracy, it is hard to ignore the penetrating recognition of the power that formative texts possess over Judeo-Christian conceptions of temporality. By positing the Bible as the ground on which temporality on its various dimensions was cultivated, Rosenzweig was able to weave a compelling religious fantasy on veritable themes.

As he confessed in later years, his knowledge of Jewish sources at the time of writing the *Star* was partial, exiguous even.[49] Nevertheless, at the time of writing the *Star* he already had a firm grasp of the main historical processes in the evolution of Jewish calendar and cult.[50] Therefore, while it is not always easy to distinguish honest mistake from intentional fiction in his liturgical calendar, it is safe to assume that Rosenzweig's pastiche of biblical and rabbinical elements is more calculated than capricious.

---

[47] *Zweistromland*, 156/Theological Writings, 132. Rosenzweig indeed provides a sociological analysis of the Christian calendar in the *Star* in the section "*Christliche Zeitrechnung*" (Christian Time-Reckoning, SE, 375–378/SR, 338–340), asserting that the sibling/rival faith of Judaism was excluded from the formative process of temporal perception described in *Star* III:1.

[48] For assessments of Rosenzweig's use of biblical quotations in the *Star* see M. Benjamin 2009, 26–64, esp. 28–29, 32,38; Sax 2008, 244–284; Schweid 1985, 311–322; and Turner 2004.

[49] Rosenzweig wrote to Isaak Breuer that part of the reason why his treatment of halakhah in the *Star* was sketchy was his lacking knowledge, which only a decade of "learning and living, learning and learning", would be sufficiently corrected to allow him to write a book about "*das Gesetz*" (BT II, 951). To Richard Koch he confided that the ideas he had jotted down on postcards in World War I (which formed the basis for the *Star*) had been intended for a book he were to write at age 70, "before which [age] I would not have acquired the necessary knowledge" (BT II, 1196).

[50] This, as the student of Elbogen, who produced a monumental study on the history of ancient Jewish prayer (Elbogen 1913; trans. Elbogen 1993), and an admirer of Leopold Zunz, pioneer of the academic research of the history of synagogue liturgy. For Elbogen's influence on Rosenzweig see Sax 2008, 197–243; Sax 2018.

4.2.1.1 Time reckoning–Cosmology

The links between the division of time and the liturgical calendar, basic in modern conceptions of temporality, were far from obvious in antiquity.[51] Rosenzweig appears to be aware of the problems this creates for him as a modern thinker, as he attempts an elegant detour. He separates his discussion of time reckoning (worldly time) from the analysis of the liturgical calendar (human time),[52] and begins the ontological analysis of time units with an original poetic description of the hour as a human construct devised to imitate eternity:

> [The hour's] ... end can merge back into its beginning because it has a middle, indeed many middle moments between its beginning and its end ... When an hour is up, there begins not only 'new' hour, much as a new moment relieves the old one. Rather, there begins 'again an hour.'" Human perception of the notion of eternity is drawn from the idea behind the time unit – "hour". The time that elapses between its beginning and end creates the possibility of an infinity of unique events, while its recurrence establishes the constancy of the perpetual (SE, 323/SR, 290).

The Bible enters the picture with the move from hour to day and week. The Sabbath is the hinge upon which the transition from cosmology to calendar revolves, as it is both the marker of the end of the week, and the first and fundamental ritual in Jewish liturgy. Originally, God instituted the Sabbath to commemorate His work of creation in Genesis 2:1–3, celebrating the establishment of worldly temporality, which is regulated by the two luminaries (Genesis 1:14–18). After the flood, God aligned worldly time (day, season, year) with human temporality (Genesis 8:22). Rosenzweig summarises:

> The two luminaries, the greater and the lesser, mark time for man not because of the orbits which they describe in the heavens ... the repetition which occurs in circling the orbit becomes perceptible only as this point, [the Sabbath], is fastened. These times are turned into hours, into guarantors of eternity within time, not by the celestial orbit but by the terrestrial repetition. When God laid the first and most universal basis for his covenant with the new generation of mankind, he promised the father of that generation that the alternation of

---

[51] Sacha Stern notes that having been asked to deliver a paper on the Jewish conception of time, he discovered during its preparation that, "the relationship between the Jewish calendar and the concept of time was actually only tenuous" (S. Stern 2001, 1). He demonstrates the very loose notion of time units in Rabbinical literature through a convincing terminological analysis in ibid, 26–45, where he shows that זמן (zman) in the ancient sources he surveys, "is not a self-standing or 'pure entity, a universal dimension, a flow, or a continuum" (29).

[52] Time reckoning is addressed in SE, 303, 321–324/SR, 272–273, 289–292, while the calendar is described in SE, 342–364/SR, 308–328.

'seedtime and harvest, cold and heat, summer and winter, day and night,' would never cease (SE, 321/SR, 290–291).

If God were a creating *deus absconditus*, the intertwining of worldly and human temporalities would have been trivial, a self-evident fact grounded in empirical experience and expressible in scientific terms. A point that has eluded most scholars, however, is that Rosenzweig grounds both temporal dimensions in interpretations of the Bible's instituting their regulated cycles.[53] Notably, he argues that the constitutive moment in which God lays down the cycle of times [*der Kreislauf der Zeiten*] does not take place during the six days of creation; it is bound up with God's first covenant with humanity in the wake of the Flood. Since the Bible itself does not prescribe a commemorative event of this covenant, however, the celebration of the work of creation had to be attached to a different covenant between God and humanity.

Earlier on in the *Star*, Exodus 20:2 – "I am YHWH your God" – served Rosenzweig to explain God's transition from transcendence (as hidden creator) to immanence (as eternally revealed). The verse's protasis, "who has brought you out of Egypt, out of the house of bondage", however, was left out.[54] In *Star* I:3, Rosenzweig demonstrates how divine transcendence and immanence are bound up together, by invoking this very protasis in the recapitulation of the Ten Commandments in Deuteronomy (5:14):

> Remember that you were a slave in the land of Egypt, and YHWH your God brought you out thence with a mighty hand and an outstretched arm; therefore YHWH your God commanded you to keep the Sabbath day.[55]

The verse's linking of the remembrance of the Exodus with the Sabbath has puzzled traditional exegetes because it deviates from the ubiquitous designation of the Sabbath as celebrating the completion of the work of creation, and clashes with the prescription of the Sabbath in the original version of the Ten Commandments.[56] But Rosenzweig employs it to clinch together God's transcendence and immanence, the eternal and providential aspects of His essence:

---

53 See e.g., Mosès 1992, 186–200. Ehrlich is an exception, although his conclusion that "[Rosenzweig's] principal project ... was to articulate the Hebrew Bible's primordial temporalization [*Zeitigung*] of the Truth", is not developed any further. See Ehrlich 1988, 742.
54 Mara Benjamin noticed Rosenzweig's "elimination" of the protasis of Exodus 20:2 from the *Star*, but missed his emphasis on the dramatic importance of the exodus from Egypt to Jewish history and identity. See M. Benjamin 2009, 50.
55 Paraphrased in Rosenzweig, SE, 324/SR, 291.
56 See, e.g., Maimonides, *Moreh* II:31; Ibn Ezra on Exodus 20:1.

> [The Sabbath] was instituted primarily to commemorate the work of Genesis and thus forms the solid grounding of the spiritual year ... The creation of a people into a people takes place in its liberation. And so, the feast that comes at the beginning of its national history is a feast of liberation. Therefore the Sabbath can justly be taken to be a reminder of the Exodus out of Egypt (SE, 352/ SR, 317).[57]

The benediction read on Sabbath eve in the *Siddur*, one of Rosenzweig's favourite Jewish texts, has made its dual recognition of the work of creation and the exodus from Egypt natural to generations of Jews. Yet, the benediction's core, designating the Sabbath as, "A day commemorating the work of Creation, for it is a day beginning holy convocations, reminder of the Exodus from Egypt", is, plain and simple, a paradox. How can these two distinct divine acts, one of universal importance, the other the establishment of a particular ethnic-national group, coexist?[58] Rosenzweig sees this multiplicity of functions as an opportunity rather than a hindrance. In his eyes, the Bible's instituting the Sabbath as the conclusion of the work of creation, a holy day of rest that vouchsafes for the Sinai covenant and (as we will see below) the first event prescribed in the most comprehensive versions of the biblical calendar, threads together the three immanent aspects of temporality—time reckoning, cosmology and calendar—with the transcendence of the Eternal.

4.2.1.2 Calendar and Worship

As noted, Rosenzweig's use of biblical and rabbinical elements in his calendar is by no means consistent or historically exact. In addition to the Sabbath, the dominance of biblical materials is evident from the rather unexpected description of the course of the spiritual year, based on the Bible's most detailed versions of the liturgical calendar in Leviticus 23 and Numbers 28–29. A few minor changes notwithstanding, Rosenzweig's calendar faithfully reflects the order of feasts and holy days laid down in the desert for the People of Israel. He omits the counting of seven weeks from Passover to Shavuot, ספירת העומר (*Sefirat Ha-Omer*), appearing in Leviticus, and the beginning of the month, ראש חדש (*Rosh Hodesh*), appearing in Numbers. Otherwise, his calendar is faithful to bib-

---

57 Translation altered. This interpretation of the difference between the two versions of the Decalogue resembles Nachmanides' commentary on Deuteronomy 5:15. For a critique of this view see *Ha-tur Ha-aroch* on Deuteronomy 5:5.

58 Hermann Cohen, for example, vehemently opposed the emphasis on the Sabbath's relation to the act of creation, and concentrated on the ethical merits of its commemoration of the Exodus through the inclusion of all household members, including slaves and foreigners, in the rest. See H. Cohen 1924a, 24–25.

lical prescription: the first and most important calendrical event is the Sabbath; the spiritual year begins with Passover and ends with Sukkot; the historical feasts of Hannukah, Purim and the Ninth of Av are not acknowledged as an organic part of the calendar, and dismissed as lacking the spiritual essence of their biblical counterparts (SE, 410/SR, 368–369).[59] In customary fashion, Rosenzweig does not justify his presentation of the calendar, nor does he even hint that it is based on the archaic, pre-rabbinical ordering of the months and high holidays.

Tab. 4.4: Numbers 28–29 and the Liturgical Calendar in the *Star*

Star of Redemption	Numbers	Event
	(28:2) Command the people of Israel, and say to them, 'My offering …you shall take heed to offer to me in its due season.'	Introduction
(p.310) … the reading of the Torah becomes the liturgical focus of the holiday on which the spiritual year is founded, of the Sabbath.	(28:9) On the Sabbath day	Sabbath
----	(28:11) At the beginnings of your months	Rosh Hodesh
(p.317) Among the many meals of the spiritual year, the evening meal of the Passover … is the meal of meals.	(28:16–18) On the fourteenth day of the first month is the LORD's Passover … And on the fifteenth day of this month is a feast; seven days shall unleavened bread be eaten. On the first day there shall be a holy convocation	Passover
(p.319) Among the three feasts of the people of revelation, the feasts of the revelation in a narrower sense lasts only two brief days	(28:26) On the day of the first fruits, when you offer a cereal offering of new grain to the LORD at your feast of weeks, you shall have a holy convocation	Shavuot
	(29:1) On the first day of the seventh month you shall have a holy convocation … It is a day for you to blow the trumpets	Rosh Hashanah

---

59 This approach is surprisingly consistent with contemporary scholarship on biblical calendars. While the relationship between calendar and worship was clear enough, the connection between chronology and worship in biblical times appears to have been minimal. See Beckwith 2003, 1–4.

(p.324) ... the Days of Awe, New Year's Day and the Day of Atonement, place the eternity of redemption into time.	(29:7) On the tenth day of this seventh month you shall have a holy convocation, and afflict yourselves	Yom Kippur
(p.320) The Feast of Booths is the feast of both wanderings and rest.	(29:12) On the fifteenth day of the seventh month you shall have a holy convocation; you shall do no laborious work, and you shall keep a feast to the LORD seven days	Sukkot
(pp. 327–328) ... it is most significant for the structure of the spiritual year that the festivals of immediate redemption do not conclude the feast month of redemption that closes the annual cycle of Sabbaths. For after them comes the Feast of Booths ... [which] reinstates the reality of time. Thus the circuit of the year can recommence, for only within this circuit are we allowed to conjure eternity up into time".	(29:35) On the eighth day you shall have a solemn assembly	Simchat Torah

While the Bible's prescription of feasts and holy days still forms the backbone of the Jewish year to this very day, several crucial additions were made in later periods. The main structural changes are the following: (1) The cryptic feast of "a memorial day of blowing the trumpet" (יום תרועה [*Yom Teru'ah*]) was designated Rosh Hashanah, literally – head of the year[60]; (2) consequently, the beginning of the year was moved from the springtime month of Nissan to the autumnal month of Tishrey; (3) several festivals of historical commemoration were added, the important of which are Hannukah, Purim, and the Ninth of Av.[61] Based on these changes, the official meaning of some of the festivals changed as well, most significantly Rosh Hashanah, which was made the first of ten days of repentance leading to the Day of Atonement, or Yom Kippur; and Shavuot was transformed from the feast of offering the first fruits to the feast of the giving of the Torah. This version of the liturgical calendar was sanctified in the rabbinic corpus and has been used since (with minor changes) by Jews the world over as their only calendar. It is therefore striking that Rosenzweig, who was well aware that Jewish praxis follows the rabbinical calendar, chose to present its biblical version in the *Star*.

---

60 *Mishnah*, Rosh Hashanah 1:1
61 *Bavli* Shabbat 21b (Hannukah); *Mishnah* Megillah (Purim); *Mishnah*, Ta'anit 4:6 (Ninth of Av).

But this is where the idiosyncrasy of Rosenzweig's liturgical calendar only begins. Instead of basing his interpretation of all feasts on the meaning that the Bible ascribes to them, Rosenzweig follows Scripture only in relation to the Sabbath, Passover and Sukkot; while his account of Shavuot, and most dramatically, of Rosh Hashanah and Yom Kippur, is wholly derived from their rabbinical interpretations.

According to Rosenzweig, the three festivals of pilgrimage, Passover, Shavuot and Sukkot,

> ... only seem to be feasts of commemoration. In reality, the historical element in them is living and present, and what is said to every participant at the first festival holds for them all: that he must celebrate the feast as though he himself had been delivered from Egypt (SE 352/SR, 317).[62]

As the first festival of the calendar, Passover is presented as the feast of creation. But since Jewish tradition associates with creation the liberation from Egyptian slavery in the Sabbath ritual, Rosenzweig focuses on Passover's reflection of all three divine acts:

> Like the creation of the world, the creation of a people contains the final goal, the final purpose for which it was effected. So it is that the people have come to feel this feast as the most vivid of the three, including the meaning of the two others (SE, 325/SR, 317).

Rosenzweig's presentation of Shavuot as the feast of the giving of the Torah, and hence as the feast of revelation, reflects a rabbinical innovation. In the Bible, it is strictly a festival of offering of first fruits of the produce of the land, ביכורים (*bikkurim*), to God. The transition from a feast of offering to a feast of revelation took place after the destruction of the Second Temple, when it became necessary to adapt the feast to a reality in which Jews lack a central site of worship and offer-

---

62 In his essay "The Builders" of 1923, Rosenzweig elaborated this notion drawn from the famous dictum in the Passover Haggada, a rabbinical work, emphasizing that it is grounded in Deuteronomy 5:3: "It was not with our fathers that the Lord made this covenant, but with us, the living, every one of us who is here today". For this dictum charging Israel to experience anew the constitutive events of the Jewish nation, Rosenzweig coined the term *Heutigkeit*, the "todayness" of the covenant between God and Israel. *Zweistromland*, 708–709/Glatzer 1955, 85–87. For the alignment of Rosenzweig's notion of *Heutigkeit* with classic rabbinic approaches to halakhah see Wiener 2017, 179–201.

ing. The Talmud therefore established that the Torah was given at Sinai on the 6th of Sivan, the date on which Shavuot is to be celebrated.[63]

Rosenzweig's description of Rosh Hashanah and Yom Kippur is also unabashedly rabbinical: "The horn blown on New Year's Day at the peak of the festival stamps the day as a 'day of judgment'" (SE, 360/ SR, 324). In the Bible, Rosh Hashanah (a name first introduced in the eponymous mishnaic tractate), is an enigmatic day of remembrance, holy convocation and of blowing the trumpets. It became a celebration of the New Year only once Tishrey replaced Nissan as the first month in the calendar. Its association with Yom Kippur came with the advent of the Ten Days of Awe, ימים נוראים (*Yamim Nora'im*), leading from the New Year to the Day of Atonement, also a Talmudic innovation.[64]

In contradistinction to Shavuot, the centrality of the temple to rite and worship on Yom Kippur did not change the practice of the festival after 70 CE. Prescribed as a day of repentance and self-affliction in Scripture, a "Sabbath of solemn rest" (Leviticus 23:32), in the Mishnah it became the only day of the year on which the House of Israel stood in the presence of God, symbolically attested by the High Priest's pronouncement of the divine name, which could not be uttered in any other way. Rosenzweig's description, which is a paraphrase on Mishnah Yoma 3:9, conveys the spirit of the festival:

> The congregation now rises to the feeling of God's nearness as it sees in memory the Temple of old, and visualizes especially the moment when the priest pronounces the ineffable name of God, which is always paraphrased [*unumschrieben*] and the assembled people fall on their knee (SE, 359/SR, 323–324).[65]

The utterance of the name of the God of eternity who had promised Moses eternal "being there" resounds in the festival that brings the spiritual year to its

---

[63] *Bavli*, Yoma 4b. Rachel Elior has recently claimed that the construction of Shavuot as the festival of the giving of the Torah was a development in several post-biblical traditions to which the tannaites opposed and tried to silence in the Mishnah. See Elior 2012.

[64] *Bavli*, Yoma, 16b: א"ר יוחנן שלשה ספרים נפתחין בר"ה אחד של רשעים גמורין ואחד של צדיקים גמורין ואחד של בינוניים צדיקים גמורין נכתבין ונחתמין לאלתר לחיים רשעים גמורין נכתבין ונחתמין לאלתר למיתה בינוניים תלויין ועומדין מר"ה ועד יוה"כ זכו נכתבין לחיים לא זכו נכתבין למיתה. (Said R. Yohanan. Three books are opened on Rosh Hashanah: one of the utterly evil and one of the utterly righteous and one of the moderate. The utterly righteous are immediately written and signed to life, the utterly evil are immediately written and signed to death, and the moderate remain suspended between Rosh Hashanah and Yom Kippur: if they are received favourably they are signed to life; if they are not received favourably they are signed to death.)

[65] Translation altered.

close. Sukkot, then, is a festival of repose⁶⁶ and *Heutigkeit:* recollection of the perpetual presence of the formative past in Jewish life. Finally, as the feast of redemption, Sukkot is also charged with the task of bringing back the celebrating congregation from the heights of the spiritual elation accompanying the contemplation of eternity to the ground of reality: "... so this close of the spiritual year is not permitted to be actual closure but must flow back to the beginning" (SE, 349/ SR, 320 – 321). At this juncture, the Bible's cultic function in the reading of weekly Torah portions and prophetic lections, הפטרות (*haftarot*), which accompanied the description of the calendar, reveals its contribution to the Sabbath's temporal nexus:

> ... redemption does not conclude the feast month of redemption which closes the annual circuit of Sabbaths ... In the common unity of man, the soul was alone with God. To neutralize this foretaste of eternity, the Feast of Booths reinstates the reality of time. Thus the circuit of the year can recommence, for only within this circuit are we allowed to conjure eternity up into time" (SE, 364/SR, 327–328).

4.2.1.3 From Sanctifying Proclamation to Holy Writ

A unique feature of the biblical calendars in Leviticus and Numbers is their designation of all calendrical events (the Sabbath and the festivals) as מקרא קדש (*mikra kodesh*). The phrase, appearing only in these documents and in Exodus 12:16 (the first prescription of the Passover festival) (Licht 1978, 437– 438), is understood as denoting a summoned assembly for a sacred purpose.⁶⁷ Although Rosenzweig does not mention it in the *Star*, he surreptitiously binds the ancient prescription with the meaning *mikra* assumed during the return from Babylonian exile: the Bible.⁶⁸ The ordering of the spiritual year according to the listing of

---

66 Rosenzweig appears to echo Rashbam's commentary on Leviticus 23:43, which links the timing of the festival at the end of the agricultural year to the symbolic function of the sheds: "'I made the children of Israel to dwell in booths' [Leviticus 23:43] refers to [the Israelites'] forty years without settlement and their having arrived at an estate due to which you shall give thanks to the one who gave you an estate and affluent homes and do not say in your hearts my own strengths and the power of my hand has yielded this success".

67 Fabry & Ringgern, vol. 7, 145. According to Licht, modern scholars accept the interpretation of Nachmanides (commentary on Leviticus 23:2) for *mikra kodesh* as denoting an announcement of assembly to sanctify the day in question. Compare Rashi's commentary on Exodus 12:16, which cites *Sifra*, Emor 12, where the event is defined by *kodesh* (sacrosanct) rather than *mikra* (reading), sanctified by eating, drinking and clean garments. Cf. the earlier version in *Mekhilta de-Rabbi Ishmael*, de-Pesach 9:30 (commentary on Exodus 12:16).

68 Fabry & Ringgern, vol. 7, 146, based on Nehemiah 8:8: "And they read from the book [*mikra*], from the law of God [*Torah*]". Eliezer Ben Yehuda understands *mikra* in this verse as referring to

mikra'ei kodesh (the plural of *mikra kodesh*), combined with references to the lectionary readings on the high holidays as reflecting the essence of each feast, undergird Rosenzweig's emphasis on the centrality of the assembly of the congregation to hear the words of Scripture on the Sabbath and high holidays. From the outset of the discussion of the spiritual year, Rosenzweig emphasises the performative power of the public reading of Scripture. Torah readings before the congregation are the means to attaining collective silence, which is posited as the final end of liturgical praxis[69]:

> ... only this connection with a text that secures 'devout' listening [*"andächtige" Zuhören*] by all ... the text that the assembled congregation accepts [*gilt*] as the word of its God secures [*schafft*] to the one who reads it, the collective listening of all of the assembled (SE, 343/SR, 309–310).[70]

In other words, as long as the congregation accepts its scriptures as divine, it will remain open to the possibility of practicing silence as the ultimate devotional act, and will preserve its integrity. Rosenzweig concludes:

> The public reading [*Verlesung*] of the words of Scripture is the main thing [*ist die Hauptsache*]; for in that [reading] the communion of listening [*die Gemeinsamkeit des Hörens*] and thereby it establishes the solid ground of any and all communion among the assembled [*aller Gemeinsamkeit der Versammelten geschaffen*] (SE, 344/SR, 310).[71]

The practice of Torah readings is not only the phenomenological manifestation of the ontological foundations of temporality, it is a recurreing generation (*Be-Zeugung*) of the experience of creation through the living members of the community (Ehrlich 1988, 735). The institution of reading weekly portions of the Torah in an infinite cycle of repetition exposes the dialectics of the Heraclitan and Parmenidean elements of temporality: the unresolved and unavoidable clash between flux and stasis: "Precisely the regularity of the sequence of Sabbaths, precisely the fact that other than the weekly Torah portion each resembles the other, makes the Sabbaths the cornerstone of the [spiritual] year" (SE, 345/SR, 310).

The implicit presence of *mikra* as the reading of Scripture in Rosenzweig's adumbration of *mikra'ei kodesh* was further developed in his translation of the

---

the reading of any book: Ben Yehuda 1980, 3289. The first occurrences of the term in the Mishnah denote either a passage from the Bible (e. g., Sotah 7:2) or the biblical corpus (e. g. Nedarim 4:3).
69 Rosenzweig will disclose his systematic considerations for this move in III:3. See chapter 3.
70 Translation altered.
71 Translation altered.

term in *Die Schrift*. Notoriously difficult to translate since antiquity,[72] German translators diverged on how it should be understood. Table 4.5 below shows that Buber and Rosenzweig were closer to, yet distinct from, their Jewish predecessors. Instead of translating *kodesh* as *Heiligtum* and have the verse describe the festivals as assemblies at the site of holiness (sanctuary or temple, as *Heiligtum* denotes both), they opted for the verbal noun *Heiligung*, the act of sanctification. And rather than Zunz's and Hirsch's summons or an appeal to assemble (*Berufung*), following Mendelssohn they translated *mikra* as *Ausrufen*: a proclamation, or literally – calling out. And so, the events of the biblical calendar become a "sanctifying proclamation":

Tab. 4.5: *mikra kodesh* – Exodus 12:16

B–R	Luther	Mendelssohn	Zunz	Hirsch
Ausrufen von Heiligung am ersten Tag und Ausrufen von Heiligung sei euch am siebenten Tag	Der Tag soll heilig sein, daß ihr zusammenkommt; und der siebente soll auch heilig sein, daß ihr zusammenkommt	Am ersten Tage soll die Ausrufung der Heiligkeit geschehen, und am siebenten Tage soll bei euch eine Ausrufung der Heiligkeit geschehen	Und am ersten Tage ist Berufung in's Heiligthum, und am siebenten Tage soll auch Berufung in's Heiligthum seyn	Und am ersten Tage soll Berufung zum Heiligtume und am siebenten Tage Berufung zum Heiligtume euch sein

וּבַיּוֹם הָרִאשׁוֹן מִקְרָא־קֹדֶשׁ וּבַיּוֹם הַשְּׁבִיעִי מִקְרָא־קֹדֶשׁ יִהְיֶה לָכֶם

The emphasis on the sanctity of the event and its auditory nature, rather than its location and social function, remains faithful to the original context of the phrase while resonating with the emergence of the Bible as a ritual artefact. Therefore, it not only offers an important example for the continuity between Rosenzweig's work in the *Star* and *Die Schrift*; it also illustrates the unique ability of the language of the Bible to comport with the philosophical concerns of modern Jewish thought.

4.2.2 Eternal Life in Our Midst

Since recording in 1914 the powerful impression that the thanksgiving to God who "planted eternal life in our midst" had made on him, Rosenzweig's fascina-

---

[72] Licht 1988, 438.

tion with this expression only intensified. So much so, that in the *Star* it became a leitmotif for the actualisation of the organic connection of between eternity and the present. If its first appearance, in the Threshold between Parts II and III, refers to the progression from revelation to redemption, the transition to Part III lifts the thin veil of systematic impartiality and asserts the uniqueness of the Jewish people in light of their privileged access to eternity in the present.[73] A full quotation of the line, "Blessed be He, who has planted life in our midst" opens and closes *Star* III:1,[74] framing the presentation of the liturgical calendar and announcing the crucial function of Torah readings in bridging between eternity and the present:

> [Sabbath] morning becomes a celebration of revelation ... the joy of [Moses], the great recipient of revelation, to whom God "spoke face to face ."… is followed, in the order of the day, with the public reading [*Verlesung*] of the weekly portion to the congregation by its representatives. On Sabbath eve it was the knowledge of the origin in creation [*Geschaffenheit*] of all things earthly [*alles Irdischen*], which the consecrating locution [*den Spruch der Weihe*] formed; in the morning, it becomes the awareness [*Bewußtsein*] of the people's election [*der Erwähltheit des Volks*] through the Giving of the Torah, in which *the gift of planting eternal life in their midst* takes place. With this awareness of election the man called forth to the Torah from the congregation approaches the book of revelation, and with the awareness of eternal life he returns and merges back with the congregation. But with this awareness of eternal life he rises [*steigt er*] within the Sabbath over the threshold [*über die Schwelle*] separating both revelation and creation from redemption.[75]

The trope of eternal life planted in the midst of the Jewish people joins together neatly with the God of revelation and the eruption of eternity into the present. And yet, it is far from exhausting the discussion. The shift from *der Ewige* to ICH BIN DASEIN as the translation of God's proper name, and the translation of *mikra kodesh* as *Ausrufen von Heiligung* in *Die Schrift*, which I have examined above, exemplify Rosenzweig's continuous efforts to refine his ideas outside of the systematic setting of the *Star*. And indeed, "eternal life" expands the possibilities of venturing beyond the system while remaining firmly anchored in it. In

---

[73] The ritual reading of the Torah portion on the Sabbath, which the Church did not retain in its own weekly service, is, according to Rosenzweig, among other factors, linked to a fundamental ontological difference between Jews and Christians. Though they are both communities of revelation, as God's elect, the Jews are privileged with the seed that kindles in our hearts the fire of the Star (of Redemption) of God's truth (SE, 462/SR, 415).

[74] Rosenzweig, SE, 331/SR, 298; SE, 372/SR, 335, respectively. Rosenzweig makes slight variations that are difficult to reflect in translation: he opens with *in mitte unter uns* and concludes with *in unsrer Mitte*.

[75] Rosenzweig, SE, 346–347/SR, 312. Translation altered, my italics.

the original setting of the benediction, the eternal life motif acquires additional meanings that lie at the core of Jewish religious life, enhancing Rosenzweig's exposure of the dialectic between transcendence and immanence.

This expansion of the trope occurs in spite of, rather than thanks to, his translation of its Hebrew origin, the phrase חיי עולם (*hayey olam*).[76] Other than in the benediction itself (which is one of the earliest documents in which *hayey olam* appears),[77] the phrase is used in rabbinical sources mainly in two contexts: (1) as the study and contemplation of divine lore, which is contrasted with the preoccupation with the trivialities of mundane existence[78]; (2) as the afterlife – חיי עולם הבא (*hayey ha-olam ha-ba*).[79] *hayey olam* in the sense of existence outside of the exigencies of time (=immortality), appears less common.[80] It is not unreasonable to think that in his translation and adaptation of *hayey olam* Rosenzweig tapped into the religious imagination of early rabbinical literature, relying on a combination of knowledge and intuition. For, he not only invokes the stock-in-trade allegory of the Torah as a seed planted into the people of Israel that grows into a tree[81]; he employs it to thread together revelation (to which the "one People" may became privy through reading its scriptures – (*torat emet*), and redemption (*hayey olam*):

> In eternal life, indeed, redemption was already anticipated for the world in revelation which, after all, contains everything; eternal life was planted in the revelation to the one people, so that it itself would no longer change; this eternal life will one day return in the fruit of redemption as it was once planted. Thus, a piece of redemption is here already really placed into the world, the visible world, and it shall be true that, seen from the world, revelation shall actually already be redemption (SE, 466/SR, 419).

---

76 His rather orthodox formulation resonates with other Jewish translations of the benediction. Cf. "*Gelobt seist du, Ewiger, unser Gott, König der Welt, die Lehre der Wahrheit gegeben und ewiges Leben in uns gepflanzt hat*" (Einstädter 1910, 38). Incidentally, the publisher of this siddur will publish eleven years later the first edition of the *Star*.
77 David Flusser considers the benediction to date much earlier than Tractate Sofrim, based on parallels he has found between the benediction read *before* Torah readings and fragments of daily liturgies from Qumran. Flusser 1989, 148–150.
78 See *Bavli* Berachot 21a; Shabbat 10a, 33b; Betza 15b; *Yerushalmi* Berachot ch.3 6 col. 1:1; Mo'ed Katan ch.3 82 col.2:5. Rashi on *Bavli* Shabbat 10a.
79 *Bavli* Berachot 48b; Ta'anit 21a (where *hayey ha-olam ha-ba* denotes the afterlife and is also contrasted with *hayey sha'ah*); *Mekhilta deRabbi Ishamel*, Yitro, Tractate Amaleq, 2:5. Flusser 1989, 152–153, considers this meaning to be central.
80 *Sifra on Leviticus* (Weiss) Nedava 1:2. *Numbers Rabba* (Vilna) 14:22.
81 On the centrality of the analogy between the Torah and the tree of life see Flusser 1989, 150–151. Rosenzweig invokes a similar image of seed and tree in SE, 291; 384/SR, 261; 335. He also invokes Yehudah Halevy's later variation on this theme in SE 421/SR, 379.

In a letter to Gertrude Oppenheim written two years before the *Star* was completed, Rosenzweig articulated in shorthand the ideas posited in Part I in order to move beyond them in Part III. Conflating idolatry with revelatory faith (in both its Christian and Jewish manifestations), he observed that while the idolatrous culture spanning Babylonian priests and the Monists of Jena (i.e., Hegel) preoccupied itself with the frivolities [*Seitensprüngen*] of the gods, revelatory religions followed the ways of God (*BT* I, 412–413). "Revelation", he tells his cousin, "grounds the above and below, Europe and Asia, etc., earlier and later on the one hand, past and future on the other hand" (*BT* I, 413). The name (i.e., God's name), is not echo and smoke [*Schall und Rauch*] but rather word and fire:

> ... the Word reverberates through time, from mouth to mouth, and the fire stretches across space. For, the penetration of the *Name* through the chaos of the un-named, that which can be named thus or otherwise ... has formed the stage and content of world-history (*BT* I, 413).[82]

Resorting to the firm barrier he had identified between revelation and reason (*Tagebücher* VI, 24),[83] he concludes: "Neither Plato nor Aristotle had known anything [of this sort]. 'The entire earth' ['*die ganze Erde*'] and ,'The End of Days' [*das 'Ende der Tage'*] are absent from their vocabulary" (*BT* I, 413).

Even the founding fathers of Western philosophy could not pluck from the tree of Torah the fruits of revelation: recognition of God's work,[84] and the anticipation of its consummation.[85] At a relatively early stage, before completing the blueprint of his system, Rosenzweig was acutely aware that it would ultimately shed its philosophical scaffolding and plumb the depths of Jewish religious imagination. And indeed, through the climactic ending of his tome he would eventually do just that.

---

82 Italics in the original.
83 I discuss this entry in chapter 2.
84 With *Die ganze Erde* Rosenzweig probably referred to Psalm 89:12: " The heavens are yours, the earth also is yours: as for the world and the fullness thereof, you have founded them".
85 *Ende der Tage* alludes to the popular prophetic trope אחרית הימים (*aharit ha-yamim* [End of Days]). See e.g., Isaiah 2:2; Jeremiah 23:20, 30:24, 48:47, 49:39; Ezekiel 38:16, etc.

Chapter 5:
Im Angesicht Gottes bewährt: From Truth to the Divine Face

Franz Rosenzweig's death on December 10, 1929, came as no surprise, bringing to a close an eight-year battle with amyotrophic lateral sclerosis. And yet, it shocked the circles of his admirers and colleagues, within the Jewish community in Frankfurt am Main and throughout Germany. Within several months, two commemorative volumes were published (E. Mayer 1930; H. Mayer 1930), both containing a vignette penned by Martin Buber, grieving the loss of his close friend and venerated partner to the task of translating the Bible. With uncharacteristic conciseness Buber captured the essence of the life and thought of his deceased friend by telling the story behind the motto of the *Star:* צלח [ו]רכב על דבר אמת (*tzelah [u-]rehav al dvar emet*), an excerpt from Psalms 45:5. The two editions of the work, published in 1921 and 1930, display two variations on the verse, which originally reads:

וַהֲדָרְךָ, צְלַח רְכַב-- עַל-דְּבַר-אֱמֶת, וְעַנְוָה-צֶדֶק; וְתוֹרְךָ נוֹרָאוֹת יְמִינֶךָ.

(*ve-hadrach tzelah rechav al dvar emet ve-anavah tzedek; ve-torach noraot yeminecha*)

Neither variation, however, cites the source accurately.

As recorded in his 1922 notebook, Rosenzweig chose *rechav al dvar emet* as the *Star*'s motto when it first came out, as it reflected his conviction that *tzelah*, the wishing for full success, cannot be met in relation to the attainment of truth (*Tagebücher* VII, 10). This, thought Rosenzweig at the time, is only possible at the moment of consumation (*Voll-endung*) of one's life in death.[1] As the *Star* ends with a call to enter into life—*ins Leben*—Rosenzweig wished to avoid this contradiction, despite the urgings of Hermann Cohen to cite the verse in its entirety, as he had in *Religion of Reason* (E. Mayer 1930, 21). To justify his dismissal of Cohen's suggestion, Rosenzweig concludes the notebook entry with the saying *nemo ante mortem beatus:* None are blessed before death (*Tagebücher* VII, 10).

According to Buber, Rosenzweig's comment preceding this Latin aphorism is the "innermost intention" (*die innerste Absicht*) of the *Star* as a whole, which Ro-

---

[1] "The concept of the verification of truth becomes the basic concept of this new epistemology ... the way leads, over those truths for which man is willing to pay, to those he cannot verify in any other way than with the sacrifice of his life". *Zweistromland*, 158–159/*Theological Writings*, 135–136. On Rosenzweig's linking of verification (*Bewährung*) and death see Kavka 2012.

senzweig duly recorded in his notebook: "Indeed, I ought to advance into life" (*Die mich ja doch, ins Leben führen sollte*) (E. Mayer 1930, 21). This advancement into life, Buber adds, took place in the *Star*, "From the gate of that Temple, in which the divine truth in the *Mysterium* of the image [*Ebenbildlichkeit*] as face [*Antlitz*] has been seen" (E. Mayer 1930, 21).

The shift in Rosenzweig's perspective that led him to add *tzelah* to the motto of the *Star*'s second edition, Buber relates, found expression in "The New Thinking". With "unsurpassable accuracy", the eulogising friend muses, Rosenzweig described the *Star*'s ending as, "stepping into the everyday of life". The consummation of one's life, he realised, need not wait for one's moment of death; it can take place in one's encounter with the Almighty in everyday life. In Buber's words: "Standing before the Temple's exit is where truth as the illumination of the divine face is seen, the author transforms, for he is no longer an author, but a living human" (E. Mayer 1930, 21). In the eight years of his illness, Buber continues, Rosenzweig did just that: "The truth that he had seen he verified in the face of God [*in Angesicht Gottes bewährt*]" (E. Mayer 1930, 22).

In Buber's hands, the concluding pages of the *Star* become a record of a life of faith in awe of the mystery of the divine. As a self-standing statement, it even resists the kind of systematic development of ideas to which it serves as a climactic conclusion in the work. Hence, from Buber's personal perspective, this presentation of his friend's life's work made perfect sense. And yet, Buber's point of departure, the *Star*'s motto, beckons from the work's title page, forcing us to backtrack from the foray into the mystery of God's face to the precise moment in which Rosenzweig oversteps the limits of discursive thinking.[2] The idiosyncratic concept of truth articulated in *Star* III:3 is that precise moment. The cause common to philosophy and theology, searching for the truth, is the point of their simultaneous convergence and separation: by definition, the ultimate truth must include the logically- and empirically-verifiable truths that philosophy pursues; at the same time, it must extend beyond those categories and encompass non-discursive, non-rational knowledge.

---

[2] I am following here Stéphane Mosès' distinction between the discursive and non-discursive elements in the *Star*: "… this ultimate form of Truth is not graspable by discursive thought, and in order to evoke it, Rosenzweig must have recourse to the system of images and representations offered by the mystical traditions of Judaism and Christianity. In this form, Truth is not anymore given to conceptual knowledge or even to collective religious experience, but only to imagination … In spite of this, in order to speak of Truth we are forced to use discourse, whether it is the conceptual discourse of philosophy or the metaphorical discourse of religious tradition. See Mosès 1992, 263–271; here at 263. My discussion of Rosenzweig's engagement with mysticism in Part II differs substantially from Mosès' reading.

A leap from the discursive to the non-discursive would have undermined the entire systematic structure. The continuity between these two purportedly incompatible modes of thinking, then, had to be established on a ground common to both. Consistent with his strategy up to this point in the *Star*, Rosenzweig structures the discussion on a rhetoric that sustains a self-sufficient argument that can be construed in philosophical terms exclusively.[3] As we have seen in the previous chapters, this rhetoric is nonetheless undergirded by biblical prooftexts that Rosenzweig translated and inscribed into the systematic discussion. The function of these prooftexts in the expansion of the system from discursive- to non-discursive thinking is to support the smooth transition from the former to the latter, by proving equally essential to both.

The current chapter will expose the biblical infrastructure that supports the extension of the system to the realms of the ineffable, by situating it between two interlocutors. Hermann Cohen represents the farthest outpost in the engagement of discursive thinking with the sources of Judaism. As we will see, Rosenzweig bases his own truth concept on the very same sources Cohen interprets in *Religion of Reason*, and addresses very similar concerns, and yet he ventures way over and beyond what Cohen's system could tolerate. Martin Buber, the future friend and partner to the task of translating the Bible, is anticipated in the vision of the divine face. In his reading of the *Star*, however, the author of *Ecstatic Confessions* (Buber 1909, 1996) was a bit too keen to read past Rosenzweig's systematic edifice and concentrate on the foray into the mystery of the divine; whereas the author of the *Star* continued to exercise the epistemic prudence he demonstrated throughout the work, inspired by Maimonides.[4]

At this juncture we may discern what perhaps is the most ingenious aspect of Rosenzweig's system: its openness. That the discursive is open to the non-discursive, the philosophical to the theological, the systematic to the scriptural, the ideational to the real, saves the *Star of Redemption* from the fate of the imperious philosophical projects of German Idealism on which it is modelled. Once the system is complete, the cogitative process is not locked within a closed circuit; redemption as the pinnacle of the architectonic structure is not *only* absolute, but also partial. This seemingly contradictory notion is in fact what saves Rosenzweig from dogmatism: the full disclosure of truth as inhering in God, which

---

3 See Wolfson 1997, 2010; Mosès 1992, 262–286; G. Greenberg 1978a and 1978b; Freund 1959, 170–185).
4 See chapter 3 for a discussion of Rosenzweig's championing of Maimonides' adage, "His ways are not our ways, and His thoughts are not our thoughts". Elliot Wolfson's understanding of Rosenzweig's adoption of Maimonides' negative philosophy as a limiting principle is, in my view, too radical. See Wolfson 2010, 112–114.

is the consummation of the redemptive process, is not the ultimate, but pen-ultimate stage in the system's unfolding. The subjective encounter with the divine face, in the wake of which the subject is led *by the system itself* back into life, concludes the system and simultaneously directs the subject to that which still lies beyond it, until final redemption will take over in the coming of the kingdom.

5.1 From the Truth to God

The encounter between Cohen and Rosenzweig at the Berlin Lehranstalt in winter 1913 proved decisive for both thinkers, intellectually as well as personally. Though impressed, Rosenzweig strictly separated between his admiration for Cohen the teacher and his ambivalence toward Cohen the philosopher (Fiorato-Wiedebach 2012, 139). It was the ecounter with Cohen's conception of correlation (*Korrelation*) between God and humans that left an indelible impression on Rosenzweig (Schmied-Kowarzik 2006b, 120–121), and induced him to remain in contact with Cohen after leaving the Lerhanstalt for the war in September 1914 (Bienenstock 2009, 38–39). Initially visiting Cohen's class out of sheer curiosity, Rosenzweig began regularly attending the course "The Concept of Religion in the System of Philosophy" (Schmied-Kowarzik 2006b, 116), as the encounter with the retired philosophy professor left him with "unparalleled astonishment" (*Zweistromland*, 239). Cohen's system inspired Rosenzweig to resolve the problem of creation *ex nihilo*, but he ultimately "availed himself" from its grip in order to add a speculative element that Cohen could never tolerate (Gibbs 1989, 639). Cohen's posthumous masterpiece, *Religion of Reason*, undoubtedly had the greatest impact on Rosenzweig, who described it as "the philosopher's homecoming" (*Zweistromland*, 227). The old philosopher entrusted a carbon copy of the book's manuscript in Rosenzweig's hands circa January–February 1918, who in turn was thrilled to find between its pages the lecturer he had met in winter 1913–1914, instead of the author of a flawed philosophy of religion (Schmied-Kowarzik 2006b, 120–121). Quite plausibly, *Religion of Reason* inspired the young thinker, among other things, thanks to its heavy reliance on Cohen's prowess as a translator of Jewish sources. Rosenzweig had already become privy to this talent at the Lehranstalt, as Cohen shared with his class original traslations of Psalms (*Zweistromland*, 216). The book's analysis of the rational foundations of Judaism bedecked with innumerable translations of biblical verses, rabbinic dicta and aphorisms, and arguments of medieval Jewish philosophers, seems to have motivated Rosenzweig to outdo his teacher.

5.1.1 Riding in the Cause of Truth

Indented to the right, in typeface size smaller than the perfunctory line stating ERSTE AUFLAGE/ZWEITE AUFLAGE (first/second edition), stands the motto of the *Star*. Its Hebrew characters are bereft of vocalisations; its provenance inscrutable to the German reader lacking knowledge of Hebrew. And even when its meaning and provenance become clear, צלח [ו]רכב על דבר אמת remains a seemingly disjointed prelude to the opening line of the *Star:* "*Vom Tode, von der Furcht des Todes, hebt alles Erkennen des All an*"; "From death, from the fear of death, rises all cognition of the All". Yet, the existential dread that goads us to strive for knowledge of the All is in fact the negative to the positive of the Psalmist's call to ride in the cause of truth. This call renders itself to be read as a Hebraic replica of a Platonic aphorism; but it bespeaks the biblical provenance of the underframe supporting the entire edifice of the *Star:* from the depths of *Die immerwährende Vorwelt*, via *Die allzeiterneuerte Welt* to the soaring heights of *Die ewige Überwelt*.[5]

In order to expose this underframe, let us perform the following thought experiment: omitting the text beginning with the *Star*'s opening line, we will skip from the motto directly to the opening sentences of *Star* III:3, "The Star, or the Eternal Truth", and then to the opening of the *Star*'s postlude, "Gate":

> *tzelah u-rechav al dvar emet*
>
> God is the truth. Truth is his signet.[6] By it he is known, also when one day all that in which he had let his eternity known within time, all eternal life, all eternal way, finds its end, the same place where the eternal finds its end: in eternity (SE, 423/SR, 380).[7] [...]
>
> The eternal had become figure in the truth. And the truth is none other than the face of this figure. Truth alone is its face. And take much heed for the sake of your soul: you saw no form; you heard only speech, – this is how it is called in the mid- and surrounding world of revelation. But in the redeemed world of above and beyond, brought over in the right time and at the right place by the blessing uttered with yet higher powers, the word is silent. Of that consummated-pacified [world] it is said: He make his face [*Antlitz*] shine upon you.

---

5 In Hallo's translation: "The ever-enduring proto-cosmos", "The always-renewed cosmos", and "The eternal hyper-cosmos"; in Barbara Galli's translation: "The everlasting primordial world", The ever renewed world", and "The eternal supra-world", respectively.
6 Cf. *Bavli*, Shabbat 55a: "The signet of the blessed Holy One is truth". Compare H. Cohen 1987, 487; and Rashi ad loc.: "[the letter *mem*] is the middle between the first [letter, *aleph*] and the last [letter, *tav*], after 'I am First and I am Last'" (Isaiah 44:6). On the centrality of this verse to Rosenzweig's concept of God see chapter 3.
7 Translation altered.

> This shining of the divine face [*Angesicht*] alone is the truth ... But he to whom He shall make his face [*Angesicht*] shine, is also he to whom He shall turn it (SE, 465/SR, 418).[8]

The transition from the motto to the opening of our hypothetical *Star of Redemption* appears seamless. This is so, first and foremost, because the passage constructed above is made up of six verses that Rosenzweig weaves together:

Tab. 5.1: Biblical Citations in "Buber's" *Star of Redemption*

Verse	RSV	Rosenzweig (*SE*)	Luther
Psalms 45:5	In your majesty ride forth victoriously for the cause of truth	tzelah u-rechav al dvar emet*	Zieh einher der Wahrheit zugut (Ps. 5:4)
Jeremiah 10:10	But the LORD is the true God	Gott ist die Wahrheit	Aber der HERR ist ein rechter Gott
Deuteronomy 4:9	Only take heed, and keep your soul diligently	Und hütet euch sehr um eurer Seele willen*	Hüte dich nur und bewahre deine Seele wohl
Deuteronomy 4:12	[You] saw no form; there was only a voice	Gestalt habt ihr keine gesehn, Sprache allein vernahmet ihr	aber keine Gestalt saht ihr außer der Stimme
Numbers 6:25	The LORD make his face to shine upon you	Er lasse dir leuchten sein Antlitz	der HERR lasse sein Angesicht leuchten über dir
Numbers 6:26	The LORD lift up his countenance upon you	Wem er aber sein Angesicht leuchten läßt, dem wendet er es auch zu†	der HERR hebe sein Angesicht über dich

Notes:
* Reference not provided.
† Translation is a paraphrase on the text of the original verse; reference provided.

Under our reading, the *Star* becomes surprisingly amenable to Buber's account: an inventive modern theology of faith suffused with biblical references, tinged with mystical curiosity. The absence of the slightest reference to the German Idealist tradition implies the redundancy, irrelevance even, of philosophical inquiry to the discussion. And yet, it is impossible to conceive of such a large part of the *Star* as redundant. We must therefore re-examine those 90 % that stretch between the motto and Part Three Book Three of the *Star* and rediscover their ne-

---

8 Translation altered.

cessity in the light of the verses with which Rosenzweig frames them: Psalms 45:5 and Jeremiah 10:10. As noted above, *tzelah u-rechav al dvar emet* leaves the question open as to the nature of the truth in the cause of which, using the Psalmist's words, Rosenzweig urges us to ride forth. The answer to this question is suspended through Parts I–III:2, until Rosenzweig states in the opening of Part Three: *Gott is die Wahrheit*; God is the truth. Thus placed, this citation functions as the conclusion of the unfolding of the *Star* as a discursive system, and as the beginning of its unfolding as a non-discursive system. Rosenzweig justifies this move by claiming that the positing of truth as the ground of philosophical discourse, rather than its final destination, is one of the fundamental errors of the philosophical heritage (SE, 436/SR, 392; *Zweistromland*, 157–159/ *Theological Writings*, 135–156). As Stéphane Mosès notes, in order to rectify it the system must acknowledge that it "is nonetheless constantly outspanned by its own beyond" (Mosès 1992, 267). In other words, it must acknowledge that ultimate truth cannot be attained by reason alone, as its source lies outside of its limits.

Rosenzweig asserts that in this extra-rational realm truth may only be contemplated in silence, requiring "leaping beyond the world of words" (SE, 428/SR, 385), to the ultimate silence that stands for the "true depth of the deity" (SE, 427/ SR, 384). Truth "is one with all that is real" (SE, 427/SR, 384), i.e., it is organically connected with the truths that we encounter within the limits of the sayable. And yet, the truth does not verify [*bewährt*] reality; reality maintains [*bewahrt*] truth (SE, 16/SR, 14). Nor can the designation of truth as fact support our attempt to establish a concept of eternal truth, because truth and untruth are equally factual. Hence, instead of fact, Rosenzweig contends, we must base our concept of truth on trusting faith [*Vertrauen*]: "All trust in the truth rests upon an ultimate trust that the ground on which truth places itself with its own two feet is capable of supporting" (SE 431/SR, 388). In "The New Thinking" Rosenzweig hints that the ground upon which trusting faith stands is actually the words of Scripture, as he confesses that in order for his book "to say what it has to say, especially the new thing it has to say, the old Jewish words come" (*Zweistromland*, 155/ *Theological Writings*, 131). However, the evidence from the *Star* makes it amply clear that the Bible is for Rosenzweig more than a mere repository of suitable vocabulary for articulating his system.[9] Crucially, the vocabulary of the Jewish

---

9 Rosenzweig makes this comment in order to explain his claim at the beginning of the essay that the *Star* is not a Jewish book. Norbert Samuelson cautions against literal readings of this statement: "What Rosenzweig meant [by making this statement] is that this book is a serious work in a tradition of serious academic theology and philosophy that is not to be confused with the kinds of popular books for religious and Jewish masses current both then and now"

sources that Rosenzweig uses does not appear in the original Hebrew, but in translation; and not just any "authoritative" or literal translation, but in Rosenzweig's own subversive rendition. Hence, the necessity of the "old Jewish words" for the articulation of the *Star* does not stem from their ancient Semitic origin. It is chiefly in virtue of the scriptures comprised of the "old Jewish words", which, through our acceptance of their authority with *Vertrauen*, or trusting faith, which is itself derived from Rosenzweig's translation of the Hebrew root ב.ט.ח. (*b.t.h.*),[10] become the only medium at our disposal for articulating that which lies beyond words, in the realm of silence.[11]

And so, as Rosenzweig's answer to the question "What is the truth", his translation of Jeremiah 10:10 emerges as the linchpin that holds together the entire system of the *Star:* it is the system's final destination, which marks the conclusions of its discursive part and the beginning of its non-discursive part. Indeed, the sources index in the *Star*'s second edition indicates that the verse is not only cited in the chapter's opening statement, but that it also applies to the discussion of truth in chapter sections *Gott und die Wahrheit* ("God and the Truth") through *Das Erleben der Wahrheit* ("The Experiencing of Truth".) (SE, 428–439/SR, 385–395). These sections constitute Rosenzweig's two-tiered interpretation of the proclamation "God is the truth": (1) a self-contained epistemological claim, interpreted analytically; (2) the conclusion of the discursive part and the beginning of the non-discursive part of the system of the *Star*, interpreted metaphorically.

(Samuelson 2010, 575). Indeed, this statement has been misread and misunderstood by many a Rosenzweig scholar due to the sophisticated rhetoric he employs. The same rhetorical strategy appears to have led Rosenzweig to remains completely silent on the matter of his extensive reliance on translation in the *Star*. The considerations that led Roesnzweig to develop his rhetoric are a topic worthy of further investigation, which exceeds the scope of the current book.

10 The *Star's* sources index lacks any references in relation to the pages in question. But in the grammatical analysis of Psalms 115, the source text analysed in *Star* II: 3, Rosenzweig asserts: "Hopeful trust [*Hoffendes Vertrauen*] is the key word [*Grundwort*] in which the anticipation of the future into the eternity of the moment occurs" (SE, 280/*Star*, 252). *Hoffendes Vertrauen* is Rosenzweig's variation on the translations of Psalms 115:9 ("O Israel, trust in the LORD! He is their help and their shield") by Zunz ("*Jisraël vertraue dem Ewigen*") and Philippson ("*Jisrael, vertrau' auf den Ewigen*"). Compare Luther ("*Aber Israel hoffe auf der HERR*") and Buber ("*Jisrael, sei sicher an IHM!*).

11 In *Star* III:1, public Torah readings are the means for facilitating worship in silence by the congregation. See chapter 4.

5.1.2 The Truth: Tiers I & II

The first tier of Rosenzweig's interpretation shows that "God is the truth" functions simultaneously as premise: "God is the truth. Truth is his signet. By it he is known" (SE, 423/SR, 380);
Proposition:

> For truth is the only thing which is wholly one with reality ... And is then truth—God? No ... Truth is not God. God is the truth ... The proposition 'God is the truth' differs from other propositions of the same kind, even from the proposition that reality is truth, since its predicate is not the general concept under which the subject is subsumed (SE, 428–429/SR, 385–386) ...

And conclusion:

> 'God is the truth' means that he bears it within himself, that it is imparted to him. The whole truth is imparted only to God. Man partakes in the truth, and verifies as much with his Truly [*Wahrlich*] which is the veritable countersignature to the document, emanating from the truth of the Lord (SE, 439/SR, 395).

The second tier of the interpretation draws the bridge between the self-contained concept of truth, which belongs to the realm of silence, and the *Star*'s three discursive parts. It does so by assigning to God a different image through which He is manifest at each of the stages on the path creation–revelation–redemption: death, love and light, respectively.

> God is not life: God is light (SE, 423/SR, 380).

> We experience his existence directly only in virtue of the fact that he loves us and awakens our dead Self to a beloved and requiting soul. The revelation of divine love is the heart of the All. [*Die Offenbarung der göttlichen Liebe ist das Herz des All* (SE, 424/SR, 381).

> Though the God of the *Vorwelt* had not himself been dead, he was, as Lord of dead matter, himself like this Nothing [*Nichts*] ... And the Lord of dead matter, though he is not part of that matter, is in essence akin to it and thus a Nothing like it (SE, 427–428/SR, 384–385).

> God's truth is none other than the love with which he loves us. The light with which the truth illuminates is none other than the word to which our Truly makes answer (SE, 436/SR, 392).

5.1.3 Truth in *Religion of Reason*

Rosenzweig's acquaintance with the sources of Judaism is usually considered one of his main weaknesses. As noted in the previous chapters, the sources that he cites in the *Star* were shown to have been derived from the writings of his two venerated teachers at the *Lehranstalt*: Ismar Elbogen and Hermann Cohen. Despite his astounding intellectual voracity, it was impossible for the graduate of a German *Gymnasium* and universities to have established a firm grip on the "Jewish bookcase" in the course of one year's study and several years of active military service. Still, even where Rosenzweig is clearly basing his discussion on the sources appearing in his teachers' treatment of the same subject, the interpretation is entirely his own.

Such is the case with the concept of truth, which is based on the same sources that Hermann Cohen includes in the *Religion of Reason*. This observation goes well beyond the biographical anecdote: the differences in the function of the sources within each system, in the way in which they are interpreted, and the use of translation as the element that transforms the nature of philosophical discourse from analytical to hermeneutical, allow us to appreciate the daring originality of Rosenzweig's invention of a new dynamic between the traditions of German Idealism and Judaism. A comparison of Rosenzweig's discussion with Cohen's clearly shows that the former student developed his ideas as a counter-response to the master's attempt to establish a neo-Kantian conception of Judaism.[12]

The essential difference between Rosenzweig's conception of truth and that of Cohen, to use Stéphane Mosès' term, is that it outspans the system by drawing a bridge between its tight-knit structure of the infinity of knowledge at which that structure is pointing, thus announcing its inability to articulate that infinity. Cohen, on the other hand, insists on a closed system within which the sources of Judaism offer the optimal articulation of its purely rational synthesis of ethics and nature.

Both discussions are anchored in an interpretation of Jeremiah 10:10, presenting it as the *summa* of their argument and repeatedly invoking it to reiterate their point. But while Rosenzweig uses it as his opening, Cohen first describes the philosophical problem that the concept of truth out of the sources of Judaism purportedly resolves.

---

[12] Out of the texts that both thinkers draw on in their discussion, Rosenzweig's interpretation of *Bavli* Shabbat 55a is the most similar to Cohen's in the sense that they both employ it as an interpretation of the ontological relations between God and the truth as they are described in Jeremiah 10:10. See Rosenzweig, SE, 427–429 /SR, 384–386; and H. Cohen 1987, 487.

We may therefore read Rosenzweig's severing of the Gordian knot between reality and truth, as a direct critique of Cohen, who, by positing truth as the *Urproblem* of philosophy, is repeating philosophy's perennial error that Rosenzweig criticises. Hence, "For the world, truth is not law but content. The truth does not verify [*bewährt*] reality; reality maintains [*bewahrt*] truth" (SE, 16/SR, 14), is Rosenzweig's counter-argument to Cohen's "Truth alone is the law of the necessary connection of natural cognition with moral cognition" [*Wahrheit ist allein das Gesetz des notwendigen Zusammenhangs der Naturerkenntnis mit der sittlichen Erkenntnis*".] (H. Cohen 1987, 476).

5.1.3.1 Jeremiah 10:10

Both Rosenzweig and Cohen offer original translations of Jeremiah 10:10, shaping them in the mould of their argument, making the biblical prooftext reflect it. As Table 5.2 below shows, Rosenzweig and Cohen retain the original function of אמת (*emet*) as a noun, which the Christian translations turned into an adjective (Kautzsch: *wahrhaftig*; Luther: *rechter*). But, while Cohen reads the verse in the context of its literary setting, as the conclusion of a prophetic assault against idolatry, Rosenzweig isolates it and extrapolates a universal proposition: God is the truth.[13] Paradoxically, Cohen's historical reading subjects the Bible to the dictates of his closed rational system, while Rosenzweig's ignoring the verse's original setting opens up the system of the *Star* to the rich, non-rational imagination of the Bible, which he will explore in his portrait of the divine face. Like Cohen, he sees in idolatry a problem that should be addressed in the context of truth, but he does that by emphasising the fundamental difference between the relative nothingness of the God of the Bible in the *Vorwelt*, and the absolute nothingness of pagan idols.[14]

---

[13] A few verses earlier (10:2), Jeremiah warns his audience not to follow the ways of the foreign nations ("Thus says the LORD: "Learn not the way of the nations, nor be dismayed at the signs of the heavens because the nations are dismayed at them") in order to conclude in 10:10 that, "As the God of truth, YHWH will shake the earth with His wrath, and the foreign nations will not bear His fury".

[14] Cf. His translation of Psalms 96:5, "For all the gods of the peoples are idols": "'*Die Götter der Heiden sind Nichtse,*' ruft der Psalmist", ("For the gods of the idolaters are nothings, calls the Psalmist"; SE, 425/SR, 382). Compare Luther's: "*Denn alle Götter der Völker sind Götzen*". In *Die Schrift* Rosenzweig took this interpretation one step further, translating אלילם (*elilim*, in Leviticus 19:4 and Isaiah 2:8) as *Gottnichtsen* – "God nothings".

Tab. 5.2: Jeremiah 10:10

Rosenzweig	Cohen	Luther	Kautzsch	Zunz	Philippson
Gott is die Wahrheit	Aber der Ewige is ein Gott der Wahrheit	Aber der HERR ist ein rechter Gott	Jahve jedoch ist wahrhaftiger Gott	Aber der Ewige, Gott ist Wahrheit	Aber der Ewige, ist Gott in Wahrheit
וַיהוָה אֱלֹהִים אֱמֶת הוּא					

On this particular point, Rosenzweig's position is much closer to Maimonides' reading of Jeremiah 10:10 in *Hilkhot Yesodei Ha-Torah* 1:3–4. Even though the verse is cited in the original Hebrew, Maimonides' excerpting of *Adonai Elohim emet* (The Lord God [is] truth) is identical with Rosenzweig's excerpting and his translation of the verse as an equation of God with truth, as opposed to Cohen's more conservative translation according to which, "The Eternal is **a** God of the truth". The affinity between Rosenzweig's reading and Maimonides' is strengthened when their commentaries are compared:

Tab. 5.3: Maimonides and Rosenzweig on Jeremiah 10:10

Maimonides *Hilkhot Yesodei Ha-Torah* 1:3–4	Rosenzweig SE, 429/SR, 385
Therefore His truthfulness is unlike the truthfulness of any of them. This is what the prophet says: "And the Lord God is truth" (Jeremiah 10:10), He alone is Truth, and none other has truth as His Truth.	Truth is enthroned above reality. And is then truth – God? No. Here we ascend to the pinnacle seen from which the entire traversed path lies at our feet. Truth is not God. God is truth … It is not truth that sits enthroned above reality but God, because he is truth".

5.1.3.2 Psalms 45:5

In contradistinction to Jeremiah 10:10, the contribution of Psalms 45:5 to the discussion is more subtle. Cohen cites it twice in two different translations.[15] In both instances Cohen's citation serves to illustrate a point, rather than form the core

---

[15] (1) "*schreite, reite für die Sache der Wahrheit* "(Come forth, ride in the cause of truth), H. Cohen 1987, 490; (2) "*Gürte dein Schwert um die Hüfte, du Held, deinen Glanz und deinen Hoheit!, dringt durch, fahre einher für Wahrheit!*" (Gird your sword on your hip, you, Hero, your glory and your majesty! **Advance directly, fare ahead for truth**), ibid, 495.

of the argument itself. But as shown above, his encouraging Rosenzweig to use Psalms 45:5 as the motto of the *Star* indicates that he likely considered it to genuinely reflect the *Star* as a whole.

Micah 6:8, the fourth source common to both discussions also appears at a late stage in the presentation of their respective arguments. If Jeremiah 10:10 is the final destination of the discursive development of the Star of Redemption, Micah 6:8 is the destination of the system's non-discursive progression. Appearing on the *Star*'s penultimate page, it is the very last source to which Rosenzweig refers in the source index. Rosenzweig emphasises the biblical provenance of this verse by placing it in quotation marks and translating it in full, in contradistinction to *Gott is die Wahrheit*.[16]

Cohen uncharacteristically breaks up the verse into two parts, which he places in different parts of his work. The first partial quotation appears in the introduction as prooftext for the assertion that "Reason with its principle of the good connects God and man, religion and morality" (H. Cohen 1987, 39). Hence, Cohen sees it as the ground upon which the God of the Bible may cohabit with truth as the *Urlösung* (fundamental solution) to the *Urproblem* (fundamental problem) of philosophy. The verse's second part appears toward the end of the chapter on virtues, in conclusion of Cohen's discussion of the virtue of humility – *Demut* – which follows his discussion of truth.

5.1.3.3 Micah 6:8

The opening declaration of Micah 6:8 has much greater systematic importance for Cohen than its conclusion. The connection between God and man, grounded in reason qua the good, is reiterated in his definition of truth: "Only in the unification of theoretical and ethical cognition, only in the unification of the two power sources (*Kraftquellen*) of scientific consciousness, the God idea may be fulfilled (*kann die Idee Gottes erfüllen*). "Intuition, like any form of mysticism", he adds, "is in conflict with logical reason" (H. Cohen 1987, 480). Consequently, the non-rational and irrational forms of religious consciousness—intuition and mysticism—do not partake in the truth. As a side remark, Cohen adds that research should be made into the Kabbalah's stance in relation to truth, and whether it "makes do with the truth, with its multifaceted dialectic, or whether it seeks to outflank and oust it (*überflügeln und entsetzen*)" (H. Cohen 1987, 480).

In perfect asymmetry, Rosenzweig emphasises the ending of Micah 6:8, וְהַצְנֵעַ לֶכֶת עִם-אֱלֹהֶיךָ (*ve-hatzna' lechet im elohecha*), restating his translation, "*einfältig*

---

[16] On Rosenzweig's selective use of quotation marks see M. Benjamin 2009, 42–45.

wandeln mit deinem Gott", three times. Like the theme of the last movement of a Romantic symphony, Rosenzweig has *"einfältig wandeln mit deinem Gott"* chime in mounting crescendo, leading to the grand finale that blares in double fortissimo with the call—*INS LEBEN*—printed in block letters at the bottom of the funnel-shaped paragraph with which the closing lines of each of the *Star*'s three parts close.[17] The prophet's call, enshrined in English translations as a plea to "walk humbly" with the Almighty, is not teleological like its antecedent instruction to "do justice and be good in your hearts", (*Recht tun und von Herzen gut sein*; SE, 472/SR, 424) in Rosenzweig's rendition; it is an expression of the unmediated partaking of the eternal truth (*unmittelbar der ewigen Wahrheit teilhaft*), which is precisely the opposite of Cohen's grounding of human access to the truth in virtue of the perfect correspondence of reason with God. Rosenzweig is not opening up truth to the insights drawn from intuitive or mystical cognition against which Cohen cautions; but he is certainly appealing to a religious form of cognition that is beyond the pale of philosophising. It is useful to describe this form of cognition with Stéphane Mosès (1992, 266) as "religious imagination" (although unlike Mosès, we will conceive of this imagination as nurtured primarily by the Bible, rather than by Kabbalistic and Christian mystical literature). Rosenzweig's religious imagination is inspired by the "old Jewish words" of the Bible and opens up new possibilities for systematic thought, which his translations of the words of Scripture articulate.

5.2 From Thinking Into Life

"*Einfältig wandeln mit deinem Gott*" defies the consensus on the translation of *ve-hatzna' lechet* as *demütig sein* (be humble) or *demütig wandeln* (walk hum-

---

17 Rosenzweig describes *Star* III:3 as the *ritardando* (gradual slowdown of tempo) before the final rise of the apotheosis. Rosenzweig, letter to Margit Rosenstock-Huessy dated 1.2.1919, "The 'Gritli' Letters (1914–1929)", Eugen Rosenstock-Huessy Fund. http://www.erhfund.org/the-gritli-letters-gritli-briefe/.

bly),[18] which like the Hebrew root צ.נ.ע. (*tz.n.a*) strictly expresses humility and modesty, both as moderate conduct (as opposed to vanity or arrogance) (Fabry & Ringgern 1989, 1079). *Einfältig* is proximate to *demütig* in its denotation of credulity and innocence,[19] and even childlike simple-mindedness.[20] Yet, its semantic field is far wider, as it includes simplicity, directness, unmediated contact and wholeness, which is denoted in biblical Hebrew by the root ת.מ.מ. (*t.m.m.*).[21]

The subversive originality of Rosenzweig's translation of Micah 6:8 goes almost unnoticed in the climactic excitement of the *Star*'s conclusion,[22] and it does not appear to have caught the attention of any critic of the *Star*. Rosenzweig's supplanting of *demütig* with *einfältig* makes a very powerful statement on the nature of the human experience of the encounter with the divine: one need not feel humbled, but whole and pure. His insistence on drawing this insight from a biblical prooftext not only attests to Rosenzweig's prowess and ingenuity as a translator at this stage in his career; most importantly, it sheds light on the sources and intertextual dialogue that nourished his religious imagination.

18

Zunz	Philippson	Luther	Kautzsch
Er hat dir kund gethan, o Mensch, was gut ist; und was fordert der Ewige von dir, als: auf Recht halten, Liebe üben, und demüthig wandeln vor deinem Gott.	*Verkündet hat er dir, o Mensch, was gut, und was der Ew'ge von dir fordert: nur Recht zu üben, und Huld zu lieben, und demüthig zu wandeln vor deinem Gott.*	*Es ist dir gesagt, Mensch, was gut ist und was der HERR von dir fordert, nämlich Gottes Wort halten und Liebe üben und demütig sein vor deinem Gott*	*Er hat dir gesagt, o Mensch, was frommt! Und was fordert Jahwe von dir außer Recht zu thun, sich der Liebe zu befleißigen und demütig zu wandeln vor deinem Gott?*

19 E.g., in Luther's translation of וְהֹלְכִים לְתֻמָּם (*ve-holchim le-tummam*) in II Samuel 15:11 as "*sie gingen in ihrer Einfalt*".
20 E.g., in Luther's translation of שֹׁמֵר פְּתָאיִם (*shomer peta'im*) in Psalms 116:6 as "*behütet die Einfältigen*" and פְּתָאיִם (*peta'im*) in Psalms 119:130 as "*Einfältigen*".
21 Grimm 1971, Band 3, 173. The examples in the *Grimm Wörterbuch* for the occurrence of *einfältig* in German letters indicate that it was Luther's translation that introduced it into literary usage (Genesis 20:5; Psalms 116:6, 119:6). Rosenzweig could have drawn further encouragement from Zunz's translation of בְּתָם־לְבָבִי (*be-tom levavi*) in Genesis 20:5 as "*der Einfalt meines Herzens*" and קֹרָאיִם וְהֹלְכִים לְתֻמָּם (*keru-im ve-holchim le-tummam*) in 2 Samuel 15:11 as "*in ihrer Einfalt gegangen*".
22 Both English translations replicate the conventional rendition of the verse, "walk humbly with your God" (SR, 424; Galli 2005, 447), whereas Amir's citation of the verse (*Kokhav*, 437) makes it impossible for the Hebrew reader to be aware of Rosenzweig's original rendition.

Unfortunately, evidence that may explain Rosenzweig's opting for *einfältig* is limited to the circumstantial sort, as there is no record available of his translation work process in the *Star*.²³ I will begin with the conclusion to which the evidence has led me: In all likelihood, Rosenzweig's translation of *ve-hatzna' lechet* as *einfältig wandeln* was inspired by Luther's translation of the Greek adjective απλους (*haplous*) in Matthew 6:22 and Luke 11:34: "*Wenn dein auge einfältig ist, so wird dein ganzer Leib leicht sein*".²⁴

Rosenzweig's high regard for the New Testament is evident from his forthcoming approach to Christianity. His thorough knowledge of Christian scriptures is evident from his early diaries.²⁵ In his heyday as a student at the *Lehranstalt* he even notes that the New Testament is on a par with the Talmud, considering both as prophetic texts manifesting two different aspects of revelation (*Tagebücher* VI, 19). Rosenzweig, then, transforms the original lexical meaning of humility into simple wholeness and clarity, which re-translated into Hebrew would read וְהִתְמֵם דרך עם אלהיך (*ve-hatmem derech im elohecha*; And walk innocently with your God).²⁶ Far from whimsical or philologically reckless, this translation emerges as attuned to the ambience of the ancient religious imagination of biblical scribes and the authors of the Gospels, while remaining connected to the philosophical and extra-philosophical search for the truth in God. Its brazen, defiant ingenuity demarcates a clear and distinct framework for exploring the realms of religious imagination open to the reader of the Bible, which is much closer to Cohen's description of Kabbalah as a multifaceted dialectic than to the outflanking and ousting of truth.

Recalling that Rosenzweig embraces Maimonides' cautioning that God's ways are not our ways and His thoughts are not our thoughts, this unmediated, wholesome walking with God that Rosenzweig portrays requires a very clear de-

---

23 Even in Ephraim Meir's close reading of the Gritli Letters and their documentation of the composition of the *Star*, translation is brought up conceptually, as a framework facilitating cross-cultural encounters between two "others": Rosenzweig's Jewish and Margit Rosenstock-Huessy's Christian perspectives. Like Batnitzky, however, Meir refers to Rosenzweig's German rendition of the *Tischdank* blessing as his first attempt as translator. Meir 2006, 13–17.
24 "The eye is the lamp of the body. So, if your eye is sound, your whole body will be full of light" (RSV).
25 See his interpretation of Matthew 25:40 discussed in chapter 1 and of 1 Corinthians 15:28 discussed in chapter 2.
26 Delitzsch's Hebrew translation of *haplous*, which Luther translates as *einfältig* offers further substantiation for these semantic possibilities. In Matthew 6:22 and Luke 11:34 he translates ὁ οφθαλμός σου 'απλους (*o opthalmos sou haplous*) as נֵר הַגּוּף הָעַיִן וְאִם־עֵינְךָ תְמִימָה כָּל־גּוּפְךָ יֵאוֹר. See also, Romans 12:8 *Gibt jemand, so gebe er einfältig* הַנּוֹתֵן יַעֲשֶׂה בְתָם־לֵבָב; Romans 16:19 *aber einfältig zum Bösen* וּתְמִימִים לִבְלְתִּי הָרֵעַ; James 1:5 *der da gibt einfältig jedermann* הַנּוֹתֵן לַכֹּל בִּנְדִיבָה.

scription of the nature of the possibility of encountering God, one which would also have to correspond and support the proposition "God is the truth".

5.2.1 The Divine Face

We may now resume our inquiry into Buber's description of Rosenzweig's ultimate achievement as "to verify truth in the face of God—*im Angesicht Gottes bewährt*" (E. Mayer 1930, 22.) As Buber notes, the system of the *Star* attained its final fulfillment in the transformation of its author into a living person who no longer promulgates his thoughts, but lives; who knows God not through the written word, but through action (E. Mayer 1930, 21–22). Rosenzweig carries out this final move in the postlude to *Star* III:3—*Tor*—or Gate, embodying this final stage by switching to the first person singular for the rhapsodic encounter with the face of God. The subtle interplay of metaphor and substance we have identified as Rosenzweig's second-tier analysis of the concept of truth is distilled to utmost refinement. The geometrical representation of the system as a Star of David is superimposed unto the contour-less notion of the divine face, which is then encountered in a vision. Enhancing the occult effect yet further, the *Star* ends at the open doors of the temple through which the person experiencing the vision is to step over the threshold from the systematic reflection INTO LIFE.

Rosenzweig's staging of the encounter with the divine face is anticipated by a long process which is one of the *Star*'s best-kept secrets.[27] Rosenzweig makes a categorical distinction between two manifestations of the human face – the passive *Antlitz* and the active *Angesicht*.[28]

---

[27] The only studies that I have found analysing the face motif in the *Star* do not appear to have identified the trope of the dichotomy between *Antlitz* and *Angesicht* as leading to the concluding vision of the work. See Samuelson 1996; R. Cohen 1994, 241–273; Wolfson, 1997; 2010. The only exception is Brasser 2006. Yet, as I show below, he also misses Rosenzweig's grounding of this dichotomy in his interpretation of face-to-face encounters in the Bible.

[28] According to the *Grimm Wörterbuch*, Luther uses *Antlitz* (Grimm 1971, Bd. 1, 501–502) very often, noting that today it has a more solemn and poetic ring than *Angesicht* or *Gesicht*. But with the exception of Leviticus 17:10, Luther reserves *Angesicht* exclusively for the divine face, using it in the context of God's direct revealment of His face (in the Leviticus example, God's words make figurative use of the face, and do not denote actual revelation of it). As for *Angesicht* (Grimm 1971, Bd. 1, 350–352), the Grimm divides it into active (look, eyes, the presence of an onlook *an-gesicht*, as in "*er meidet mein Angesicht*" [he avoids my eyes (lit. my look, my face)], and passive meanings (the face observed, synonymous with *Antlitz*), observing that in its passive form, it also assumes the meaning of a mask.

Tab. 5.4: פנים in Translation

Verse	Hebrew Bible	Rosenzweig	Luther
Gen. 32:31	כִּי־רָאִיתִי אֱלֹהִים פָּנִים אֶל־פָּנִים (For I have seen God face to face)	Gottes Antliz (SE, 470/SR, 422)) Ich habe Gottheit geschaut, Antlitz gegen Antlitz (B–R)	denn ich habe Gott von Angesicht gesehen
Gen. 33:10	כִּי עַל־כֵּן רָאִיתִי פָנֶיךָ, כִּרְאֹת פְּנֵי אֱלֹהִים־וַתִּרְצֵנִי (for truly to see your face is like seeing the face of God, with such favor have you received me)	Denn ich habe nun doch einmal dein Antlitz angesehen, wie man Gottesantlitz ansieht (B–R)	... denn ich sah dein Angesicht, als sähe ich Gottes Angesicht
Gen. 43:3	הָעֵד הֵעִד בָּנוּ הָאִישׁ לֵאמֹר לֹא־תִרְאוּ פָנָי (The man solemnly warned us, saying, You shall not see my face)	Nicht sollt ihr mein Antlitz sehn (B–R)	... Ihr sollt mein Angesicht nicht sehen
Ex. 25:20	וְהָיוּ הַכְּרֻבִים פֹּרְשֵׂי כְנָפַיִם לְמַעְלָה סֹכְכִים בְּכַנְפֵיהֶם עַל־הַכַּפֹּרֶת וּפְנֵיהֶם אִישׁ אֶל־אָחִיו אֶל־הַכַּפֹּרֶת יִהְיוּ פְּנֵי הַכְּרֻבִים (The cherubim shall spread out their wings above, overshadowing the mercy seat with their wings, their faces one to another; toward the mercy seat shall the faces of the cherubim be)	Und die Cheruben seien Flügel breitend nach oben hin, mit ihren Flügeln schirmend über dem Verdecke, das Antlitz jeder zum Bruder, nach dem Verdecke zu seien die Antlitze der Cheruben. (B–R)	Und die Cherubim sollen ihr Flügel ausbreiten von oben her, daß sie mit ihren Flügeln den Gnadenstuhl bedecken und eines jeglichen Antlitz gegen das des andern stehe; und ihre Antlitze sollen auf den Gnadenstuhl sehen
Ex. 33:11	וְדִבֶּר יְהוָה אֶל־מֹשֶׁה פָּנִים אֶל־פָּנִים כַּאֲשֶׁר יְדַבֵּר אִישׁ אֶל־רֵעֵהוּ (Thus the LORD used to speak to Moses face to face, as a man speaks to his friend)	Mit dem Gott redete von Angesicht zu Angesicht wie ein Mann redet mit seinem Freund (SE, 346/SR, 312) So redete ER zu Mosche, Antlitz zu Antlitz, wie ein Mann zu seinem Genossen redet (B–R)	Der HERR aber redete mit Mose von Angesicht zu Angesicht, wie ein Mann mit seinem Freunde redet
Ex. 33:20, 23	וַיֹּאמֶר לֹא תוּכַל לִרְאֹת אֶת־פָּנָי כִּי לֹא־יִרְאַנִי הָאָדָם וָחָי. 	Mein Angesicht kannst du nicht schauen, denn nicht	Mein Angesicht kannst du nicht sehen; denn kein

Tab. 5.4: פנים in Translation *(Continued)*

Verse	Hebrew Bible	Rosenzweig	Luther
	(But," he said, you cannot see my face; for man shall not see me and live) וַהֲסִרֹתִי אֶת–כַּפִּי וְרָאִיתָ אֶת–אֲחֹרָי וּפָנַי לֹא יֵרָאוּ (then I will take away my hand, and you shall see my back; but my face shall not be seen.)	schaut mich der Mensch und lebt. Hebe ich dann meine Hand weg, schaust du meinen Rücken, aber mein Angesicht wird nicht erschaut. (B–R)	Mensch wird leben, der mich sieht. Und wenn ich meine Hand von dir tue, wirst du mir hintennach sehen; aber mein Angesicht kann man nicht sehen
Lev.17:10	וְנָתַתִּי פָנַי בַּנֶּפֶשׁ הָאֹכֶלֶת אֶת–הַדָּם (I will set my face against that person who eats blood)	mein Antlitz gebe ich wider die Seele die Blut ißt (B–R)	wider den will ich mein Antlitz setzen
Num.6:25 (Priestly benediction)	יָאֵר יְהוָה פָּנָיו אֵלֶיךָ וִיחֻנֶּךָּ. (The LORD make his face to shine upon you, and be gracious to you)	Er lasse dir leuchten sein Antlitz (SE, 465/SR,418) helle ER sein Antlitz dir zu und begünste dich (B–R)	der HERR lasse sein Angesicht leuchten über dir und sei dir gnädig
Deut.5:4	פָּנִים בְּפָנִים דִּבֶּר יְהוָה עִמָּכֶם בָּהָר מִתּוֹךְ הָאֵשׁ (The LORD spoke with you face to face at the mountain, out of the midst of the fire)	Angesicht an zu Angesicht redete ER mit euch am Berg aus mitten dem Feuer (B–R)	Er hat von Angesicht zu Angesicht mit euch aus dem Feuer auf dem Berge geredet

Martin Brasser's recent article about the philosophical implication of this distinction does not delineate in full the unique epistemological status that Rosenzweig ascribes to *Angesicht* in the work.[29] Rather, he characterises the "Theory of the face" in the *Star* as "empirical through and through" (Brasser 2006, 125). Briefly mentioning Rosenzweig's citation of Numbers 6:25, Brasser fails to account for the rich biblical tradition on which Rosenzweig draws in his portrayal of the face, and of the human experience of the divine face. In particular, he

---

29 He does however identify Rosenzweig's use of Reason as a "limit of knowledge" (*Erkenntnisgrenzen*). Brasser 2006, 135.

misses Rosenzweig's selective use of *Angesicht* and *Antlitz* in his translation of verses narrating encounters with the divine face.[30]

Indeed, Rosenzweig does not articulate the function of the two epistemological categories philosophically; he does so *philologically*. He had already identified in the *Urzelle* the systematic function of philology once the system crossed the limits of discursive reflection:

> The eternal occurrence in God can be understood ... on two grounds: from the basis of the fulfilled philosophy (Schelling) and on the basis of revelation (mysticism). Thus theosophy —I am myself still astonished and resistant to this thought—is joined to *theo*logy and philo*sophy*, concluding the triangle of the sciences.
>
> **The remainder is philo-logy**, i.e. silence. But seriously, what do you say to it? (*Zweistromland*, 137/*Theological Writings*, 70).[31]

Read in the context of Rosenzweig's translations in the *Star*, and crucially, in reference to the *Antlitz–Angesicht* dialectic, Rosenzweig's rather cryptic conclusion of the *Urzelle* acquires a decisive meaning. In the previous part we have followed the philological[32] consideration that supported the translation of *ve-hatzna' lechet*. Rosenzweig's most explicit account of the personal experience of revelation is grounded in the same methodology. The patent difference between *ve-hatzna' lechet* and פנים (*paneem* = face), is that the former is a singular term in the Bible, whereas the latter is used frequently and in different contexts. As such, it has broader implications in Rosenzweig's system, and accordingly, the impact of conceptual considerations (as opposed to strictly philological ones) is more pronounced.

Throughout the *Star*, Rosenzweig's first choice for translating *paneem* in general, and *paneem el paneem* (face-to-face) in particular is *Antlitz* (see Table 5.4 below). *Angesicht* is reserved for specific instances. By comparing the contexts in which Rosnzweig uses *Antlitz* and *Angesicht* to translate *paneem*, we may see that encounters, interpersonal and human-divine, are on most occasions be-

---

30 One interesting source he does refer to is Matthew 5:29 ("If your right eye causes you to sin, pluck it out and throw it away; it is better that you lose one of your members than that your whole body be thrown into hell"), on which Rosenzweig probably drew for the distinction between the weak and strong eyes, see Brasser 2006, 130.
31 My emphasis.
32 Rosenzweig's use of the term exceeds the strictly technical discipline of historical analysis of etymology. He describes himself as practicing philology while working on the dissertation (*BT* I, 115). From his letters in the 1920s that mention the topic, Rosenzweig appears to think of the "philology" he practices as modelled on lower criticism (*BT* II, 875), and he describes himself as "*als alter Philologe der ich bin.*".. (*BT* II, 970).

tween the external appearances of the parties, their *Antlitz*. But not all human-divine encounters are like that.

When God descends in a pillar of cloud on the Tent of Meeting (Exodus 33:11), Moses speaks to him פנים בפנים (*paneem be-faneem*) – *von Angesicht zu Angesicht*. This privileged encounter, in which the intimate features disclosing the thoughts and feelings behind the external appearance, or mask, as Rosenzweig calls it (SE, 470/SR, 423), was reserved for Moses alone. Moses' privilege is emphasised further in the portrait of the human face (SE, 470–471/SR, 423), which hails him as having concluded his life by being sealed with a divine kiss. To compare: Jacob the Patriarch sees only the divine *Antlitz* at the Yabbok River; the Priestly Benediction in Rosenzweig's translation permits only God's *Antlitz* to shine and bless the collective you it addresses.

The occurrences of *von Angesicht zu Angesicht*, far and few between numerous appearances of *Antlitz*, serve Rosenzweig to criticise misguided epistemologies of revelation. Thus, Nietzsche, "never before whom a philosopher stood eye to eye with the living God, so to speak ... was the first to see God face to face [*von Angesicht zu Angesicht*] ..." (SE, 20/SR, 18),[33] at the very same moment denied God's existence. Idolaters, posited as ancient precursors of Nietzsche's conception of God,[34] take the impossible leap over the chasm which no understanding of the understood, no wisdom of the wisdoms, may yield, to meet God, *von Angesicht zu Angesicht* (SE, 43/SR, 39). Finally, and most importantly, the encounter *von Agensicht zu Angesicht* is experienced by the Christian who must greet at mass the Head Bloodied and Wounded (SE, 406/SR, 365).[35] The immanent possibility of meeting *von Angesicht zu Angesicht* God's human incarnation guided Martin Luther in translating *paneem be-faneem* and *paneem* as *Angesicht zu Angesicht* almost categorically (see Table 5.4 below). Therefore, Rosenzweig's philological work appears to have been structured as a counter-response that tempers Luther's epistemological recklessness. He demonstrates the appropriate prudence through the application of *von Angesicht zu Angesicht* in the Jewish experience of revelation. The necessary and sufficient conditions for the attainment of this intimacy are silence and worship: (1) Moses' encounter at the Tent of Meeting is recreated, according to Rosenzweig, in the public Torah reading at syna-

---

33 My translation.
34 Rosenzweig entitles the section concluding his discussion of idolatrous deities *Götter Dämerung*, after Nietzsche's *Twilight of the Idols*.
35 A direct reference to *O Haupt voll Blut und Wunden*, Paul Gerhardt's German translation of the Latin poem *Salve mundi salutare*, which became a famous hymn in the Lutheran Church, set to music by Johann Sebastian Bach in the St. Matthew Passion and in the Cantata *Sehet, wir gehn hinauf gen Jerusalem* (BWV 159).

gogue, where the congregation exercises collective silence and the reader articulates its yearning for the divine with the words of scripture (SE, 346/SR, 312); (2) In the silent greeting of God, on bent knee (i.e., on Yom Kippur) permits encounter Him *von Angesicht zu Angesicht* (SE, 359/SE, 323). The silent encounter, structured by worship practices, creates a deliberate tension with the individual's experience of the revealment of truth in the divine face. The vision, intense and tantalising as it might be, is nevertheless related with cool sobriety that eschews mystical intoxication. The person who has ascended to the divine temple and discerned the figure of the face in the superimposed triangles that for the Star of Redemption, encounters an *Antlitz*, not an *Angesicht*.

5.2.2 The Kabbalistic Enigma

"Was Franz Rosenzewig a Mystic?" Nahum Glatzer explored this question in an essay thus entitled, and reached a negative conclusion (Glatzer 1979). Indeed, Rosnzweig's poetic, overflowing religious imagination, and sporadic, enigmatic references to kabbalistic ideas and texts have sparked the imagination of many a scholar. Three generations of Kabbalah scholars have mused over this possibility (Scholem 1971; Idel 2010; Wolfson 2010), as well as Rosenzweig experts.[36] But while they hunt for possible allusions and parallels with the Jewish mystical tradition of the middle ages and onwards, none of their studies have given due consideration to the sources Rosenzweig actually cites and adapts in the *Star*. As we have seen throughout this chapter, Jeremiah 10:10, Micah 6:8, and a host of verses describing face to face encounters serve Rosenzweig to bring his system to the farthest limits of discursive thinking, and lead to its completion in the realm of non-discursive thinking. In the realm of the ineffable, the cultic function of Scripture as the articulation for the congregation's worship in silence, which I have explored in chapter 4, was expanded to include the articulation of the system itself, with the "old Jewish words" of the Bible.

In conclusion, I will now argue that there is stronger evidence to suggest that the literature that served as chief inspiration for Rosenzweig's vision of the divine face in the *Star* is post-biblical; that is, it is chronologically proximate to the redaction of the Bible and was conceived as an elaboration on, or expansion of, biblical themes and narratives. By making this argument I would like to emphasise Rosenzweig's profound commitment to the discursive knowledge and re-

---

[36] Horwitz 2006; Bertolino 2006b; R. Cohen; Mosès 1992, 279–286; Galli 2006; Kornberg Greenberg 1996, 35–50, 115–121; Scholem 1930, 1988, 2018.

ligious inspiration he drew from the Bible, expressed by subscribing to what he saw as a biblical mindset. The first, and most compelling, evidence for basing my argument is the role of the temple in Rosenzweig's vision. As far as I have been able to determine, no scholarly consideration has been given to its meaning or possible sources. I have already noted in chapter 4 the potency of Rosenzweig's allusion to the mishnaic account of the High Priest's declamation of the divine name at the Temple as the pinnacle of worship on Yom Kippur. In Gate, the temple reappears, once again heightening the drama of the moment. The gate of God's sanctuary, and the face (*Antlitz*) encountered therein, are evocative of the vision related in Ezekiel 10:22–11:1.[37] But while Ezekiel relates God's message while undergoing an ecstatic experience, Rosenzweig sees what he had already heard from within life: "the height of the redeemed world-of-beyond" (*der Höhe der erlösten Überwelt*), seen by "walking in the light of God's face", (*im Lichte des göttlichen Antlitzes zu wandeln*) (SE, 471/SR, 424).[38] Moreover, the reader of Rosenzweig's vision need not muse on the possible appearance of the divine face, as she is forced to do in Ezekiel; Rosenzweig had already provided a detailed account of what can be known of the divine face.

Crucially, the account of the divine face was an integral part of the systematic discussion based on the analysis of the star figures conveyed by a juxtaposition of the three elements on the three divine actions. The encounter with the divine face that follows it is explicitly and intentionally based on Jewish sources. The ascension to higher realms and entry into God's innermost sanctum appears to be inspired by the early mystical tradition known as Hekhalot literature.[39] The likelihood that Rosenzweig was familiar with at least some of the works attributed to this corpus is quite high, particularly in light of his discussion a few pages earlier of Merkavah mysticism (SE, 454–456/SR, 408–410), whose lore is to be found mainly in the Helkhalot corpus. Zunz, Graetz, and most importantly Elbogen, wrote about this literature, and its major works appeared in Aharon Jellinek's compilations of lesser known midrashim, *Beit Hamidrasch*.[40]

---

37 "And as for the likeness of their faces, they were the very faces whose appearance I had seen by the river Chebar. They went every one straight forward. The Spirit lifted me up, and brought me to the east gate of the house of the LORD, which faces east." In Buber's translation: "*Und die Gestalt ihrer Antlitze: dies waren die Antlitze, deren Ansehn ich am Stromarm Kebar gesehen hatte. Und sie, jeder in der Richtung seines Antlitzes, gingen sie. Mich aber schwang ein Geistbraus empor und ließ michan das östliche Tor SEINES Hauses kommen.*" My emphasis.
38 My translation.
39 For key studies on Hekhalot literature relevant to Rosenzweig's vision see: Scholem 1965, esp. 1–19; Gruenwald 1980, esp. 73–123; Schäfer 1988, 234–249.
40 I have not found any references by Rosenzweig to this work or its author; however, his familiarity with Merkavah mysticism and especially the year he spent at the *Lehranstalt* in Berlin

Tab. 5.5: Rosenzweig's Vision of the Temple and Parallels in Hekhalot Literature

	Star of Redemption (SE, 472/ SR, 424)	Hekhalot Rabati 23:1	Book of Enoch[41]
Temple/ Temple doors	Im innersten Heiligtum der göttlichen Wahrheit er schloß mir die Pforten des Heiligtums auf, das in der innersten Mitte erbaut ist So mußte jenes Heiligtum [...] in der Welt selber ein Stück Überwelt, ein Leben Jenseits des Lebens sein die Worte stehen über dem Tor, dem Tor, das aus dem geheimnisvoll-wunderbaren Leuchten des göttlichen Heiligtums Wohinaus aber öffnen sich die Flügel des Tors?	היה ענפיאל פותח לו דלתות פתח היכל השביעי (Anfi'el would open for him he doors of the seventh hall)	הייתי נכנס בששה היכלות חדר בתוך חדר וכיון שהגעתי בפתח היכל שביעי עמדתי בתפלה לפני הקב"ה (I walked into six *heichalot* room within room and as I arrived in the entrance of the seventh *heichal* I stood in prayer before the Blessed Holy One)
Mirror	erblickt so der Mensch nichts andres als ein Antlitz gleich dem eigenen [...] Nicht Gott, aber Gottes Wahrheit ward mir zum Spiegel	והיו אותן עינים כל אין ועין אחת מעיני הקודש פקועה (And those eyes, each and every one of the sacred eyes was agape)	
The world on-high	So mußte jenes Heiligtum [...] in der Welt selber ein Stück Überwelt, ein Leben Jenseits des Lebens sein		אמר רבי ישמעאל: כשעליתי למרום להסתכל בצפיית המרכבה (Said Rabbi Ishmael: When I ascended on-high to be-

---

make it highly unlikely that he was unaware of its existence, and did not at least browse through its pages. *Beit Hamidrasch* became the standard text of the works it contained, until the publication of more modern critical editions. On Jellinek's contribution to the study of Jewish mysticism see Idel 2004; on Jellinek's scientific-theological agenda in the *Beit ha-Midrasch* project see Niehoff 1998.

41 Parallels of Rabbi Ishmael's ascent and observance of the *merkavah* in *Heichalot Rabati* 1:1, 2:3, 18:1.

	Denn die Schau auf der Höhe der erlösten Überwelt zeigt mir		hold the sight of the *merkavah*)
God/celestial beings	und im Lichte des göttlichen Antlitzes zu wandeln, wird nur dem, der den Worten des göttlichen Mundes folgt	היה ענפיאל פותח לו דלתות פתח היכל השביעי (Anfi'el would open for him he doors of the seventh hall) ומראה עיניהם כברקים ירוצצו חוץ מעיני כרובי גבורה ואופני שכינה שהן דומות ללפידי אור ושל שלהבות גחלי רתמים (And their eyes appeared to flicker like lightening, apart from the eyes of the Cherubim of Valour and the Spheres of the Shechinah that resemble torches of light and flaming embers)	

As Table 5.5 above illustrates, Rosenzweig's description of his ascent to the heavenly temple bears substantial similarities to R. Ishmael's entry to the seventh *hekahl* in *Hekhalot Rabbati* and to the opening verses of *The Book of Enoch*, both published by Jellinek. The patent differences between the conclusion of the *Star* and these works are just as telling. Rosenzweig is careful to exclude any other mediating figures (or angeology), avoids hyperbolic descriptions of celestial grandeur, or relate any experience that smacks of religious ecstasy. This attests to his consistent application of epistemic prudence befitting of a philosopher, and wholly uncharacteristic of a mystic.

Rosenzweig's selective assimilation of Hekhalot-like imagination emerges, then, as an expansion of the religious mindset he had heretofore developed based on his reading, translation and inscription of biblical verses in and into the *Star*. By choosing to conclude his vision with the divine call to "walk wholly with your God" as he, the subject relating the vision, stands before the open gate of the temple (evoking Ezekiel 11:1), and is about to leave the realm of speculation and step into life, Rosenzweig once more sets himself apart from any form of mysticism. Instead, he makes it amply clear that the sure footing that the *Star* purports to offer is to be found on the firm ground of the Hebrew Bible.[42]

---

42 Rosenzweig's relation to Jewish mysticism in general and Kabbalah in particular, has intrigued scholars for many years. While Glatzer 1979 remains scpetical about such an affinity,

5.3 In Life Itself

Lamenting the loss of his close friend, Buber wrote that in the eight years of his illness, Rosenzweig verified truth in God's face—"*die Wahrheit ... im Angesicht Gottes bewährt*". The truth that Buber had in mind was of the type that Rosenzweig pursued after the completion of the *Star*, i.e., after his transformation from author (as distinct from thinker or philosopher), to living man. The intimacy of encountering the divine face in its genuine posture (*Angesicht*), rather than its aloof facade (*Antlitz*) as attained *ins Leben*, in life itself. This meant for Rosenzweig, as much as for Buber, encountering God in the undertaking of translating the Bible. Hence, if Cohen translated the object of the *Star*'s motto, על דבר אמת, as "*für die Sache der Wahrheit*", Buber concluded his eulogy with the following translation of the verse from Psalms: "*Heil dir, reite für die Sache der Treue*" (E. Mayer 1930, 23). *Treue*, which directly translates as faithfulness or fidelity, is strongly associated in German with these acts in a religious context. But as opposed to *Glaube*, which is straightforward faith, *Treue* also resonates with truthfulness.[43] And so, if we think of Buber's translation of the *Star*'s motto as "riding in the cause of true faith", and conflate it with Cohen's "riding in the cause of truth", we may delineate a dialectic that is fundamental to Rosenzweig's project as a whole. That Cohen read in the verse the philosophical side of the dialectic, and Buber the side of faith, shows the necessity of a system sustained by both, and the inevitability of stepping out of the system and into its living sources: The Hebrew Bible in its entirety and integrity.

Grözinger, Harvey 2003 and Idel 2010 insist on Rosenzweig's indebtedness to Kabbalistic ideas. Most recently Lucca 2012 and Lucca & Wygoda 2018 confirm that Gershom Scholem remains the most persistent interpreter of Rosenzweig's work as underpinned by Kabbalistic inflections, relying on two manuscripts they printed for the first time: Scholem 2012 and a transcription of a 1936 talk published in Lucca & Wygoda, where Scholem makes the following observation: "Rosenzweig's fundamental position is mystical. Here is a mysticism of religious revelation primarily based on a philosophy of language and on elements that could be termed secrets and mysteries of the Torah" (in Lucca & Wygoda 2018, 215).

43 Grimm 1971, Bd. 22, 282–283. The etymology of *Treue* overlaps with the English True. Compare the first definition of "Trust" in the *OED:* "Confidence in or reliance on some quality or attribute of a person or thing, or the truth of a statement", as well as the now rare usage as "The quality of being trustworthy; fidelity; reliability; loyalty; trustiness" ("trust, n.". OED Online. July 2018).

Chapter 6:
Redemption through Translation: *Die Schrift* as the Culmination of Rosenzweig's Quest

Simon Bernstein, author of Rosenzweig's first Hebrew biography, *The Seer from Frankfurt*, concludes his piece by asserting that, "It is in this book [i.e., *Die Schrift*], and not in any other book [he authored], that Rosenzweig found his own 'Star of Redemption'" (Bernstein 1939, 20). Unlike the hagiographic tenor of Bernstein's short work, the pathos of this particular statement is justified. Rosenzweig the "Seer"[1] found in the translation of the Hebrew Bible into German the fulfilment of redemptive yearnings, which marked the trajectories along which his thought developed in the course of some twenty-five years.[2] In the previous chapters we have seen how time and again the translation of biblical verses served Rosenzweig to address philosophical problems. While in Rosenzweig's earlier work his philological investigations were pursued in *pianissimo*, the Buber-Rosenzweig translation employed philology in *fortissimo* due to the project's very nature. Now it was philosophy that was practiced between the lines, so to speak. In consonance with this shift of emphasis, the philosophical and philological modes of thinking continued to interact and fructify Rosenzweig's work. The systematic articulation of his thinking continued to frame his engagement with translation, while acquiring new modes of expression inaccessible through philosophical formulations.

The current chapter will begin by exploring Rosenzweig's conception of translation as a redemptive act. Though unique, it was not singular in the intellectual climate of Germany in the early 1900s. The "romantic roots" of this conception,[3] ripened in Walter Benjamin's conception of the task of translation in a similar, yet strikingly distinctive way. A comparison of their conceptions of translation will highlight their common premises and significant differences, indicat-

---

[1] The letter that opens Rosenzweig's collected letters and diaries is a "prophecy" that he sent to his cousins Gertrude and Helene Frank a few weeks after his bar mitzvah. The writing already reflects a profound grasp of the rhythm of biblical prose (*BT I*, 2–3).
[2] In the context of my discussion, Rosenzweig's first major translation project of Yeudah Halevy's poems is a transitional work that has more in common with the *Star* than with *Die Schrift*. I believe that Rosenzweig's own claim in *The New Thinking* that the Halevy poems are a perfect example for the practice of New Thinking should be taken with all seriousness (*Zweistromland*, 152/*Theological Writings*, 128), as opposed to his statement in the same essay that the *Star* is not a Jewish book, (see chapter 5).
[3] I am borrowing this image from the title of Brit 2000.

ing that Rosenzweig was committed to a more robust redemptive scheme than Benjamin. Exercising the same epistemic prudence, the two thinkers-cum-translators understood their prerogative of selecting the works they would subject to translation in diametrically opposed ways: While Benjamin immersed himself in modern literature that explored the secular-profane present, Rosenzweig explored the spiritual cadences and tropes of devotional poetry, and crucially, the source of inspiration for both his and Benjamin's conceptions of translation—the Hebrew Bible.

I will then turn to examine the central redemptive dimensions of Rosenzweig's collaboration with Martin Buber in producing *Die Schrift*. I will aim to show that Rosenzweig's theory provided a broad and rather loose framework for exploring potentialities that were not expressly stated, or perhaps even contemplated, in the theoretical discussion of the redemptive arch of translation. I will present their endeavour as undergirded by a dialectic between what they regarded as the authentic or primal voice of the text and the multiplicity of readings to which it has been subjected throughout history. Thus, the attempt to distil the initial meaning of the original will emerge as a redemptive effort to echo readings that amplify its authenticity and defy putative (mis)appropriations that have become entrenched over the centuries.

6.1 The Redemptive Potential of Translation

In the latter years of the second decade of the twentieth century, unbeknownst to one another, Walter Benjamin and Franz Rosenzweig were developing very similar theologically inflected conceptions of language.[4] The prospect of redemption through the retrieval of primordial, universal language and the pivotal role that translation plays in this redemptive process, was the shared theme upon which each developed his own distinctive approach. Their modest interaction,[5] which

---

[4] In 1917, a year after Benjamin completed *On Language as Such*, Rosenzweig wrote to his cousin, Rudolph Ehrenberg: "Translation is after all the actual goal of the mind [*das eigentlich Ziel des Geistes*]; only when something is translated does it really becomes *audible* for the first time ..." *BT I*, 460–461.

[5] Benjamin became acquainted with *Star of Redemption* in 1921, after Gershom Scholem warmly recommended to him the book (Scholem 1981, 101), appears to have been more interested in Rosenzweig's work than vice versa, and he is not even listed in the index of the critical edition of Rosenzweig's letters and diaries. For a survey of Benjamin's acquaintance of Rosenzweig's work, see Mosès 1984.

took place in the 1920s at Gershom Scholem's urging,[6] was concomitant with Benjamin's admiration for Rosenzweig's analysis of Greek tragedy in the *Star*, and which subsided in wake of Benjamin's siding with Siegfried Kracauer's dismissive review of Buber's and Rosenzweig's translation of the Book of Genesis.[7] Scholars have long noted the affinity between their philosophies of language in general, and of translation in particular,[8] while several studies have been devoted to the controversy that followed the publication of the first volume of *Die Schrift*.[9] The perfect inverted symmetry between the secular and the devotional nature of the works Benjamin and Rosenzweig respectively chose to translate, however, does not seem to have been noticed, nor have its implications for the understanding of their work.

As practitioners of the art of translation who devoted considerable thought to its metaphysical presuppositions, Rosenzweig and Benjamin shared a profound scepticism regarding the prospects of translated works doing justice to their original. But equally beholden to the cultural necessity of translation, they applied their prodigious literary and philological gifts to that very task. Benjamin's perception of secular reality through the prism of theological categories, perhaps best articulated in his *The Origin of German Tragic Drama*,[10] is epitomised in his selection of Charles Baudelaire's *Tableaux Parisiens* and Marcel Proust's *Á la recherché du temp perdu* as his two major translation projects.[11]

Within the inverted symmetry of the nature of the works they chose to render into German, Benjamin's Baudelaire will be contrasted here with Rosenzweig's translations of poems by Jewish medieval luminary Yehudah Halevy,[12] while Benjamin's rendition of Proust will be compared to Rosenzweig's *Die Schrift* of the Hebrew Bible. By placing their respective translation projects in this comparative matrix, we may observe the profound differences between their understanding of the redemptive role of translation.

---

6 Benjamin reported to Scholem of his meeting with the ill Rosenzweig in a letter dated 30 December, 1922, see *Briefe*, 295–296.
7 Kracauer 1963, 173–186; translated in Kracauer 1995, 189–201.
8 Mosès 1984, 2009; Jacobson 2003; Kornberg Greenberg 1996; Britt 1996, esp. 70–90; Lambrianou 2004; Di Cesare 2005.
9 Britt 2000; Jay 1976; Rosenwald 1994; Gordon 2003, 237–245; Batnitzky 2000, 135–139.
10 See for example George Steiner's introduction in Benjamin 1977, 7–24, esp. 4–18; Jacobson 2003, 38–45.
11 For Benjamin's translation career, see Brodersen 1997, 162–168 and Scharf 2018a, 147–148.
12 First published in 1924 as *Sechzig Hymnen und Gedichte des Jehuda Halevy* (Rosenzweig 1924). A second, expanded edition was released two years later as *Zweiundneunzig Hymnen und Gedichte des Jehuda Halevy. Deutch. Mit einem Nachwort und mit Anmerkungen* (Rosenzweig 1926), containing translations of and commentaries on 95 poems.

6.1.1 Language: Edenic or Prophetic?

What is, then, the theological dimension of language according to Benjamin? In his 1916 essay, "On Language as Such and the Language of Man", Benjamin declares: "Hence, it is no longer conceivable, as the bourgeois view of language maintains, that the word has an accidental relation to its object, that it is a sign for things (or knowledge of them) agreed by some convention. Language never gives *mere* signs" (Benjamin GS II.1, 150/*Reflections*, 324). Hence, he rejects a conception of language whereby it is a system producing meaning by cross-referencing arbitrarily related "signifiers" and "signifieds" deprived of any essential connection with the ontology of the meaning-content that a said lexical system expresses. Above all else, it is important for Benjamin to emphasise that language is neither instrumental nor arbitrary; rather, it is essentially and organically related to the world it describes:

> What does language communicate? It communicates the spiritual being [*geistige Wesen*] corresponding to it. It is fundamental that this spiritual being communicates itself *in* language and not *through* language ... Spiritual being is identical with linguistic being only insofar as it is capable of communication ... Language therefore communicates the particular linguistic being of things, but their spiritual being only insofar as this is directly included in their linguistic being... (Benjamin GS II.1, 142/*Reflections*, 316). [13]

Already at this early point in the essay, Benjamin lets the theological dimension as anchored in the words of the Bible shine through the text. *Das geistiges Wesen*, which Edmund Jephcott translates in *Reflections* as "mental being", and Eric Jacobson insists on translating as "substance of the intellect" (Jacobson 2003, 89), could bear either meaning or simultaneously encompass all three: the spiritual-mental-intellectual being of entities. A careful reading of the passage in which Benjamin presents the challenge faced by any theory of language, however, clearly shows that the spiritual connotation is the dominant one, and that it subsumes the other two meanings:

> Die Ansicht, daß das geistige Wesen eines Dinges eben in seiner Sprache besteht ... ist der große **Abgrund**, dem alle Sprachtheorie zu verfallen droht!, und **über, gerade über ihm sich schwebt** (GS II.1, 141)

> The view that the spiritual essence of a thing consists precisely in its language ... is the great abyss into which all linguistic theory threatens to fall (*Reflections*, 315). [14]

---

13 Translation altered.
14 Translation altered, emphasis added.

In this context, the coupling of the noun *Abgrund* with the verb *schwebend* suggests a deliberate invocation of Luther's translation of Genesis 1:2: ... *und Finsterniß auf der Fläche des **Abgrundes**, und der **Geist Gottes schwebend** über der Fläche der Wasser.* If this were an isolated biblical reference, we could dismiss it as an incidental figure of speech. But the very *Sprachtheorie* that Benjamin discusses in the passage at hand rests in its entirety on a reading of chapters 1 and 2 in Genesis, which takes up the second half of his essay. Moreover, this passage serves as a performative demonstration of what he holds to be the correct way to consider the nature of language in light of Genesis, as "the discovery of what emerges of itself from the biblical text with regard to the nature of language", and that "the present argument broadly follows [the Bible] in presupposing language as an ultimate reality" (GS II.1, 147/ *Reflections*, 322).[15]

Once made explicit, this reading completes the argument, which up to this point was more metaphysical than theological: the spiritual essence of the entities created is the consequence of divine utterances in God's pure language, in which at the moment of creation the spiritual and linguistic essences of the entities created were fully aligned; language was given to humans as an expression of their mastery over nature, formally announced in Genesis 1:28: "Be fruitful, and multiply, and replenish the earth, and subdue it: and have dominion over the fish of the sea, and over the fowl of the air, and over every living thing that moves upon the earth". And formally manifested by Adam's naming God's creations in Genesis 2:19: "And out of the ground the LORD God formed every beast of the field, and every fowl of the air; and brought them unto Adam to see what he would call them: and whatsoever Adam called every living creature, that was the name thereof".

But sure enough, this paradisiacal state did not last very long. On Benjamin's reading, the foremost metaphysical implication of the fall from Eden was the loss of pure language, and the fragmentation of human speech into myriad tongues that preserved portions of their pure prototype to varying degrees. The fact that we know that this perfect language existed is sufficient to motivate us to try and recreate it. At the current state of affairs, the best-suited activity to attempt this is translation:

> The language of things can pass into the language of knowledge and name only through translation – as many translations, so many languages – once man has fallen from the paradisiacal state that knew only one language (According to the Bible, this consequence of the expulsion from paradise admittedly came about only later) (GS II.1, 152/*Reflections*, 326).

---

15 Translation altered.

Benjamin stresses that translation is not an "afterthought", as "it is necessary to ground the concept of translation at the deepest stratum [*Schicht*] of linguistic theory … Translation attains its full meaning in the realisation that every evolved language (with the exception of the word of God) can be considered as a translation of all the others" (GS II.1, 151/*Reflections*, 325). And so, "All higher language is a translation of lower ones, until in ultimate clarity the word of God unfolds, which is the unity of this movement made up of language" (GS II.1, 157/ *Reflections*, 332).

6.1.2 In the Tradition

It took Benjamin seven more years to develop a more comprehensive theory of translation within the framework of his earlier *reine Sprachtheorie*. "The Task of the Translator", published in 1923, is an introduction to Benjamin's translation of Baudelaire's *Tableaux Parisiens* (Benjamin 1923), the second of six parts comprising the poet's masterpiece, *Fleur du Mal*. In the tradition of great translators, Benjamin's essay offers important insights to the main challenges faced by the translator, proposing solutions that are compelling as much as they are provocative.

Throughout the essay, Benjamin stresses that translation demonstrates the kinship of languages and their shared origin from the *reine Sprache*, nonetheless beseeching translators not to strive and pretend to have produced texts that are literally faithful to the original. He asks: "If the kinship between languages is to be demonstrated by translations, how else can this be done other than by conveying the form and meaning of the original as accurately as possible?" (Benjamin GS IV.1, 12/*Illuminations*, 72). And he then answers decisively: "If the kinship of languages manifests itself in translations, this is not accomplished through a vague resemblance between copy and original" (Benjamin GS IV.1, 13/*Illuminations*, 73–74).[16] The resemblance between the two works is vague by necessity, because of their unique reciprocity: without an original, there cannot be a translation; but without translation, the original work faces the grave danger of being forgtten. And so, translation has a redemptive function not only in the linguistic sphere, but in the literary one as well: "Just as the manifestations of life are intimately connected with the phenomenon without being of importance to it, a translation issues from the original—not so much from its life as from its afterlife [*Überleben*] … the translation [of great works of world literature] marks their

---

16 Translation altered.

stage of continued life" (Benjamin GS IV.1, 10 – 11/*Illuminations*, 71). Hence the necessity of producing new translations of literary masterpiece also exposes the dialectical relationship between languages, which is framed by incommensurable differences and essential similarities.

Benjamin designates this only plausible objective of translation with the adjective *durchscheinend* (Benjamin GS IV.1, 18/*Illuminations*, 79).[17] Harry Zohn translates it as "transparency", which is actually a derivative of the literal combination of *durch* and *scheinend:* that which may be seen through, or that which *shines* through. Thus, a translation commended as purportedly superior to its original is actually unfaithful to its calling. The translation that is seen through, "… does not cover the original, does not block its light, but allows the pure language … to shine upon the original all the more fully". Almost casually, Benjamin notes in this passage that "In the realm of translation, too, the words *En arche en ho logos* [in the beginning was the word] apply" (Benjamin GS IV.1, 18/*Illuminations*, 79).[18] As we recall, in "On Language as Such", Benjamin posited *logos* as an embodiment of the overlap between spiritual and linguistic being, which is the essence of pure language. We may also recall the performative employment of Genesis that anticipates its interpretation later in the essay. Returning to "The Task of the Translator", we find that the tangential quotation of John 1:1 emerges an important performative demonstration of the operation of translation as an activity that partakes of the essence of pure language.

The citation from the original Greek, one of the most famous verses in the New Testament, is, of course, based on the Septuagint translation of Genesis 1:1: εν αρχη εποιησεν ὁ θεὸς τὸν οὐρανὸν καὶ τὴν γῆν (*en archē epoiēsen o theos ton ouranon kai tēn gēn*) – In the beginning God created the heaven and the earth. By inscribing the Jewish and Christian scriptures in a polyglot translation—from Old Testament Hebrew into New Testament Greek, and from the Greek into German—Benjamin distils a textual embodiment of his idea of *reine Sprache*—the overlap between spiritual and linguistic being, grounded in Creation—in order to demonstrate the redemptive potential of translation. Ascending from the deepest stratum of language, to which genuine translation is beholden, to the New Testament verse as an original text, the Greek forces the translator to choose between two alternatives. According to the Liddell-Scott-Jones *Greek–English Lexicon*, λογοσ (*logos*) denotes, "The word or outward form by which the inward thought is expressed", as well as "The inward thought itself, so that *logos* comprehends both *ratio* and *oratio*" (Liddell-Scott 1883, 901). By plac-

---

[17] "*Die wahre Übersetzung ist durchscheinend*".
[18] For a discussion of Rosenzweig's own interpretation on John 1:1 see chapter 2 above.

ing the standard translation of the verse in parentheses after the original Greek, Benjamin foregrounds the dialectic relations of fallen languages with their pure source: the simultaneous presence of thought and word is at once accommodated and rejected by the simultaneous presentation of *logos* and its translation as "word"; while translation's unique ability to let the essence of pure language—conceptually, as the medium of spiritual-linguistic being, and ontologically, as the origin of languages—is made to shine through the text.

For Rosenzweig, language is the medium with which God relates to the world and man on the path of creation, revelation and redemption. Moshe Schwarcz has observed that each of these three moments on the divine path has a corresponding grammatical form: (1) creation—word forms [*Wort Formen*]: the expression of the given *ontological-verbal* contents of language, in the past tense; (2) revelation—dialogue: the ever-renewing and ever-unanticipated exchange of sentences between interlocutors, which takes place in the perfect present; (3) redemption—choir form proleptically celebrated the absolute future: the sentences uttered in each of these instances serve to explicate and emphasise the meaning of God's one, overarching sentence. "These three linguistic forms —story, dialogue and choir—encompass the totality of experience, in which human thought can partake as a temporal quality. Past, present, future—the three temporal modes—constitute the fundamental laws of language on its various forms" (Schwarcz 1978, 273). Echoing Benjamin's sublation of representation and essence into the pure language of creation, Rosenzweig asserts that the structure of language perfectly corresponds with creation as the primordial symbolic system of reality itself, and therefore it is essentially identical with this reality (SE, 166–167/SR, 150). His grammatical analysis of Genesis 1 recurrently emphasises this link between representation and essence made manifest in the creative power of God's utterances.[19]

Benjamin's idea of a pure language of divine origin finds similar, though less emphatic expression in Rosenzweig. In the *Star* he describes God's *Ich* as the "pedal point" by which all human languages orient themselves; in other words, God's being, which includes a dominant linguistic element, is like the sustained note that the organist produces with the instrument's pedal as the har-

---

[19] Rosenzweig SE, 168–173/SR, 151–155. Significantly, however, this emphasis differs from Benjamin's in two respects: (1) It ignores Adam's part in the creative process through the naming of the world of objects; (2) It somewhat downplays the contrast between the purity of prelapsarian language and the fragmentation of postlapsarian language, as language continues to facilitate our very ability to relate to God: "The ways of God are different from the ways of man, but the word of God and the word of man are the same. What man hears in his heart as his own human speech is the very word which comes out of God's mouth"; *SE* 167–168/*SR*, 151.

monic substratum upon which s/he will play written (or improvised) melodies. Rosenzweig is considerably more explicit than Benjamin in his articulation of the important role that pure language will play in the final, consummated stage of universal redemption. Rosenzweig's vision extends directly from the words of the prophets—Zephaniah 3:9 (SE, 373/SR, 296), and Zechariah 14:9 (SE, 426/SR, 383).[20] In this sense, Lawrence Rosenwald's description of the motivation that Rosenzweig shared with Buber for translating the Bible as "vatic" (Rosenwald, 149) is illuminating: it presents his translation projects as partial fulfilment of the prophets' harbingering of universal redemption through the transcendence of linguistic and religious barriers to "call together in God's name and worship him shoulder to shoulder" (Zephania 3:9).

As Leora Batnitzky has observed, despite the enormous interest in Rosenzweig's *Sprachdenken*, relatively few scholars have acknowledged the fundamental role of translation within it (Batnizaky 2007, 141).[21] She herself, however, dates Rosenzweig's initial efforts at translation to his 1920 rendition of the grace after meals,[22] whereas in all of the previous chapters of this book I have argued for a much earlier dating by demonstrating the indispensability of translation for both the prose and argumentation of the *Star*. Indeed, Rosenzweig camouflaged well his reliance on translation in the composition of his tome, but stressed the fundamental role of translation in interpersonal as well as human-divine communication.[23] As Rosenzweig devoted the larger share of the limited time his fatal illness allowed to the translation of sacred Hebrew texts, the distance between his theory and the practice of the art, evident in the *Star*, was eliminated almost completely. This was in sharp contrast to Benjamin, whose foray into the field of literary translation was accompanied by a stubborn attempt to conceal the process from the public eye, in order to have his rendition of the original work appear as though it was produced *ex nihilo*.

---

20 Compare: "There is only one language ... Upon this essential oneness of all language and upon the dependent commandment, namely that of universal human mutual understanding, is based on the possibility as well as the task of translating ... Rosenzweig, "Afterword", *Jehuda Halevy*, 3; translated in Galli 1995, 171.
21 An important exception is Barbara E. Galli's translation and commentary on Rosenzweig's Yehudah Halevy translations: Galli 1995, esp. 322–398.
22 See the discussion in chapter 4 above.
23 Galli 1995, 338–359.

6.1.3 The Translator's Prerogative

Both Benjamin and Rosenzweig chose to translate poetic works based on personal admiration for their authors. Benjamin, however, does not disclose a specific reason for dedicating "a considerable time" to Baudelaire (*Briefe*, 133) while Rosenzweig provides several reasons for his preferences in the *Nachwort*, none of which appear decisive.[24]

Even though their precise considerations cannot be ascertained (not least because they seem to have occurred to Benjamin and Rosenzweig only gradually), it is clear that both sought to produce translations that would be more than mere German renditions of beloved poems. These translations were to *do* something in the world. Rosenzweig's *Nachwort* and commentary disclose some of those purposes in their content as well as by their very inclusion in the text and Rosenzweig's chosen layout (M. Benjamin 2007a, 131–133). One important echo that Mara Benjamin picks up is the anti-bourgeois streak of Rosenzweig's project.[25] In this sense, it uncannily predates Walter Benjamin's view of *Fleur de mal* as an induction into an anti-bourgeois mode of thinking that facilitates a deeper appreciation of Baudelaire's thought:

> The signature of Baudelaire's literature could have been composed in its entire essentiality, if Baudelaire had never written *Fleur du Mal* ... It stands thus, that one is not obligated to calmly drag behind the barriers of bourgeois thinking, as well as certain bourgeois reactions; to find pleasure in one or other of these poems is one thing, but [it is] hardly [possible] to feel at home in the *Fleur du Mal* (*Briefe*, 742).

In contradistinction to Rosenzweig, Benjamin appears to hide and even dissimulate the objectives of his project, and more significantly—the inner workings of his undertaking (etymological considerations, challenges dictated by structural differences between the languages, style and taste). It is neigh impossible to ac-

---

[24] Glazter takes Rosenzweig's complaint on Emil Cohn's translation of Halevy's poems (*Ein Diwan Jehuda Halevi, Übertragen und mit einem Lebensbild versehen von Emil Berhard [Cohn]* [Berlin: E. Reiss, 1920]) as the incentive for setting about the project (Glatzer 1953, 122), but Rafael Rosenzweig, who edited the poems volume for the *Gesammelte Schriften* edition remarks that it is unclear what impelled Rosenzweig to undertake the project (*Jehuda Halevy*, xxi.). Mara Benjamin suggests that "what began as a simple corrective to Cohn, grew into something much grander". M. Benjamin 2007a, 128.

[25] Rosenzweig insisted on a personal affiliation with Halevy by retrieving a Hebrew name identical with the poets' through a shaky reconstruction of his own family genealogy. This was triggered by his admiration for Halevy, as much as by his loathing for his given German name, which he considered a crude expression of his parent's bourgeois mindset. See M. Benjamin 2007a, 128–129.

cept his deprecatory observations in "The Task of the Translator" on the translator's relatively minor role in the shaping of the text as applying to his *Tableaux Parisiens*. The rhyming of the lines and retention of structure and even word placement certainly surpass Stefan George's translation, which Benjamin acquired in early 1918 (*Briefe*, 171). I believe that in this respect, the layout and design of the original printing of Benjamin's *Tableaux Parisiens* (Benjamin 1923) provides us with important clues regarding his approach to this translation. The large format (34 cm X 24 cm) of the edition and the impressive typeface size of the poems, laid out with the original French on the left-hand page and its German rendition on the right, make a clear statement: the poetry—in the original, in translation, and in the interaction between the two—is granted centre stage. Yet, the layout of "The Task of the Translator" is even more telling: using a different font than the one with which the poems are set, and in typeface size approximately one third the size of the poems', the introductory essay assumes the appearance of an instruction manual of esoteric teachings. Benjamin's complete silence on his own practice of the art of translation, which Rosenzweig is almost obsessed about sharing with his readers,[26] creates the powerful impression that Benjamin considered it to be an occult, even mystical activity, whose secrets should be guarded.[27] And if this observation is indeed correct, it reveals an important amplification of Benjamin's theology of language, which places the translator at the heart of the redemptive process, in a manner akin to a master of theurgical lore.

6.1.4 Lifting the Theoretical Veil

Prima facie, it would be reasonable to approach Benjamin's work on and in translation in light of his separation of the theory of translation from the act of translation. His theoretical reflections on language and translation are speculative, abstract; they are purged of the concrete philological problems or specific linguistic challenges that he encountered in his work on Baudelaire, Proust or other authors whose work he translated. This presupposition may lead to the misconception that his translations were refracted by a purely theoretical perspective; that their polished elegance is simply actualizing the ideational constructs that his theoretical disquisitions develop. Moreover, in writing about

---

[26] Buber assembled Rosenzweig's essays about *Die Schrift* along with his own pieces in Buber & Rosenzweig 1936.
[27] For an exploration of Benjamin's disillusionment with the possibility of translation see Scharf 2018a.

the authors whose works he translated, Benjamin made a patent effort to be perceived as a critic, whose work on their translation has no bearings on his reading and understanding of their work. Anyone who ever undertook the task of the translator knows that this is a sheer impossibility.

If the original setting of Benjamin's "The Task of the Translator" alongside his translation of Baudelaire's poetry emphasised the esoteric aspect in Benjamin's figure of the translator, his commentary on Proust, particularly in "The Image of Proust," (Benjamin GS II.1, 310–324/ *Illuminations*, 201–215) places his translation of the second, third and fourth volumes of *Recherche*—*A l'ombre des jeunes filles en fleurs*, *Le côte de Gueremantes* and *Sodome et Gommorreh* respectively—in a similar, yet distinct, context: the Bible. Perhaps unwittingly, Benjamin himself provided the link between the esotericism of "The Task of the Translator" and the scriptural quality of Proust in the closing of his introductory essay to *Tableaux Parisiens*: "… to some degree all great texts contain their potential translation between the lines; this is true to the highest degree of sacred writings. The interlinear version of the Scriptures is the prototype or ideal of all translation"(Benjamin GS IV.1, 21/*Illuminations*, 82). Merely four years after making this statement, in the midst of translating *Rechreche*, Benjamin opened his essay on Proust by describing his novel as a literary achievement of biblical proportions: "… an inconstruable synthesis in which the absorption of a mystic, the art of a prose writer, the verse of a satirist, the erudition of a scholar and the self-consciousness of a monomaniac have combined in an autobiographical work" (Benjamin GS IV.1, 310/*Illuminations*, 201). As the essay progresses, Benjamin presents a reading of the novel as inflected with theological-religious concerns: he agrees with Cocteau's interpretation of Proust's work as a frenzied quest for happiness (312–313/203); dismisses readings that laud him as elevating his reader to "'the higher regions which a Plato or a Spinoza reached" (320/210–211); and ends with a powerful biblical crescendo:

> For a second time, there rose a scaffold like Michaelangelo's on which the artist, his head back, painted the creation on the ceiling of the Sistine Chapel: the sickbed on which Marcel Proust consecrates the countless pages which he covered with his handwriting, holding them up in the air, the creation of his microcosm (324/215).

This perspective on the novel corresponds with similar intuitions that Rosenzweig had on the relations between modern literature and the Bible. In the *Star* he draws a parallel between the creative powers of poetic genius and God's act of creation (SE, 165/SR, 149). Most dramatic, however, is his comment in a letter to Gertrud Oppenheim noting that the authors of the Bible thought of

God in similar terms to Kafka, whose novel *The Castle* is the first book he has read that is so strikingly reminiscent of the Bible (*BT* II, 1152).

The nexus between modern literature, translation and the Bible illumines the parallels and dissimilarities between Benjamin's and Rosenzweig's conceptions of the redemptive dimension of translation. Their agreement on the redemptive potential of the act of translation is undercut by their contrasting conceptions of the translator's role: Benjamin's minimalisation of the individual translator's philological judgment is countered by Rosenzweig's emphasis on the importance of exercising philological discretion, which he advanced in numerous essays about *Die Schrift*.[28]

As already mentioned above, Rosenzweig's objective in undertaking the translation of the Bible have been subjected to extensive scrutiny, particularly in light of Kracauer's Benjaminian assault on the project. The overarching objective identified by Kracauer include the desire to contribute to a Jewish spiritual renaissance in Germany (Jay 1976, 6, 14), and a subversive political project of exposing the Hebraic roots of modern German culture (M. Benjamin 2009, 130 – 134; M. Benjamin 2007b, 269). Pertinent as they are, these interpretations focus on Rosenzweig's commentary on *Die Schrift* without taking sufficient note of the fundamental link that he identified between the Bible's presence in world history and the art of translation. Rosenzweig appreciated the "World-Historical Importance of the Bible" mediated by its translation, as he entitled one of his essays (*Zweistromland*, 837– 840), while considering the Bible as equally constitutive of the history of translation. Several months before commencing the writing of the *Star*, he writes to Hans Ehrenberg that, "Revelation became at home in the world for the first time with the Septuagint" (*BT* I, 461). In the *Star* itself, his most quoted passage on translation, which is the bridge between one person to another, one language to another, "The Bible is therefore the first book translated, whose translation and original [*Urtext*] were held in equal esteem" (SE, 407/SR, 366).[29]

In this context it would seem that there is every reason to translate the Bible and every reason *not* to translate it. Benjamin told Scholem that the Buber-Rosenzweig translation was a mistake:

---

[28] Compare Caroline Sauter who forcefully argues for the centrality of the Bible to Benjamin's theory of translation (Sauter 2014, 38), and for the support of this theory to his messianic theory (218 – 222). Sauter stresses, however, that the Bible remained in Benjamin's view a conceptual model for "Scripture" or "Scriptures", while he rarely dwelt on the interpretation of specific verses (39).

[29] Translation altered.

> I have no idea who or what at this time might be justly interested in a translation of the Bible into German. Isn't this translation ultimately a highly questionable exhibition of things which, being exhibited, immediately disavow themselves in the light of this German – particularly at a time when the contents of Hebrew are being discussed anew, when the German on the other hand is in a rather problematic state, and especially when fruitful mutual relations between the two seem only latently possible, if at all (Benjamin, *Briefe*, 432/Jay 1976, 20).

At the same time, Benjamin's own immersion in the translation of Proust's masterpiece was partly due to its defilement by the inadequate German translation of Rudolph Schottlaender (Brodersen 1997, 165–166). Benjamin's equation of Proust's *Recherché* to Michaelangelo's "Creation" can therefore be read as an expression of admiration for the type of literary works that merit consideration as a "modern Bible", based on a clear and distinct division that he makes between the secular present, the sacred past, and the redemptive future.

This triadic division evokes a Platonic epistemology of the Parable of the Cave: in the present, we can only see the shadows and reflections of God's work, and hence we are confined to engage with those shadows and reflections. In Benjamin's "cave", we can only practice a secular, laicised form of theology; not because he dismisses the validity of religious knowledge, but rather because we are not in a position to ascend to the theological "realm of ideas" and engage them directly. In this sense, there is no material difference between the concerns of a Proust, Baudelaire or Michelangelo and those of a Talmudic sage or medieval Kabbalist (as may be surmised from his Kafka essays)[30]; yet, they direct their inquiries at two different realms of knowledge: the former, within the cave of the present, the latter, in the realm of ideas of the Edenic past and the redeemed future.

For Rosenzweig, this form of redemption will obtain once the prophecy described in Zephaniah 3:9 is actualised. As we have seen in chapter 3, Zephaniah's vision has a pride of place in Rosenzweig's redemptive scheme as marking the penultimate stage of the redemptive process, and facilitating the final dissolution of all barriers separating God from world and humanity. For Benjamin, the lightning that flashes during the act of translation and shines through pure language makes us aware of the primeval bond between words and the objects they denote. This conception of language, despite Benjamin's unsystematic articulation of his messianic scheme posits translation as instrumental for har-

---

[30] Benjamin GS IV.1, 421–424/*Illuminations*, 122–126; Benjamin *Briefe*, 756–644/*Illuminations*, 141–145.

bingering the messianic age.³¹ This must not blur the focus of both thinkers on the redemptive dimension of translation on the linguistic plane and its vital importance in the life and afterlife of texts.³² Hence, though they diverged considerably in their project choices, both Rosenzweig and Benjamin hoped to reach biblical proportions.

And so, we may conceive of the fundamental difference between Benjamin's and Rosenzweig's respective conceptions of translation as deriving from a disagreement on the epistemological possibilities available to humans in relation to the redemptive future. While Benjamin is convinced that our fallen state chains us to the present, Rosenzweig is determined to break those chains and overcome this epistemological barrier. This difference manifested itself in the choice of works that each of them translated, and in their presentation of the task of the translator. Benjamin's "fallen epistemology" was complemented by his exclusive focus on works of literature that deal with modern existence and its profaning effect on human life; Rosenzweig's cleaving to redemptive hopes found expression in his rendition of Yehudah Halevy's devotional poetry and of the Hebrew Bible. Unbridgeable as this disagreement may seem, it is nonetheless grounded in an important concord in relation to the privileged metaphysical role of the translator, which she performs by exercising her prerogative of choosing the works that should be translated. As we have seen, once exercised, the question whether this prerogative contributes to the promotion or occlusion of redemption through translation itself engenders an intense spiritual quandary. Rosenzweig was certainly prepared to face the consequences of this challenge.

6.2 Redeeming Words, Redeeming Worlds

When Martin Buber came with the offer to produce together a new German translation of the Bible, Rosenzweig had been battling his ultimately fatal illness for

---

31 Vivian Liska convincingly demonstrates the theo-political function Benjamin reserves for translation by comparing his thesis in "The Task of the Translator" with Maurice Blanchot's meta-commentary on the translation essay. According to her, "Benjamin returns to pure language in the last notes that he wrote in 1940 in preparation for his theses on the philosophy of history. In those notes, he speaks about a universal language that can come into being only with the coming of the Messiah. If a paradisiacal state is at stake in his first references to a pure language, these last writings are essentially messianic and directed toward a future" (Liska 2017, 97).
32 "Just as the manifestations of life are intimately connected with the phenomenon of life without being of importance to it, a translation issues from the original—not so much from its life as from its afterlife". Benjamin GS IV.1, 10–11/*Illuminations*, 71.

some two and a half years. Though he did not leave a record of why he proposed this joint project to his ailing friend, it is hard to imagine that one of Buber's main reasons for approaching him was not to uplift his spirits. Once Rosenzweig agreed, however, the enterprise was anything but an act of charity. The two quickly became absorbed in the task, producing a staggering ten volumes, covering Genesis through Isaiah, in the span of just under five years.[33]

In many ways, a translation of the Bible into German could not have been a more natural pursuit for both men: it showcased their rich experience as translators;[34] it was aligned with their concerns for the spiritual decay of German Jewry; and it presented a unique opportunity to shape the Hebrew Bible in the light of theological, philosophical and aesthetic insights they shared. Indeed, Buber and Rosenzweig discussed those considerations in essays, responses to reviews and correspondence. These documents portray a complex network of objectives that coalesced into a solid aggregate of guiding considerations.[35] To this day, however, the question of *Die Schrift*'s authorship has not been clarified altogether, not least because Buber manually performed *all* of the writing and revision work due to Rosenzweig's illness. In spite of the symbiotic process they had established, Buber and Rosenzweig retained distinct, if allied conceptions of translation. What is more, recently Amy Hill Shevitz has forcefully demonstrated the indispensability of Rosenzweig's wife Edith (née Hahn) for her husband's participation in the endeavor, while giving long-overdue credit to Edith's original input in the translation process (Hill Shevitz 2015, 289–290). Bauer 1992 (7) and HaCohen (Buber 2014, 12) stress Buber's casting of Rosenzweig as in-charge of

---

[33] Buber & Rosenzweig 1926–1930. By Rosenzweig's death, he and Buber had completed Isaiah 53. In the 1930s, Lambert Schneider published the books of Jeremiah, Ezekiel and the Twelve Minor Prophets, and Schocken Verlag published Psalms and Proverbs before closing down in 1938. Buber recommenced the translation in 1950 at the behest of Jakob Hegner Verlag in Switzerland, which published *Die Bücher der Weisung* (1954), *Bücher der Geschichte* (1958), *Bücher der Kündung* (1959) and *Die Schriftwerke* (1962), which included Buber's tranlsation of the remaining books, as well as revisions and amendments of the work conducted with Rosenzweig. Republished in Buber 1992. See, Buber 2012, 143–144; 176. On Buber's completion of the translation, see Scharf 2015.
[34] Some two decades earlier, Buber had established himself as the foremost mediator of Hassidism to the liberal Jewish readership through his translation-adaptation of tales of Rabbi Nachman of Bratzlav (1906); and of the founder of Hassidism, the Ba'al Shem Tov (1908). Buber had intended to launch a collaborative effort of translating the Bible in the 1910s, but his plans were thwarted by the outbreak of World War One. See, Buber 2012, 143; 174–175. On Buber as translator see Mendes-Flohr 2007.
[35] Buber's essays are now collected in Buber 2012, Rosenzweig's are assembled in *Zweistromland*, 721–840, and appear jointly in English translation in *Scripture and Translation*.

the conceptual infrastructure upon which their translation was built. Shortly after his close friend's death, Buber conceded that it was Rosenzweig who set the tone in the intensive exchange of ideas during the production of *Die Schrift:* "'My role here,' Rosenzweig wrote me at the beginning of the work, 'will probably be that of the muse of precision (Diotima and Xanthippe united in a single person) [...] 'His role' became, though he held throughout to the image of the muse of precision, a hundred times greater than the 'example' would suggest". (Buber 2012, 144/*Scripture and Translation*, 179). Therefore, for the purposes of my discussion I will read *Die Schrift* as Rosenzweig's redemptive project in which Buber was invested (conceptually speaking) almost to the same extent.

Reflecting back on their friendship in the light of the work on the Bible a few months after Rosenzweig's death, Buber stressed that, "... belief based on language, in which all verbal language becomes language based on belief" was the "germ of our collaboration" (Buber 2012, 176/*Scripture and Translation*, 211). The subtle realisation that "One believes not *in* the Bible but *through* it, and throughout it" (Buber 2012, 176/*Scripture and Translation*, 211),[36] which they also shared, deterred Rosenzweig and Buber from treating the words of the Bible as fossils whose shape had to be recovered through careful excavation; believing *through* the Bible rather than *in* it, meant that they sought, "to draw out the elemental meaning of individual words, i.e., their original concrete sense, whenever ... here was expressed a fundamental fact of teaching and belief" (Buber 2012, 183/*Scripture and Translation*, 218). Yet, this attempt was not made by operating in a linguistic "clean room" in which the translators produced a text sterilised against the "contamination" of the pristine original by a mixed hoard of readings and misreadings. A fine balance was to be struck between the text of the Hebrew Bible and its reception through translation and commentary over the centuries. The beauty and precision of Buber's explanation on how this was achieved, merit quoting him at length:

> ... the passage of time had largely turned the Bible into a palimpsest. The original traits of the Bible, the original meanings and words, had been overlaid by a familiar abstraction, in origin partly theological and partly literary ... The Bible asks us for a reverent intimacy with its meaning and its sensory concreteness; but that has been replaced by a mix of uncomprehending respect and unthinking familiarity ... and its relation to the real Bible resembles the relation of the murdered God of our time—that is, the familiar and diffuse concept of God—to the living God of reality (Buber 2012, 68/*Scripture and Translation*, 73).
>
> Even the most significant translations of the Bible that we possess—the Greek Septuagint, the Latin Vulgate, the German of Luther—do not aim principally at maintaining the original

---

36 Italics added by English translators.

character of the book ... They aim rather at transmitting to the translators' actual community—the Jewish diaspora of Hellenism, the early Christian *oikumene*, the faithful adherents of the Reformation—a reliable foundational document (Buber, 2012, 69/ *Scripture and Translation*, 74).

The great translators were of course possessed by the inspired insight that God's word must hold for all times and places; they did not see, however, that such an insight does not diminish but rather increases the importance of viewpoint, of There and Then in all their national, personal, corporeal conditionality. Revelation is accomplished in the human body and the human voice, i.e., in *this* body and *this* voice, in the mystery of their uniqueness (Buber, 2012, 69/ *Scripture and Translation*, 74).

Our work illuminates the palimpsest; it gets beneath the waxen surface upon which nations have inscribed the "Bible" of their religious needs and expressive forms, and the original text appears. The great work of the human mind and spirit inscribed upon the waxen surface is named *history*; but the name of the original text is *the book*. To the former belongs the honour of having gathered humanity around the book; to the latter, however, belongs the right, in a late and necessarily reflective moment of that history, to be discovered and contemplated by that humanity. It will be harder to live with the book than to live with history; the book will not conceal from us that it is as contradictory and vexatious as the world itself. But even its contradiction and vexation have Instructions to dispense [*Weisungen zu verschenken*]. (Buber, 2012, 85/ *Scripture and Translation*, 89)[37]

Understanding their position as situated between "history" and "the book", Buber and Rosenzweig strove to transcend the former in order to penetrate the latter, on its contradictions and vexations. Acknowledging that these contradictions and vexations are "like the world itself", they aligned themselves with the conclusion of the *Star:* just as the system, once completed, orients the subject back into life, so the Bible orients the reader back into the world. At the same time, both the *Star of Redemption* and the Bible point at that which lies beyond worldly life, the redemptive future and divine perfection. As thinkers and as translators, Rosenzweig and Buber saw it their calling to make evident as much as possible this redemptive-divine potential. In *Die Schrift* this was to be accomplished by applying the philological means at their disposal in order to reverse the formation of the biblical palimpsest: by tracing the historical evolution of its translation from modernity back to antiquity, Rosenzweig and Buber hoped to arrive at the way in which the first readers of the Bible had read it (*Zweistromland*, 734). Rather than conjuring an imagined "first reading" of Scripture, Rosenzweig and Buber tapped into the impressions of its ancient readers whose records they could access: the rabbis and the Alexandrian authors of the

---

37 Translation altered.

Septuagint.[38] As a modern representative of the decoding of biblical palimpsest, Martin Luther's translation continued to loom large over their project. The outcome was a confluence of text–commentary–translation (and translation as commentary) from eras spanning the first millennium BCE through the end of the second millennium CE, which remained attuned to the history of the Bible's reception while producing a highly original translation of their own. Although they did not employ redemptive terminology, in attempting to penetrate the imbrications of the biblical palimpsest, Buber and Rosenzweig sought to redeem the hidden, original meaning of the words of Scripture before its obfuscation by the multiplicity of translations and readings that agglomerated over two and a half millennia. Approaching the translation of the Bible as an act of redeeming its legacy from cumulative misappropriations, opens up Buber's and Rosenzweig's joint venture to additional redemptive possibilities which, though mostly not articulated in any systematic or programmatic sense, become evident from the philological process that underlay the choice of word in *Die Schrift*. In other words, the process of finding a new German rendition for the Bible's Hebrew entailed their release from the translations that had become entrenched, not only among the readers of the translations, but within the theological and philosophical discourses that had assimilated them in a variety of ways. Specifically, the dialogue in which Buber and Rosenzweig engaged with ancient readings of the Bible generated a subversive counter-reaction to modern appropriations, raised important questions regarding the authority of interpretation and "ownership" of Scripture: who has the authority to endorse the truthfulness of one translation, or even specific translational choices, over others? On what grounds "ownership" over the Bible as Holy Scripture is staked?[39]

Some of these questions have been explored in relation to modern conceptions of the Bible in Germany, mostly within the political context of Jewish-Christian polemics.[40] As I hope to have demonstrated, these are questions of a second order, whereas the first order question that preoccupied Rosenzweig (and Buber as well, to an extent), pertained to their ancient "interlocutors". Drawing great inspiration from rabbinical literature, Rosenzweig and Buber were also compelled to question its powerful claims for religious-spiritual authority. The Septuagint, whose influence on *Die Schrift* is less direct, nevertheless served as an im-

---

38 For a detailed study of Buber's and Rosenzweig's acquaintance with the Septuagint see Scharf 2016, 120–124.
39 See Scharf 2018b.
40 On the relationship between Jewish Bible translation and politics, see Plaut 1992; Breuer 1996; Reichert 1996; Gillman 2002, 2018; Seidman 2006; Wiese 2005; M. Benjamin 2009, 107–121.

portant site for examining Christian ownership claims on the Hebrew Bible through the appropriation of the Septuagint in the New Testament.[41]

The terms that I chose to examine have a particularly prodigious and volatile resonance in a German context: רוח (*ruah*) and תורה (*Torah*). The translation of the former as *Geist* is a cornerstone of Lutheran Christology and Hegelian thought. *Gesetz*, a modern incarnation of the Vulgate's translation of the Greek νομοσ (*nomos*) as *lex*, not only served as the foundation for a long Christian tradition of accusing Judaism of a spiritually jejune legalism; for Rosenzweig, it also disclosed the overlap between the function of law in Kantian ethics and the function of the Hebrew Bible as a source of moral guidance.

In what follows, the redemptive role that Rosenzweig assigned to translation in *Die Schrift* will be explained as an attempt to resolve Jewish-Christian polemics by retrieving, if only partially, the primordial voice of the biblical text. This act of retrieval consists of two key elements: 1) a critical dialogue with the multiple layers of interpretation and representation of the Hebrew Bible agglomerated in the course of nearly two millennia; 2) an attempt to re-appropriate the Bible as Jewish Scripture, over and against Christian appropriations. The latter were attained by the production of translations that generated a theological vocabulary based on the extraction of key terms in the Hebrew Bible from their Hebrew (and hence Jewish) provenance.

Consequently, my consideration of *Die Schrift* as a redemptive project is based on a conception of redemption that is far more modest than its robust definition in the *Star*, as the final consummation of the relations between God, man and world. This attenuated redemptive form actually serves to amplify the indispensability of translation. As Rosenzweig re-directs his readers at the end of *Star* back "into life," his translation of the Hebrew Bible together with Buber may be understood as the attempted retrieval of the truths that Holy Scripture contains. As such, translation redeems the Bible from mis-readings and mis-appropriations, brings closer its readers to the eternal truths that Scripture contains, while at the same time charting the limits of human knowledge; or in other words, charting the insuperable distance between humans and God.

6.2.1 Dual Loyalties

Buber and Rosenzweig were caught between the wish to produce a manifestly Jewish translation, which by its very nature would be guided by the rich rabbinic

---

[41] For the Septuagint's influence on the Buber-Rosenzweig translation, see Scharf 2016.

traditions of exegesis and translation of Scripture, and the obligation they felt to the biblical text bared "clean" of any and all commentary (M. Benjamin 2009, 121–134). As modern thinkers immersed in German high culture and versed in the innovations of higher criticism, they openly expressed their indebtedness to giants such as Goethe, Johann Herder and Friedrich Hölderin, while heeding the contributions of Wilhelm Gesenius, Julius Wellhausen and Emil Kautzsch. Awed by Martin Luther's translation, Buber and Rosenzweig initially contemplated creating a "revised" Luther Bible: as Rosenzweig put it in a letter to Buber in early 1925, a new Jewish-German translation of the Bible was not only impossible but strictly forbidden (*BT* II, 1021). It was only after trying such revision that they were forced to concede the futility of their attempt, and began working on *Die Schrift* as we know it today (Buber 2012, 143/*Scripture and Translation*, 177–178). The Luther translation maintained its dominant presence throughout the project, however, not only as an important reference, but also as a foremost example of Christian appropriations of the Bible.

The role that traditional Jewish exegesis played in the Buber-Rosenzweig translation has received vastly different scholarly assessments. Mara Benjamin's and Benjamin Sommer's positive view, I believe, better reflects the way in which the legacy of the sages of antiquity and their successors contributed to the shaping of the *Die Schrift*. Rosenzweig, according to Benjamin, "On the one hand … wished to clear all previous interpreters from the stage of biblical interpretation; on the other, he aimed to present Jewish sources as having succeeded at the task their Christian counterparts bungled". Benjamin contends that this aim was derived from the fact that, "The rabbis, for Rosenzweig, were not 'commentators' in the pejorative sense of the word, but gifted readers who attained supra-*wissenschaftlich*, universally applicable insight into the biblical text" (M. Benjamin 2009, 120). Sommer, in turn, describes Buber's and Rosenzweig's approach (along with Abraham Joshua Heschel) as "eliminating the boundary between Oral and Written Torahs", based on the attunement to the "spokenness" of the biblical text (Sommer 2015, 181–187). I would like to take this assessment even further, and claim that the exegetical heritage of rabbinic Judaism—in its ancient, medieval and modern incarnations—permeated the translation project in virtue of the unresolved tension that Buber and Rosenzweig maintained with the exegetical and legal-halakhic authority that the rabbis of antiquity had claimed for themselves. Indeed, their declared respect for the sources of Judaism did not necessarily obviate inconsistent uses of them, some due to oversight, others due to partial or exiguous knowledge, and yet others owing to conscious "idiosyncratic" re-interpretations. And yet, I believe that Buber's and Rosenzweig's fidelity to the rabbinic exegetical tradition, though not always reflected in their final choices, left an indelible mark on *Die Schrift*.[42]

6.2.1.1 He who Translates

We may characterise Buber's and Rosenzweig's appreciation for the exegetical legacy of rabbinical sages as follows: they were happy to accommodate it as long as it did not serve to endorse the sages as the human promulgators of divine law.[43] But what would be the implications of this position when it came to the rabbinic endorsement of the translation of Scripture itself?

In Bavli Kiddushin 49a we read: "R. Judah said: If one translates a verse literally, he is a liar; if he adds thereto, he is a blasphemer and guilty of libel. Then what is meant by translation? Our translation".[44] This dictum became classic in Jewish discussions of translation throughout the ages, appearing in works as diverse as the Maharal's *Tiferet Israel* (71) and Mendelssohn's introduction to his *Be'ur* – translation and commentary on the Pentateuch (10). If the *resha* (protasis) of this *gemara* addresses a fundamental problem in the very act of translation, the *seifa* (apodosis) shifts the discussion to an entirely different realm: it posits תרגום דידן (*targum didan*)—our translation—as the standard with which all other translations of Scripture must align themselves. In other words, the exegetical authority that had been anchored in the rabbinic account of the giving of the Torah at Sinai produced the only certified access to the Bible in translation; any deviation from it, R. Judah warns, amounts to blasphemy and the contempt of scripture.

I have not been able to ascertain whether Buber and/or Rosenzweig knew this *gemara* or discussed it; nevertheless, they were clearly aware of its tenor. In "The Spirit and Epochs of Jewish History", a lecture he gave in Kassel in the autumn of 1919, Rosenzweig describes the corpus of rabbinic literature (to which he refers rather abstractedly as "the Talmud"), as the bridge over the deep rift that the destruction of the Second Temple had threatened to tear in Jewish existence. The rabbis' successful canonisation of halakhah as divine law that was first transmitted to Moses at Sinai, preserved the unique spiritual quality of the Jewish people in the course of history, he contended. Rosenzweig certainly

---

42 In one of his last diary entries, Rosenzweig notes that the rabbinic distinction between laws originating in the Torah (*d'orayta*) and laws originating from the sages (*d'rabbanan*) is completely fluid in his eyes (*BT II*, 774).
43 Compare Sommer 2015, 183.
44 ר' יהודה אומר המתרגם פסוק הרי זה בדאי והמוסיף עליו הרי זה מחרף ומגדף אלא מאי תרגום תרגום דידן
See also Tosefta, Megilla 3:21: ר' יהודה אומ' המתרגם פסוק כצורתו הרי זה בדי, והמוסיף הרי זה מגדף.

could not accept the authority claim that *targum didan* asserted. Nevertheless he did not deny the decisive contribution of the rabbis' self-ascribed epistemological privilege to the spiritual perseverance of the Jewish people throughout history.

The spirit of Judaism, Rosenzweig explains in the lecture, is inextricably bound with the rabbinic corpus and the *historical* impact of its theology. In order to recognise this, however, the original Hebraic meaning of the term spirit, רוח (*ruah*), must be reclaimed by following the development of its etymology down to the narrow and misleading usage of *Geist* in modern German (an observation equally applicable to the English "Spirit"):

> The word is ancient, but its origin can be precisely established; ... What [the nations of classical antiquity] called *pneuma, spiritus* ... indeed denoted the physical life-puff of the human, his breath ... *the word "spirit" has its origins neither in Athens nor in Rome, but rather in our midst*, in the notion of God's spirit, of the holy spirit, that God bestowed upon his prophets ... Thus, instead of being merely the physical breath of life, it becomes the "spiritual bond" that binds the parts into a community. It is in this sense that the Word, coming from its Hebrew homeland, entered by way of Christian Dogmatics into the lexicon of the nations (*Zweistromland*, 527–518/Vogel 1996, 527–529).⁴⁵

And indeed, Buber's initial translation of רוח אלהים (*ruah Elohim*) in Genesis 1:2 as *Geist Gottes* was emended several times before he and Rosenzweig chose *Braus Gottes*—"a surge of God"—in order to capture both the physical and spiritual dimensions of *ruah* with a single word.⁴⁶

Explaining this translational choice in two essays: "The Man of Today and the Jewish Bible", published in 1926, and "On Word Choice in the German Translation of the Bible", published in 1930, Buber employs Rosenzweig's etymological analysis from "Spirit and Epochs" almost word for word. He then complements it with an analysis of their translation of מרחפת (*merahefet*; translated in English as either "hovered" or "moved"), as *brütet*, or brooded:

> The second verse of the Bible says of the *ruah* of God—or the God-*ruah*—that it 'hovered,' [*geschwebt*] the way Luther translates term, above the face of the waters that were not yet divided into those of heaven and those of earth. What sort of 'hovering,' this was, however, we learn only later (if at all) from the only passage of the Bible in which this rare verb recurs in the same form: Deuteronomy 32:11. God, who takes Israel from among the peoples and leads it into the promised land, is in that passage compared with the eagle, who with

---

45 Translation altered.
46 For critical assessments of this translation see Uffenheimer 1958, 52; Askani 1997, 173–175; Gordon 2003, 265–266; and Niehoff 1993.

softly beating wings hovers over its nest to awaken [*erregen*] it, i.e, to agitate its fledgling young to flight ... (Buber 2012, 49/*Scripture and Translation*, 14–15).⁴⁷

Maren Niehoff notes that Buber's association of Genesis 1:2 and Deuteronomy 32:11 drew on the Talmud and the commentaries of Rashi and Ibn Ezra. As Buber himself acknowledged:

> After further reflection and inquiry, I have a doubt concerning 'brooding.' Rashi indeed proposes 'to brood,' but this is only because he compares it to הקן על המרחפת כיונה [*ka-yonah hamerahefet al ha-kenn*; as the dove hovering over the nest], and not, as Ben Zoma (*Bavli Hagiga* 15a), to מרחפת על בניה [*merahefet al baneah*; hovering over its fledglings], which means to hover and not to brood—actually to spread one's wings. The latter view is substantiated by Ibn Ezra who relies on כנשר יעיר קנו על גוזליו ירחף [Deuteronomy 32:11: "Like an eagle that stirs its nest, hovers over its young"]...⁴⁸

Ibn Ezra took the reference to Deuteronomy from either the version in the Tosefta (Hagaiga 2:2) or the Yerushalmi (9a; 2:1), as opposed to the version in Bavli 15a:

> I was gazing between the upper and the lower waters, and there was only a bare three fingers' [breadth] between them, for it is said: *And the spirit of God hovered over the face of the waters* – like a dove which hovers over her young without touching".

In all three versions, however, the sage drawing the parallel between the hovering or brooding *ruah* of God and the hovering or fluttering wings of the birds, is the tanna Shimeon Ben Zoma.

Ben Zoma is one of the four tannaitic sages who entered the divine *pardes* and became privy to the secrets of *ma'aseh be-resheet* and *ma'aseh merkavah* (Bavli Hagigah 14b). According to the story, Ben Zoma glanced and lost his mind (and in some versions, glanced and died). In Hagigah 15a, contemplating the secret of creation, *ma'aseh beresheet*, he was gazing at the upper and lower waters, which God separates in Genesis 1:6–7. In his vision, *ruah elohim* pervades the slight gap between the waters of the ethereal realm and the waters of the earthly realm, encompassing both the physical and the spiritual.

The three aforementioned versions of the story in Tractate Hagigah therefore express the ancient concept of *ruah* that Rosenzweig had sought to restore in his lecture from 1919, and conveyed, in consultation with Buber, in *Die Schrift*. Rather uncannily, Rosenzweig's letter to Buber in which he delights at the

---

47 Translation altered.
48 Undated letter of Buber to Rosenzweig, Martin Buber Archive, MS Var 350 4b, 301, cited and translated in Niehoff 1993, 261–262.

final form of the translation of Genesis 1:2, evokes the mystery of *ma'aseh be-resheet:*

> God's spirit is the known theological term God's *Geist*, but *Braus Gottes* is yet unknown and it anticipated all of theology and any detail [therein], determinate and indeterminate ... (*BT* II, 1052).

6.2.1.2 From Sinai to this Day

The far-reaching implications of the claim regarding the divine origin of halakhah, in both the written and the oral Torah, preoccupied Buber and Rosenzweig long before *Die Schrift* was in the works. In correspondence spanning nearly three years (from September 1922 through June 1925), each thinker tried to present to his friend the way in which he perceived the relation between divine revelation, culminating in the Giving of the Torah at Mount Sinai, and its embodiment in Jewish life by halakhah. Buber, who told Rosenzweig that he stopped putting on tefillin when he was 14, viewed with modern sobriety the halakhic claim to have its origin in divine revelation: "I do not believe that revelation is ever a formulation of law. It is only through man in his self-contradiction that revelation becomes legislation" (*BT* II, 974/*Jewish Learning*, 111). Rosenzweig, for his part, was ultimately obliged to concede that "I, too, do not know whether the Law 'is' God's law. I know that as little, and even less than I know that God 'is' ... Thus, Revelation is not Law-giving. It is only this: Revelation. The primary content of revelation is revelation itself" (*BT* II, 1040/*Jewish Learning*, 117–118).

"The Builders", a letter that Rosenzweig wrote to Buber and published in 1923 at the latter's urging, addresses the question of the divine origin of halakhah by re-visiting, as it were, its constitutive moment at Sinai, in both biblical theology and the rabbinic traditions that devolved from it. Rosenzweig offers a listing of midrashic "highlights" on the Sinaitic revelation, whereby the Torah preceded the creation of the world, 600,000 Israelites witnessed the revelation at Mt. Sinai, that the Torah was written in seventy languages, etc. (*BT* II, 703/*Jewish Learning*, 78–79). He then asserts that Jews who read those midrashim uncritically accept them as "'fact", relying on "pseudo-historical and pseudo-juridical" validations of Law and therefore must be rejected (*BT* II, 704/*Jewish Learning*, 79–80).

In these letters, Rosenzweig maintains that "It is the Law's *Heutigkeit* ['todayness'], its living, contemporary reality that grants it religious validity" (Mendes-Flohr 1991, 299). Rosenzweig coins the term drawing on Deuteronomy 5:3 ("Not with our fathers did the Lord make this covenant, but with us, who are all of us here alive this day"), and notes that "It is upon us to accept the challenge of this boldness" (*BT* II, 709/*Jewish Learning*, 87).

This exchange of ideas ultimately drew the interlocutors' views closer to one another: while the sceptical Buber managed to erode some of Rosenzweig's justifications for the validity of halakhah, he adopted the notion of *Heutigkeit*, as may be seen from the closing statement of his 1924 essay on the Ten Commandments[49]:

> Once you will not consider me anymore as lost to 'our times,' and ask me once more the question, what shall be of the Ten Commandments, I will answer: this, what I try to do on my part as well: to draw closer to them. Not to a book scroll, not once more to the stone tablets, which shortly after being spoken were engraved by the 'Finger of God,' but rather to the spokenness [*Geschprochenheit*] of the Words (Buber 1962, 899).

But that was before setting to the task of translating the Bible. Exodus 19:1, which describes the People of Israel's arrival at Sinai, posed to Buber and Rosenzweig precisely the type of challenge they had tried to overcome in their correspondence. The verse reads: "On the third month after the people of Israel had gone forth out of the land of Egypt, on the day [ביום הזה; *ba-yom ha'zeh*] they came to the wilderness of Sinai".

As their translation illustrates, Buber and Rosenzweig chose to reflect the historical value of the verse as testifying to the *reception* of the Sinaitic revelation, but not as a concrete historical event:

Tab. 6.1: Exodus 19:1

Rosenzweig – Buber	Mendelssohn
genau auf den Tag, kamen sie in die Wüste Sinai	**im ersten Tage des monates**, kamen sie in die Wüste Sinai.
On the day they came to the wilderness of Sinai	
בַּיּוֹם הַזֶּה בָּאוּ מִדְבַּר סִינָי	

By rendering the verse "precisely on the day", Buber and Rosenzweig capture both possible meanings of הזה (*ha-zeh*). *genau* conveys the equal importance of each and every day of upholding the Torah, while remaining attuned to the importance of the historicity of the event without concretising it. In comparison, the liberty that Mendelssohn takes in rendering the expression "on the first day of the month", reflects the dating according to interpretations in *Bavli* (Shabbat

---

[49] Interestingly, Sommer's interptation of *Heutigkeit* is based on Rosenzweig's discussion of the present in the *Star*. See Sommer 2015, 200–201.

86b), *Mekhilta deRabbi Ishmael* (Yitro, BeHodesh 1) and medieval commentaries,[50] producing a very narrow historicist reading. Buber and Rosenzweig have their translation resonate the *Heutigkeit* of the experience at Sinai, while rejecting the presumptuous dating offered in the Talmud and the Mekhilta. It has been rarely noticed, however, that Rosenzweig had developed the notion of *Heutigkeit* before his correspondence with Buber, based on another midrashic commentary on Exodus 19:2.

In one of the last diary entries he recorded before his rapidly developing illness left nigh paralysed, Rosenzweig argued that Kant's categorical imperative as "living the law [*Gesetz*] from the viewpoint of eternity [*aus dem Gesichtspunkt der Ewigkeit*]" stands in utter opposition to the requirement to "'fulfil the law [that is, Torah] as though it were commanded unto you today'" (*Tagebücher* VII, 6). This paraphrase on the Tanhuma[51] shows that Rosenzweig was sceptical of rabbinic dicta that had become dogma,[52] but endorsed the rabbis' exegetical imagination when it defied the conventions of religious and rational thought. His attunement to ancient hermeneutic sensibilities of rabbinic and pre-rabbinic Judaism that we have encountered in chapters 4 and 5, included Jewish Hellenistic sources, and their early Christian adaptations. Through this prism he confronted one of the most contentious debates in the Bible's history of reception and translation.

6.2.1.3 תורה – Νόμοσ – *Weisung*

The multi-valence of Torah and Law (*Gesetz*), both in relation to one another and each unto itself, preoccupied Rosenzweig many years prior to working on *Die Schrift*. In the *Star*, *Gesetz* acquired a distinctive meaning in each of the three

---

50 Cf. Ramban, Rashbam, Abrabanel, Bahya, ad loc.
51 Tanhuma (Buber) Yitro 13: "ביום הזה באו מדבר סיני, כי ביום הזה באו, אלא כשתהא לומד, אל יהו בעיניך ישנים, אלא כאילו היום הזה ניתנה, ביום ההוא אין כתיב כאן, אלא ביום הזה." "On the day [*ba-yom ha-zeh*] they came to the Sinai Desert, for they came on the day. However, when you engage in study, do not consider them as belonging to the past [*al yehu be-eynechah yeshanim*], but as though it was given on this day, it does not say here 'on that day', but rather on this day". Rosenzweig's citation is ascribed to this source in Horwitz 1988, 248, n. 2.
52 The concrete dating of the giving of the Torah at Sinai was part of the massive effort to establish the authority of the sages as successors to Moses in he chain of transmission of the divine law, enshrined in Mishnah Avot 1:1: "Moses received the Torah from Sinai and handed it down to Joshuah etc. ..."

parts (Schindler 1999),[53] whereas Torah appeared in both German designations – *Gesetz* and *Lehre* (teaching) – and was even merged in a neologism, *Gesetzeslehre*, to convey the Torah's encompassing [*umschließt*] both meanings (SE, 337/SR 304). After completing the *Star*, Rosenzweig continued to alternate between the terms according to the context, using *Gesetz* to denote either Torah or halakhah (sometimes intentionally blurring the distinction between the two), at other times opting for *Lehre* instead.[54]

He was also aware that this ambiguity did not only stem from the difficulty to translate the term from the Hebrew, but also from the different meanings of *torah* in different parts of the Bible:

> The people whose living condition is the law (a recurring motif of Deuteronomy), the people's fallen destiny (Song of Moses),[55] the focal point, the תשובה (*teshuvah*), the formation of the Remainder [of Israel] of the Pharisees (Psalms 119), out of the tension between them the fact came about (*Tagebücher* VII, 5).[56]

Yet, even when applied to the Torah, *Gesetz* defied the rational, universalistic application that the term acquired in Kant's hands: "The categorical imperative is indeed only the Law of Laws [*das Gesetz des Gesetzes*]. Whereas the Torah is in reality חרות על הלוחות (*harut al ha-luhot*)" (*Tagebücher* VII, 6). Thus, even as a book of laws, the Torah has the inimitable quality of simultaneous eternality (having been engraved on stone tablets by God at Sinai; Deuteronomy 32:16),

---

53 Schindler identifies a progression from meta-ethics (Part I), via the equation of love for one's fellow with the loving relations with God (Part II) to the holy law of the Torah (part III). On the notion of law in the *Star* see also Gibbs 2004.

54 Isaac Heinmann asserts that Rosenzweig uses in his writings *Gesetz* only as standard translation for Torah, but even in *Die Bauleute*, which Heinmann quotes in the very same passage, Rosenzweig uses *Lehre*, not *Gesetz* (Heinemann 1993, 213). In his lecture on "The Essence of Judaism", Rosenzweig posits law (*Gesetz*), spirit (*Geist*) and blood (*Blut*) as the elements comprising the essence of Judaism. *Gesetz* and *Tora* (also תורה) are distinct entities. "Other [religious] legal systems have at most the divine beginning [*die göttliche Einführung*], but they do not have the divine signature [*Unterschrift*] behind every clause". Rosenzweig's use of *Unterschrift* indicates that the Torah is Holy Scripture in the sense that it is the foundational text, or underlying scripture (the literal meaning of *unter* and *Schrift*). *Zweistromland*, 522. See also: "[Biblical narrative] offers [its readers] knowledge, teaching [*Lehre*], revelation", in ibid, 829; translated as "The Secret of Biblical Narrative Form", *Scripture and Translation*, 142; and compare Yehoshua Amir's translation of *Lehre* as *torah* in Rosenzweig 1977, 19.

55 Deuteronomy 32:1–43.

56 Rosenzweig here identifies three models also recognised in modern Bible scholarship. See M. Greenberg 1990. For the Deuteronomistic designation of *torah* and its transformation after the inclusion of Deuteronomy in the biblical canon see Finsterbusch 2011.

and versatility (according to the famous midrashic extrapolation that Rosenzweig invokes by citing the Hebrew of the midrash).⁵⁷

When the time came for Rosenzweig to translate *torah* and its correlates from the root י.ר.ה. (*y.r.h*), flexibility in rendition was no longer an option. The medium, as well as the translation policy of *Die Schrift*⁵⁸ required accuracy and consistency, in spite of the term's multiple valences. The long history of Christian translation of *torah* as *Gesetz*, and nearly as long a history of Jewish translations as *Lehre*, compounded the challenge further by effectively turning it into a binary choice. Rosenzweig and Buber, however, refused to see it as a two-pronged problem. The dilemma had to be overcome upon encountering the occurrence of the root *y.r.h.* in Exodus 4:15.⁵⁹

---

57 Avot 6:2: אל תקרא חרות אלא חירות. ("Do not read 'engraved' [*harut*] but rather 'liberty' [*herut*]"). Rosenzweig's affinity for imaginative extrapolations, noted above, received its most famous expression in the title of "The Builders", derived from *Bavli* Berakhot 64a:'וכל בניך למודי ה ורב שלום בניך, אל תקרי בניך אלא בוניך. ("'All your sons shall be taught by the LORD, and great shall be the prosperity of your sons'; Do not read ' your sons' [*banayich*] but rather 'your builders' [*bonayich*]".

58 As he worked on the translation, Buber discovered the immense importance of repetition in the biblical text. Coining the term *Leitwort* (as in leitmotif), he persuaded Rosenzweig of the necessity of consistent translation, which European translators tend to forgo for the sake of variety: "By *Leitwort* I understand a word or word root that is meaningfully repeated within a text or sequence of texts or complex of texts; those who attend to these repetitions will find a meaning of the text revealed or clarified, or at any rate made more emphatic" (Buber 2012, 183/*Scripture and Translation*, 114). Rosenzweig credits Buber with the idea in *Zweistromland*, 819/*Scripture and Translation*, 131; Buber elaborates on this concept in Buber 2012, 95–110/*Scripture and Translation*, 143–150. According to Ed Greenstein, *Leitwortstil*, or etymological translations as he calls it, proved a powerful tool in the penetration of the biblical palimpsest, and even of the essence of language itself: "Buber and Rosenzweig acknowledged that a word rarely makes a clean break with its past and for a number of reasons sought to translate words according to their etymological or root meaning ... the root meaning of a Hebrew word often clarifies the psychological or theological impulse behind a term ...; in explaining the need for etymological translation Rosenzweig ... penetrates to the philosophical core, to Language itself: at the root level of languages the diverse languages of the world share a common domain and structure. The translator must probe this most basic, universal level of language. Only at that level can translation take place. Greenstein 1983, 24–25, and see below for critiques of *Leitwort*. Askani 1997, esp. 154–160, 305–315, emphasises the centrality of word and word selection in *Die Schrift*, but does not address the importance of the *Leitwort* principle in this context. For a critique of Buber's and Rosenzweig's inconsistent application of the principle see M. Benjamin 2009, 146–154.

59 The first appearance of *torah* as a noun in Genesis 26:5 (וַיִּשְׁמֹר מִשְׁמַרְתִּי מִצְוֹ֫תַי חֻקּוֹתַי) did not prompt Rosenzweig to reflect on the broader implications of its translation. See *Arbeitspapiere*, 74.

Tab. 6.2: Exodus 4:15

B–R	Luther	Mendelssohn	Hirsch	Zunz
... Ich werde dasein bei deinem Mund und bei seinem Mund und euch **weisen**, was ihr tun sollt	Und ich will mit deinem und seinem Munde sein und euch **lehren**, was ihr tun sollt	ich will schon mit deinem und seinem Munde sein, und euch **lehren**, was ihr thun sollt.	und Ich werde mit deinem Munde und mit seinem Munde sein und werde euch das **lehren**, was ihr thun sollt.	und ich werde seyn mit deinem Munde, und mit seinem Munde und euch **unterweisen**, was ihr thun sollt.
... and I will be with your mouth and with his mouth, and will teach you what you shall do					
וְאָנֹכִי אֶהְיֶה עִם־פִּיךָ וְעִם־פִּיהוּ וְהוֹרֵיתִי אֶתְכֶם אֵת אֲשֶׁר תַּעֲשׂוּן					

Rosenzweig's *euch weisen*, "I will instruct you", makes more sense than *lehren*, "teach", which the majority of other translations have opted for. The context of the verse, God's instructions for Moses and Aaron on how to lead the manumitted People of Israel, is practical rather than educational; Moses and Aharon need practical instructions rather than learning a precept or a law. The broader implications, however, were on Rosenzweig's mind as well. In his commentary on one of Buber's earlier drafts of this verse he averred: "*Zeuger* and *Zeuge* (witness and testimony) also derive from the same root. But is it possible to call the Pentateuch "Five Books of Testimony"? We [Buber and himself] cannot coin this expression. Upon its first appearance in the Bible, Torah must be called *weisen*" (*Arbeitspapiere*, 98). This translational decision proved Rosenzweig's literary genius a few chapters later, as Luther's *Gesetz* clashed with his *euch lehren*, whereas Rosenzweig's translation retained seamless continuity:

Tab. 6.3: Exodus 12:49

B–R	Luther
Einerlei **Weisung** sei dem Sproß und dem Gast, der in eurer Mitte gastet	Einerlei **Gesetz** sei dem Einheimischen und dem Fremdling, der unter euch wohnt.
There shall be one law for the native and for the stranger who sojourns among you	
תּוֹרָה אַחַת יִהְיֶה לָאֶזְרָח וְלַגֵּר הַגָּר בְּתוֹכְכֶם	

It is almost trivial to note that the Christian designation of the Torah as law, in the major European languages at least, derives from the transformation of the Septuagint's *nomos* into the Latin *lex* in the Vulgate. This transmission had cemented the equivocation of *nomos* with law in Christian Bible translations.

Though the transition from *torah* to *nomos* in the first Greek translation of the Bible, customarily dated and ascribed to 2nd century BCE Alexandria, appears straightforward, scholars still debate the range of meanings that the Greek term had signified for the translators and readers of the Septuagint.[60] Martin Luther translated the New Testament first and approached the Hebrew Bible only later in life.[61] Therefore, his translation of Paul's *nomos* as *Gesetz*, which preceded his translation of *torah* was decisive in shaping the legalistic image of the original Hebrew term.[62] This interpretation, of course obscures, the fact that Paul's use of *nomos* pertained to a plurality of meanings, some of which are more compatible with early Protestant theology than others.[63]

This may had very well been self-evident for Rosenzweig,[64] to the extent that he deemed it unnecessary to refer to the Septuagint explicitly in his commentaries on Buber's drafts in this context. Be that as it may, the final translational choice comports with a more elastic meaning of *nomos* that may be ascribed

---

60 According to Murakoa 2009, s.v. "Nomos", *nomos* denotes: (1) "a body of normative rules prescribing man's conduct"; (2) "binding regulation and rule"; (3) "the Pentateuch". While Hermann Kleinknecht and Walter Gutbrod emphasize the initial differences between *torah* and *nomos*, which only widened from the post-exilic period onwards. Kittel 1979. Indeed, Peter Richardson, editor of the Canadian journal *Studies in Religion* 13.3 (1986) introduced a special issue that explored the incredible multi-valence of *nomos* in Jewish antiquity, noting that "The range of meanings of both *Torah* and *nomos* is notoriously slippery"; Richardson 1986, 3. See also, Segal; Reinharz; Westerholm.

61 After some experimentation with the translation of Holy Scriptures, Luther completed his setting of the New Testament into German in the timespan of three months. The translation appeared in print in September 1522. Turning immediately to the Old Testament, he published his translation in instalments between 1523 and 1532. For an overview of Luther's work on the Bible see Bluhm 1983, here at 182–183.

62 One of the fundamental concepts of Lutheran theology, the dialectic of *Gesetz und Evangelium* (Law and Gospel) is premised on the separation of divine law from Old Testament law. Since both parts in the dialectic originate in creation (rather than unfold in the course of reading the Scriptures), they are fundamental to the human condition as a struggle against sin and the Devil. For an exposition of this dialectic see Althaus 1966. For a more recent discussion see Steiger, 23–35.

63 Kleinknecht and Gutbrod differentiate between two basic usages of *nomos* by Paul: linguistic [*Sprachgebrauch*] and factual [*sachlich*]. In relation to the former, they assert that Paul's *nomos* may refer to any aspect of law or Torah in the Old Testament; whereas the latter concerns Christian theology. See Kittel 1979. Sander is considered a milestone in the scholarly appreciation of Paul's rich and complex view of *nomos*. Luther, on the other hand, is seen today as largely responsible for interpretations that stress Paul's view of *nomos* as negative as by and large, see Byrne 2000, 308–309.

64 See, for example, his reference to Paul's "attack" against Jewish law without bothering to explain what that attack consisted of in *Zweistromland*, 522.

to 2ⁿᵈ century BCE Alexandria.[65] Rosenzweig's repeated references to the Septuagint as an important resource in the attempt to decipher the text of the Hebrew Bible, make it clear that he consulted the Greek continuously throughout the work, including as a "mirror image" of the Hebrew through a reverse translation of the Greek ("*Rückübersetzung*"), which he learned from Eduard Strauß (*BT* II, 1132–1133). More than an authoritative testimony, the Septuagint appears to have served Rosenzweig as a source of inspiration as the earliest-surviving record of the Jewish interpretations of the Hebrew Bible.

The semantic affinities between Rosenzweig's *Weisung* and the Septuagint's *nomos*, even without evidence that establishes direct influence, attests to the unique, sophisticated historical multi-valence of *Die Schrift*. It not only dwells in the distant past in search of origins; it simultaneously brings the ancient polemic in dialogue with modern scholarly debates and theological apologetics.

6.3 "Curiosity Abounds and Knowledge Proliferates"

Frederick E. Greenspan's "How Jews Translate the Bible" places the Buber-Rosenzweig project at the heart of a rich tradition. Indeed, some of the most conspicuous features of *Die Schrift*, either from reading it and/or Buber's and Rosenzweig's essays, turn out to be common practice for Jewish rendition of Scripture spanning antiquity through modernity. Greenspan's comparative study, perhaps unintentionally, also illuminates the uniqueness of *Die Schrift*, both as he pertains to it as a specifically Jewish project and as its bears upon the general issues of Bible translation. In addition to the "commitment to the Hebrew form" (Greenspan 2002, 45–46), a "tendency to incorporate Jewish tradition"(52–53), "removing Christian features"(53–54), and "[making] a point of drawing on Jewish sources" (58), *Die Schrift* is infused with awareness of the "World-Historical Importance of the Bible", to borrow Rosenzweig's phrase. That is, its singular contribution to the course of history and the singular importance of its reception in the course of world history. Therefore, retracing the evolution of the palimpsest of readings and interpretations in order to reach the initial, untainted voice of the biblical text was performed not only with the awareness of the task's impos-

---

[65] "It appears that for Alexandrian Jews as well, the term *torah* was nothing but an institution of practices and traditions bound to the people's history and to the acts of its judges, kings and prophets ... The Greek *nomos* initially meant to Alexandrian Jews nothing more or less than *torah* ... But with the constant interaction with Greek culture deviation occurred from the original conception of the term *torah she-be-al peh* [oral Torah], followed by a shift in the very approach to the meaning of *torah* and its designation (Urbach 1969, 257–258).

sibility, but also with the knowledge that this entails reading as many layers of the palimpsest as possible, and, when appropriate, have them resonate through the translation, irrespective of provenance. Hence, Rosenzweig and Buber were able to admire Luther and disagree with him almost categorically, or consult Goethe, Herder or even Calvin, before deciding to follow an entirely different path. This is why their project could support so readily an elaborate constellation of redemptive aspects.

The burden of dual loyalties inherent to the act of translation is a well-known problem among the practitioners of the art. In his introduction to his translation of Maimonides' *Guide of the Perplexed*, which the author himself endorsed, Rabbi Shmuel Ibn Tibbon laments that "Not by virtue of considering myself a sage, did my heart lead me to this narrow path of translation, confined by a fence on this side and on that side" (*Moreh*, 3). The narrow path Tibbon the Younger refers to, is the rendering of a text in a way that is loyal to the original's meaning as much as it is faithful to the nature of the language it is rendered into. But in the case of *Die Schrift*, the burden grew heavier in light of the translators' reverent dialogue with their predecessors, Jewish and non-Jewish.

Rosenzweig's use of the term *torah* in his writings, and his translation of it in *Die Schrift*, demonstrate a clear wish to retain its multi-valence, rather than commit to a restricted and restricting meaning. Amazingly, Rosenzweig refrained from adopting his own translation of *torah* in *Die Schrift* as the standard term in his own writings. This semantic ambiguity, I believe, should be understood as expressing the wish to expose the metaphysical multi-valence of *torah*, and as the guiding consideration in choosing *Weisung* over the other alternatives he had in mind. Concurrently, it can also be seen to reflect a fundamental perplexity that Rosenzweig confesses to Ernst Simon in relation to the Hebrew text of the Bible; a perplexity that can also be pointed out in relation to his understanding of revelation.[66]

When placed within the broader context of Rosenzweig's use and designation of *torah* in his writings, his translation of the term as *Weisung* exemplifies the multifaceted implications of the translation of the Bible as a redemptive act. Most acutely, it shows that Rosenzweig never considered himself as having attained a full and complete understanding of Being, or having been redeemed of the gnawing doubts that haunted him since his intellectual youth. His correspondence at the final stage of his life portrays a man who is fully aware of the

---

[66] In the same letter to Ernst Simon (*BT* II, 1132–1133), Rosenzweig confessed to the enormous difficulty he experiences upon trying to understand the Bible's Hebrew, even though the readings are explained by the men he holds in the highest esteem: Rabbi Nehemia Nobel, Hermann Cohen, and Simon himself, making two exceptions: Buber, and Eduard Strauß.

partiality of his knowledge and of his inability to attain full answers to the ultimate questions that the practitioners of philosophy and theology aspire to expose by practicing their respective disciplines. At the same time, Rosenzweig's views had clearly undergone a genuine, fundamental transformation. Intellectually, this transformation had taught him that his quest is worthwhile, and it is to take place in the study and interpretation of Jewish texts, and their ultimate origin – the Bible. The intellectual activity most suitable for this endeavour—translation—does not obligate him to feign completeness or force upon the text a restrictive reading. By having the German resonate the Hebrew, translation may highlight, rather than overshadow, the multi-valence of Scripture and open it up to new interpretational possibilities. This translational approach is consistent with the conception that Rosenzweig shared with Walter Benjamin regarding the redemption of the text subjected to translation from its time and place of origin, by re-introducing it to the present, in a different culture by means of a different language. At the same time, Rosenzweig significantly expanded the redemptive possibilities of translation by adapting a more optimistic epistemological approach than Benjamin. Refusing to settle for the shadows in the Platonic cave of the present, Rosenzweig confronted the challenge head-on by daring to translate the very source of the redemptive scheme he and Benjamin shared, instead of opting for modern, secular incarnations like Proust and Baudelaire. The philological investigation became for Rosenzweig the primary tool for exposing, and as much as possible, fulfilling the redemptive potentialities he discerned in the act of translation.

A similar appreciation of the reciprocity between the translation of revelatory sources and the endurance of their original texts was articulated by R. Yehuda Ibn Tibbon, father of Shmuel. In his introduction to the translation of Bahya Ibn Paquda's *Hovot Ha-Levavot* he states:

> And there we see, that several exegetes and translators interpreted and translated the books of the Bible and the orders of the Mishnah and the Talmud in foreign tongues, and how much the opinions presented therein vary from one another—one says this way and one says another way—and because those books are available to us in the original and in themselves, without additions and abbreviations and the commentaries and translations also stand in their own right, this has proved beneficial and did no damage; curiosity abounds and knowledge proliferates (*Hovot Halevavot*, 4).

Conclusion

> Time present and time past
> Are both perhaps present in time future
> And time future contained in time past.
> If all time is eternally present
> All time is unredeemable
> (T.S. Eliot, "Burnt Norton", *Four Quartets*)

There is every reason to translate the Bible and every reason not to translate it. There is every reason to harbour hopes for redemption and every reason not to. Standing at the crossroads between relativistic pessimism and spiritual optimism, Franz Rosenzweig chose to heed the words of the Psalmist and "ride forth in the cause of truth", rather than follow Nietzsche's freefall to the abyss of existentialist despair. He scoffed at Hegel's absolutist philosophy in *Phänomenologie des Geistes* and sought to realise Schelling's incomplete project in *Die Weltalter*. He saw in the Talmud the bridge that carried the Jewish people through the crisis of the destruction of the Second Temple, and considered the claims to religious and spiritual authority by the rabbis of antiquity untenable. He admired midrash and read modern Bible scholarship voraciously, if critically.

These ostensibly irreconcilable tensions were in fact the driving force of Franz Rosenzweig's lifelong search for redemption. The disappointments he experienced in the early stages of this search proved equally conducive to his project as his later discoveries. Within his economy of ideas, the historian's scepticism guided his confrontation with the question of dating the Israelites' arrival at Mount Sinai in Exodus 19:1; whereas classical Jewish exegesis was preferred over the Platonic and Kantian translations of Luther and Mendelssohn, respectively, of Exodus 3:14. For this reason, Rosenzweig was also able to demonstrate simultaneous affinity and disagreement with the ideas of contemporaries such as Hermann Cohen, Walter Benjamin and Martin Buber, who, amongst themselves, were critical of each other's work. And for this reason also, his conception of temporality, which on my reading is modelled on the biblical calendar of Leviticus 23 and Numbers 28–29, can find a poetic correlate in the opening lines of T.S. Eliot's *Burnt Norton*, published in England a mere six years after Rosenzweig's death.

The aim of this book has been to offer an interpretation of Rosenzweig's life's work as a paradigmatic modern Jewish thinker: espousing a deep commitment to the Jewish sources, discourses, hermeneutics and ideas, while being acutely aware of the dangers of trenchant traditionalism; announcing the collapse of the Western philosophical tradition while acknowledging the indispensability of its legacy: the tools of critical inquiry and the concept of system. By structuring the book's chapters according to the chronological development of Rosenzweig's ideas and works, I have sought to show that his radical shift from assimilated dilettantism to Jewish devotional life did not suppress certain fundamental intuitions and sensibilities, which persisted until the end of his short life. The conclusion to which this process led him was that Judaism and modernity need one another in order to survive—intellectually and spiritually. The eternal truths ensconced in the Hebrew Bible, which the Jewish exegetical tradition has been exploring for many centuries, offer a remedy to the ailments of philosophical discourse. But in order to retrieve these truths from Scripture, religious dogmatism must be circumvented by exercising epistemological prudence and systematic rigour. To be sure, a task on such a scale could not be completed in a single work. In the *Star of Redemption* Rosenzweig articulated those insights within a theoretical framework that he believed was exhaustive and conclusive. In this sense, it is the *summa* of his reflections on the mutual problems faced by Judaism and (Christianity) in modernity. In acknowledgment of its importance, this book focuses on the *Star* despite the fact that in terms of the work's rhetoric and presentation, the Hebrew Bible and translation do not figure prominently in its programme. But as I have emphasised, the *Star*'s concluding words, *INS LEBEN*, were written out of the conviction that the complete unfolding of the theoretical system marks the beginning of the implementation of its ideas in reality. Therefore, my interpretation of the *Star* suggests that it should be read as a transitional work, which marks an important, albeit intermediate stage in Rosenzweig's thought. The final destination of his journey, the translation of the Hebrew Bible, embodies the insight in the light of which the *Star* was shaped, but did not articulate explicitly: that the ideal mode of reflection and expression for engaging with the challenges faced by modern thought and faith is translation.

Rosenzweig's translations have attracted the attention of both readers and scholars since the time of their initial publication until today. Still, his subtle incorporation of translation and citation in his work have been recognised and explored mainly in the last decade or two. The title of this book, *Thinking in Translation*, suggests that Rosenzweig's rendering of Hebrew texts into German, and his theoretical writings on translation, provide a partial account on his use of the craft; it indicates that Rosenzweig's use of translation is not only more pervasive than what is commonly recognised, but also essential for understanding his thought as a whole. To demonstrate this claim, I have focused on Rosenzweig's translation methodology, arguing that it is based on consummate philological analyses upon which he based his translation choices. In the theoretical discussions, I have insisted on the links between the practice of translation and

Rosenzweig's systematic project as a whole. Contrary to the prevalent approach to the study of his translations, which pigeonholes this activity within the discourses of the philosophy of language and the theory of translation, I have attempted to present the ways in which the embedment of biblical prooftexts in the *Star* and the reliance on ideas drawn from his reading of Scripture were instrumental for shaping the structure and substance of the system of the *Star*. And in turn, how these insights articulated in his philosophical tome are reflected in his work on *Die Schrift*.

To be sure, the work presented here leaves many questions regarding Rosenzweig's legacy unaddressed, and many issues that call for further research. The structure of the argument within the confines of a book did not allow me to do justice to his translation of Yehudah Halevy's poems. A tour de force of literary, exegetical and philosophical ingenuity, this project merits a dedicated study, which thanks to the methodological approach to Rosenzweig's work proposed here, is sure to yield interesting results. The presentation of Rosenzweig's dialogue with rabbinic exegesis and the legacy of the Septuagint barely scratches the surface of what needs to be done. In this area, I have explored further the biographical background and underlying motivations for Rosenzweig's and Buber's interest (Scharf 2016) and the place of their project within Jewish-Christian biblical polemics (Scharf 2018a). Rosenzweig was certainly not the only Jewish thinker in the early 20th century in whose thought translation figured prominently. This book can be the stepping stone for further reflection on the importance of translation in the writings of other thinkers, especially Hermann Cohen and Gershom Scholem. As discussed here, Cohen also relied on original translations of verses in his work as part of his philosophical argumentation. Whereas Scholem, who corresponded with Rosenzweig on the latter's translation efforts, also produced translations of his own which are yet to receive their due recognition.

★ ★ ★

Throughout this book, I have repeatedly contrasted Rosenzweig's statement in "The New Thinking" that the *Star* is not a Jewish book, with the copious evidence that shows the profundity of his commitment to the sources of Judaism. I hope to have succeeded in demonstrating that Rosenzweig's literary sophistication, intellectual eclecticism and striving for universality of spirit and thought, should not obscure his fundamental commitment to his calling as a *Jewish* thinker.

One's moment of death can sometimes disclose basic truths about the core of one's being, which various factors prompt one to downplay or conceal when one is still alive. The headstone on Rosenzweig's grave at the new Jewish cemetery in Frankfurt is inscribed at the bottom with three lines of German, stating his name and dates. The lion's share of the inscription reads as follows:

פ]ה]"ט]מן]
מורנו
ר' לוי בן ר' שמואל
ראזענצווייג
נולד כה' כסלו התרמ"ז
בק]הילת]"ק]ודש] קאסעל והלך
לעולמו ה' כסלו התר"צ
פראנקפורט פה ק]הילת] "ק]ודש]
תנצב"ה

It is preceded by an epitaph from Psalms 73:23 that is set in an arch:

ואני תמיד עמך

Bibliography

Primary Sources

Franz Rosenzweig's works

Rosenzweig's collected works:

Eds. Rachel Rosenzweig and Edith Rosenzweig-Scheinmann. *Der Mensch und sein Werk. Gesammelte Schriften I: Briefe und Tagebücher. Band I: 1900–1918; Band II: 1918–1929.* The Hague: Martinus Nijhoff, 1979.
Eds. Reinhold and Annemarie Mayer. *Der Mensch und sein Werk. Gesammelte Schriften III: Zweistromland: Kleinere Schriften zu Glauben und Denken.* Dordrecht: Martinus Nijhoff, 1984.
Ed. Rafael N. Rosenzweig. *Der Mensch und sein Werk. Gesammelte Schriften IV: Sprachdenken. 1. Band. Jehuda Halevi. Fünfundneunzig Hymnen und Gedichte, Deutsch und Hebräisch mit einem Vorwort und mit Anmerkungen.* The Hague: Martinus Nijhoff, 1983.
Ed. Rachel Bat Adam. *Der Mensch und sein Werk. Gesammelte Schriften IV: Sprachdenken. 2. Band. Arbeitspapiere zur Verdeutschung der Schrift.* Dordrecht: Martinus Nijhoff, 1984.

Other works:

Das älteste Systemprogramm des deutschen Idealismus. 1914. Franz Rosenzweig Collection, AR 3001, Series II, Subseries III. Leo Baeck Institute, Center for Jewish History, New York. http://www.archive.org/stream/franzrosenzweig_03_reel03#page/n661/mode/1up.
Das älteste Systemprogramm des deutschen Idealismus. Ein handschriftlicher Fund, mitgeteilt von Franz Rosenzweig. Vorgelegt von Heinrich Rickert. Sitzungsbericht der Heidelberger Akademie der Wissenschaften. Philosophisch-historische Klasse. Vol. 5. Heidelberg: Carl Winter, 1917.
Das Büchlein vom gesunden und kranken Menschenverstand. Düsseldorf: J. Meltzer, 1964.
Der Stern der Erlösung. Frankfurt a. M.: J. Kauffmann Verlag, 1921.
Der Stern der Erlösung. 2nd Auflage. Heidelberg: Lambert Schneider, 1954.
Der Stern der Erlösung. Mit einer Einführung von Reinhold Mayer und einer Gedenkrede von Gershom Scholem. Frankfurt a. M.: Suhrkamp, 1988.
Der Tischdank. Berlin: Fritz Gurlitt, 1920.
Hegel und der Staat. Heruasgegeben von Frank Lachmann. Mit einem Nachwort von Axel Honneth. Berlin: Suhrkamp, 2010.
Sechzig Hymnen und Gedichte des Jehuda Halevy. Konstanz: Oskar Wohrle, 1924.
Tagebücher. Typescripts I–III, 14 December, 1905–4 March, 1908. Franz Rosenzweig Collection, AR 3001, Series II, Subseries I. Leo Baeck Institute, Center for Jewish History, New York. http://www.archive.org/stream/franzrosenzweig_01_reel01#page/n1016/mode/1up.
Tagebücher. Typescripts IV–V, VII and Notebook, 6 March, 1908–13 September, 1922. Franz Rosenzweig Collection, AR 3001, Series II, Subseries I. Leo Baeck Institute, Center for

Jewish History, New York. http://www.archive.org/stream/franzrosenzweig_01_reel01#page/n1097/mode/1up

The Gritli Letters (Gritli Briefe). Eugen Rosenstock-Huessy Fund. http://www.argobooks.org/gritli/index.html.

Zweiundneunzig Hymnen und Gedichte des Jehuda Halevy. Deutch. Mit einem Nachwort und mit Anmerkungen. Berlin: Lambert Schneider, 1926.

Buber, Martin and Rosenzweig, Franz. *Die Schrift und ihre Verdeutschung*. Berlin: Schocken, 1936.

Franz Rosenzweig's works in translation:

English

Cultural Writings of Franz Rosenzweig. Trans. and ed. Barbara E. Galli. Syracuse NY: Syracuse UP, 2000.

Judaism Despite Christianity: The 'Letters on Christianity and Judaism' between Eugen Rosenstock-Huessy and Franz Rosenzweig'. Ed. Eugen Rosenstock-Huessy. University, AL: University of Alabama, 1969.

Franz Rosenzweig's The New Thinking. Ed. and trans. Alan Udoff and Barbara E. Galli. Syracuse NY: Syracuse UP, 1999.

On Jewish Learning. Trans. N. N. Glatzer. New York: Schocken, 1965.

Philosophical and Theological Writings. Trans. Paul W. Franks and Michael L. Morgan. Indianapolis IN: Hackett, 2000.

The Star of Redemption. Trans. William Hallo. London: Routledge & Kegan Paul, 1971.

The Star of Redemption. Trans. Barbara E. Galli. Madison WI: University of Wisconsin Press, 2005.

Understanding of the Sick and the Healthy: A View of World, Man and God. Trans. Nahum Glatzer. Cambridge MA: Harvard UP, 1999.

Buber, Martin and Rosenzweig, Franz. *Scripture and Translation*. Trans. Lawrence Rosenwald with Everett Fox. Bloomington IN: Indiana UP, 1994.

Galli, Barbara E. *Franz Rosenzweig and Jehudah Halevy: Translating, Translations, and Translators*. Montreal & Kingston: McGill–Queen's UP, 1995.

Hebrew

(*Kochav Ha-Ge'ula*) **כוכב הגאולה**. תרגם יהושע עמיר. ירושלים: מוסד ביאליק, 1971.

(*Naharaim*) **נהריים: מבחר כתבים**. תרגם יהושע עמיר. ירושלים: מוסד ביאליק, 1977.

(*Briefe und Tagebücher*) **פרנץ רוזנצווייג. מבחר אגרות וקטעי יומן**. ההדירה והוסיפה מבוא והערות רבקה הורביץ. ירושלים: מוסד ביאליק, 1987.

(*Jehuda Halevi*) **פירושי פרנץ רוזנצווייג לתשעים וחמישה משירי רבי יהודה הלוי**. תרגמם ואיתר פסוקי מקרא ואמרות חז"ל המאוזכרים בשירים מיכאל שורץ. ירושלים: מאגנס, 2011.

Primary Sources

Bible Translations

German

Buber, Martin. *Die Schrift: Aus dem Hebräischen verdeutscht von Martin Buber gemeinsam mit Franz Rosenzweig.* 4 Vols. Deutsche Bibelgeselleschaft, 1992.
Buber, Martin and Rosenzweig, Franz. *Die Schrift.* Vols. I–X (i) *Im Anfang*; (ii) *Namen*; (iii) *Er Rief* (iv) *In der Wüste*; (v) *Reden* (vi) *Jehoschua*; (vii) *Richter* (viii) *Schmuel* (ix) *Könige* (x) *Jeschajahu.* Berlin: Lambert Schneider, 1926–1930.
Hirsch, Samson Raphael. *Der Pentateuch. Übersetzt und erklärt von Samson Raphael Hirsch.* 5 vols. 3rd Auflage. Frankfut a. M.: J. Kauffmann, 1899.
Kautzsch, Emil. *Die Heilige Schrift des Alten Testaments.* 2 vols. Ed. U. Bertholet. Tübingen: J.C.B. Mohr (Paul Siebeck), 1922.
Luther, Martin. *Die Bibel oder die ganze Heilige Schrift des Alten und Neuen Testaments nach der deutschen Übersetzung D. Martin Luthers. Nach dem 1912 vom Deutschen Evangelischen Kirchenaussuchß genehmigten Text.* Stuggart: Privilegierte Wüttembergische Bibelantalt. [no year indicated].
Mendelssohn, Moses.
ספר נתיבות השלום והוא חבור הכולל חמשת חומשי תורה עם תקון סופרים ותרגום אשכנזי ובאור.5 כרכים.
ברלין:G.F. Starcke , תקמ"ג.
Philippson, Ludwig. *Die Israelitische Bibel. Enthaltend: den Heiligen Urtext, die deutsche Uebertragung, die allgemeine, ausfürliche Erläuterung mit mehr also 500 englischen Holtzschnitten.* 2nd ed. 2 vols. Leipzig: Baumgärtners Buchhandlung, 1858.
Weibel, Alois Adalbert. *Historische Volks-Bilder-Bibel aus dem alten und neuen Testamente für katolische Christen. Erstes Buch.* Gräz: Franz Ferstl, 1839.
Zunz, Leopold. Ed. *Die vierundzwanzig Bücher der Heiligen Schrift nach dem masoretischen Texte.* 17th ed. Trans. H. Arnheim, Julius Fürst, M. Sachs. Berlin: Leo Alterthum, 1935.

English

Douay Rheimes Bible. http://biblehub.com/drb/genesis/1.htm.
King James Version Bible. http://biblehub.com/kjv/genesis/1.htm.
JPS Hebrew–English Tanakh. The Traditional Hebrew Text and the New JPS Translation. 2nd ed. (Philadelphia: The Jewish Publication Society, 1999).
Revised Standard Version Bible. National Council of Churches of Christ in America. http://quod.lib.umich.edu/r/rsv/browse.html.

Jewish Sources

(Pentateuch) מקראות גדולות. חמשה חומשי תורה עם פירושים והוספות רבות. ניו יורק: אברהם יצחק פריעדמאן, תשל"א.

(Mishnah) משניות. ווארשא: תרכ"א.
(Tosefta) תוספתא על פי כתבי יד ערפורט וינה (מהדורת צוקרמנדל). ירושלים: ספרי ואהרמן, תש"ל.
(Bavli) תלמוד בבלי (מהדורת וילנה). תרס"ח.
(Yerushalmi) תלמוד ירושלמי. זיטאמיר: תרכ"ה.
(Avot de-Rabbi Natan) מסכת אבות דרבי נתן בשתי נוסחאות. עורך ומבוא שניאור זלמן שעכטער. מהדורה שלישית מתוקנת. ניו יורק: פעלדהיים, תשכ"ז.
(Mekhilta) מכילתא דרבי ישמעאל (מהדורת איש שלום). וינה: תר"ל.
(Sifra) ספרא הנקרא תורת כהנים. וילנא. הדפסה מחודשת, ירושלים. תש"ל.
(Midrash Raba) מדרש רבה על חמשה חומשי תורה וחמש מגלות (מהדורת וילנה). תרס"ח.
(Tanhuma) מדרש תנחומא על חמשה חומשי תורה (מהדורת בובר). וילנה: תרמ"ה.
(Tiferet Israel) ליווא, יהודה בר' בצלאל. ספר תפארת ישראל. (ווארשא: תרל"א).
(Hovot Halevavot) בן יוסף אבן פקודה, בחיי. ספר חובות הלבבות בתרגומו של ר' יהודה אבן תבון. מבוא והערות א. צפרוני (ירושלים: הספריה הפילוסופית, תרפ"ח).
בן מימון, משה (רמב"ם). משנה תורה הוא היד החזקה לרבינו משה בר מימון זצ"ל. 5 כרכים. ווארשא: תרמ"א.
---. משנה תורה הוא היד החזקה לרבינו משה בן מימון ז"ל. המהדורה חדשה מצולמת מדפוס רומי ר"מ עם מבוא מאת הרב יהודה ליב הכהן מימון. 2 כרכים. ירושלים: מוסד הרב קוק, תשט"ו.
(Moreh) ספר מורה נבוכים להרב רבינו משה בן מימון הספרדי זצ"ל בהעתקת הרב ר' שמואל אבן תיבון ז"ל.ירושלים, תש"ך. הדפסה מחודשת של מהדורת לבוב, התרכ"ב.
(Mishneh Torah) משנה תורה הוא היד החזקה לרבינו משה בן מימון. מהדורה מנוקדת עם פירוש לעם. מפורש על ידי הרב שמואל תנחום רובינשטיין. 14 כרכים. ירושלים: מוסד הרב קוק, תשכ"ב.
---. משנה תורה להרמב"ם. דפוס קושטא רס"ט (1509). 4 כרכים. דברי מבוא מאת הרב ש.ז. הבלין. ירושלים: מקור, תשל"ג.
---. מורה נבוכים לרבנו משה בן מיימון. תרגום, הערות, נספחים ומפתחות מיכאל שורץ. 2 כרכים. תל אביב: אוניברסיטת תל אביב, 2002.
Jellinek, Adolph. *Bet ha-Midrasch. Sammlung. Kleiner Midraschim und vermischler Abhandlungen aus der ältern jüdischen Literatur.* 6 Vols. Jerusalem: Wahrmann, 1967. Reprint of Leipzig: 1853; Vienna: 1878.

Translations of other Jewish sources

Buber, Martin. *Die Geschichten des Rabbi Nachman.* Frankfurt a. M.: Rütten und Loening, 1906.
Buber, Martin. *Die Legende des Baal-Schem.* Frankfurt a. M.: Rütten und Loening, 1908.
Cohn, Emil. *Ein Diwan Jehuda Halevy, Übertragen und mit einem Lebensbild versehen von Emil Berhard [Cohn].* Berlin: E. Reiss, 1920.
Einstädter, Heinrich. *Deutsche Übersetzung zum hebräischen Gebetbuche.* 3rd ed. Frankfurt a. M.: J. Kauffmann, 1910.
Maimonides. *Guide of the Perplexed.* Trans. Shlomo Pines. Chicago: Chicago UP, 1963.

Other Primary Sources

Benjamin, Walter. *Charles Baudelaire Tableaux Parisiens. Deutsche Übertragung mit einem Vorwort über die Aufgabe des Übersetzers.* Heidelberg: Richard Weissbach, 1923.
Benjamin, Walter. *Ursprung des deutschen Trauerspiels.* Frankfurt a. M.: Suhrkamp, 1963.

Benjamin, Walter. *Gesammelte Schirften* IV.1. Ed. Tillman Rexroth. Frankurt a. M.: Suhrkamp, 1972.
Benjamin, Walter. *Gesammelte Schriften* II.1. Eds. Rolf Tiedemann and Hermann Schweppenhäuser. Frankfurt a. M.: Suhrkamp, 1977a.
Benjamin, Walter. *The Origin of German Tragic Drama*. Trans. John Osborne. London: Verso, 1977b.
Benjamin, Walter. *Briefe I–II*. Eds. Gershom Scholem and Theodor W. Adorno. Frankfurt a. M.: Suhrkamp, 1978.
Benjamin, Walter. *Reflections: Essays, Aphorisms, Autobiographical Writings*. Ed. Peter Demetz. Trans. Edmund Jephcott. New York: Harcourt Brace Jovanovich, 1978.
Benjamin, Walter. *Gesammelte Schriften. Supplement III*. Ed. Hella Tiedemann-Bartels. Frankfurt a. M.: Suhrkamp, 1987.
Benjamin, Walter. *Gesammelte Schriften. Supplement I*. Ed. Rolf Tiedemann. Frankfurt a. M.: Suhrkamp, 1999.
Benjamin, Walter. *Illuminations: Essays and Reflections*. Ed. Hannah Arendt. New York: Schocken, 2007.
Bloch, Ernst. *Geist der Utopie*. Munich & Leipzig: Von Dunckner & Humblot, 1918.
Buber, Martin. *Ekstatische Konfessionen gesammelt von Martin Buber*. Jena: Eugen Diederichs, 1909.
Buber, Martin. *Werke. Zweiter Band. Schriften zur Bibel*. Munich and Heidelberg: Kösel & Lambert Schneider, 1962.
Buber, Martin. *Briefwechsel aus sieben Jahrzehnten. Band II: 1918–1938*. Ed. Grete Schaeder et al. Heidelberg: Lambert Schneider, 1972.
Buber, Martin. *Ecstatic Confessions Collected and Introduced by Martin Buber*. Ed. Paul Mendes-Flohr. Trans. Esther Cameron. Syracuse NY: Syracuse UP, 1996.
Buber, Martin. *Martin Buber Werkausgabe 14. Schriften zur Bibelübersetzung*. Herausgegeben, eingeleitet und kommentiert von Ran HaCohen. Gütersloh: Gütersloher Verlag, 2012.
Buber, Martin. *Martin Buber Werkausgabe 5. Vorlesungen über Judentum und Christentum*. Herausgegeben, eingeleitet und kommentiert von Orr Scharf. Gütersloh: Gütersloer Verlag, 2017.
Cohen, Hermann. "Die Bedeutung des Judentums für den religiösen Fortschritt der Menschheit". *Hermann Cohens jüdische Schriften I: Ethische und religiöse Grundfragen*. Ed. Bruno Strauß. Berlin: C.A. Schwetschke & Sohn, 1924a. 18–35.
Cohen, Hermann. "Das Gottesreich". *Hermann Cohens jüdische Schriften III: Zur jüdischen Religionsphilosophie und ihrer Geschichte*. Ed. Bruno Strauß. Berlin: C.A. Schwetschke & Sohn, 1924b. 169–175.
Cohen, Hermann. *Religion der Vernunft aus den Quellen des Judentums*. Wiesbaden: Fourier, 1988.
Elbogen, Ismar. *Der jüdische Gottesdienst in seiner geschichtlichen Entwicklung*. Leipzig: Gustav Fock, 1913.
Elbogen, Ismar. "Ein Jahrhundert Wissenschaft des Judentums". *Festschrift zum 50 Jährigen Bestehen der Hochschule für die Wissenschaft des Judentums in Berlin*. Berlin: Philo, 1922. 130–135.
Elbogen, Ismar. *Jewish Liturgy: A Comprehensive History*. Trans. Raymond Scheindlin. Philadelphia: Jewish Publication Society, 1993.

Goethe, Johann Wolfgang. *Goethes Gedichte, Erster Teil*. Berlin: Gustav Hempel, 1882–1884.
Goethe, Johann Wolfgang. *Faust*. Ed. Erich Trunz. München: C.H. Beck, 1984.
Hegel, Georg Friedrich. *Phänomenologie des Geistes*. Werke 3. Frankfurt a. M.: Suhrkamp, 1970.
Hegel, Georg Friedrich. "The Oldest Program Towards a System in German Idealism". Trans. David Farrell Krell. *The Owl of Minerva* 17.1 (1985): 5–19.
Hegel, Georg Friedrich. *Miscellaneous Writings of G.W.F. Hegel*. Ed. Jon Stewart. Evanston, IL: Northwestern UP, 2002.
Hegel, Georg Friedrich. *The Phenomenology of Spirit*. Trans. Terry Pinkard. *Cambridge Hegel Translations*. Cambridge: Cambridge UP, 2018.
Kant, Immanuel. *Critique of the Power of Judgment. The Cambridge Edition of the Works of Immanuel Kant*. Trans. Paul Guyer & Eric Matthews. Cambridge: Cambridge UP, 2000.
Kaufmann, David. "Der 'Führer' des Maimonides in der Weltliteratur". *Archiv für Geschichte der Philosophie* 9.2 (1898): 335–373.
Mayer, Eugen. Ed. *Franz Rosenzweig: Eine Gedenkschrift*. Frankfurt a.M: Israelitische Gemeinde, 1930.
Mayer, Hermann. *Franz Rosenzwweig: ein Buch des Gedenkens*. Berlin: Aldus, 1930.
Meinecke, Friedrich. *Weltbürgertum und Nationalstaat: Studien zur Genesis des deutschen Nationalstaates*. (München: Oldenburg, 1908/1911/1922);
Meinecke, Friedrich. *Strassburg, Freiburg, Berlin, 1901–1919. Erinnerungen*. Stuttgart: Koehler, 1949.
Meinecke, Friedrich. *Cosmopolitanism and the National State*. Trans. Robert B. Kimber. Princeton, NJ: Princeton UP, 1970.
Schelling, Friedrich Wilhelm Joseph. *Sämmtliche Werke* I/5. Ed. K.F.A. Schelling. Stuttgart/Augsburg: J.G. Cotta, 1859.
Schelling, Friedrich Wilhelm Joseph. *Sämmtliche Werke* I/6. Ed. K.F.A. Schelling. Stuttgart/Augsburg: J.G. Cotta, 1860.
Schelling, Friedrich Wilhelm Joseph. *Sämmtliche Werke* I/8. Ed. K.F.A. Schelling. Stuttgart/Augsburg: J.G. Cotta, 1861.
Schelling, Friedrich Wilhelm Joseph. *The Ages of the World*. Trans. Jason M. Wirth. Albany NY: SUNY Press, 2000.
Spengler, Oswald. *Der Untergang des Abendlands*. 2 vols. Munich: Oskar Beck, 1920.
Steinheim, Salomon Ludwig. *Die Offenbarung nach dem Lehrbegriffe der Synagoge: ein Schiboleth*. Frankfurt a. M.: Siegmund Scherber, 1835.
Tillich, Paul. *Mystik und Schuldbewußtein in Schellings philosophischer Entwicklung*. Halle-Wittenberg: Bertelsmann, 1912.
Tramer, Hans. *Franz Rosenzweig: Entwicklung und Leben*. Unpublished and undated typescript. AR 3001, Series I. Franz Rosenzweig Collection, Leo Baeck Institute, New York. http://www.archive.org/stream/franzrosenzweig_01_reel01#page/n636/mode/1up.
Wittgenstein, Ludwig. *Tractatus Logico-Philosophicus*. Trans. D.F Pears and B.F. McGuinness. London: Routledge Kegan & Paul, 1966.

Secondary Sources

Alexander, Philip S. "Retelling the Old Testament". *It is Written: Scripture Citing Scripture. Essays in Honour of Barnabas Lindars*. Eds. D.A. Carson and H.G.M. Williamson. Cambridge: Cambridge UP, 1988. 99–121.

Althaus, Paul. *The Theology of Martin Luther*. Trans. Robert C. Schultz. Philadelphia: Fortress, 1966.

Altmann, Alexander. "Franz Rosenzweig and Eugen Rosenstock-Huessy: An Introduction to Their 'Letters on Judaism and Christianity". *Judaism Despite Christianity: The 'Letters on Christianity and Judaism' between Eugen Rosenstock-Huessy and Franz Rosenzweig'*. Ed. Eugen Rosenstock-Huessy. University, AL: University of Alabama, 1969. 26–47.

Altmann, Alexander. "Maimonides on the Intellect and the Scope of Metaphysics". *Von der mittelalterlichen zur modernen Aufklärung: Studien zur jüdischen Geschichte*. Tübingen: Mohr Siebeck, 1987. 60–129.

Altmann, Alexander. "Rosenzweig and History". *The Philosophy of Franz Rosenzweig*. Ed. Paul Mendes-Flohr. Hanover: Brandeis UP, 1988. 124–137.

Amir, Yehoyada. *Reason out of Faith: The Philosophy of Franz Rosenzweig* (Hebrew). Tel Aviv: Am Oved, 2004.

Amir, Yehoyada. "Religion and Religions in *The Star of Redemption*". *The Legacy of Franz Rosenzweig. Collected Essays*. Ed. Luc Anckaert et al. Leuven: Leuven UP, 2004. 199–210.

Amir, Yehoyada. "Introduction: 'Toward the Source of a Life of Truth', – Franz Rosenzweig's Encounter with R. Judah Halevy's Poetry". *Jehuda Halevi Fünfundnenzig Hymnen und Gedichte Deutsch und Hebräisch* (Hebrew). Trans. Michael Schwartz. Jerusalem: Magnes, 2011.

Amir, Yehoyada, Turner, Yossi, and Brasser, Martin, eds. *Faith Truth and Reason: New Perspectives on Franz Rosenzweig's 'Star of Redemption'*. Freiburg: Karl Alber, 2012.

Askani, Hans Christoph. *Das Problem der Übersetzung – dargetellt an Franz Rosenzweig. Die Methoden und Prinzipien der Rosenzweigischen und Buber-Rosenzweigischen Übersetzungen*. Tübingn: Mohr Siebeck, 1997.

Avineri, Shlomo. "Rosenzweig's Hegel Interpretation: Its Relationship to the Development of His Jewish Reawakening". *Der Philosoph Franz Rosenzweig (1886–1929). Internationaler Kongreß – Kassel 1986. Band II: Das neue Denken und seine Dimensionen*. Ed. Wolfdietrich Schmied-Kowartzik. Freiburg: Alber, 1988. 831–838.

Batnitzky, Leora. "Dialogue as Judgment, Not Mutual Affirmation: A New Look at Franz Rosenzweig's Dialogical Philosophy". *The Journal of Religion* 79.4. (1999): 523–544.

Batnitzky, Leora. *Idolatry and Representation: The Philosophy of Franz Rosenzweig Reconsidered*. Princeton NJ: Princeton UP, 2000.

Batnitzky, Leora. "Franz Rosenzweig on Translation and Exile". *Jewish Studies Quarterly* 14 (2007): 131–143.

Bauer, Anna Elisabeth. *Rosenzweigs Sprachdenken im "Stern der Erlösung" und in seiner Korrespondenz mit Martin Buber zur Verdeutschung der Schrift*. Frankfurt a. M.: Peter Lang, 1992.

Baeumer, Max L. "Hölderlin und das Hen kai pan". *Monatshefte* 59.2 (1967): 131–147.

Beckwith, Roger T. *Calendar, Cosmology and Worship Studies in Ancient Judaism and Early Christianity*. Leiden: Brill, 2003.

Ben Yehuda, Eliezer. *A Complete Dictionary of Ancient and Modern Hebrew*. 16 vols. (Hebrew). Jerusalem: Makor, 1980.

Benjamin, Mara H. "Building a Zion in German(y): Franz Rosenzweig on Yehudah Halevy". *Jewish Social Studies* 13.2 (2007): 127–154.

Benjamin, Mara H. "The Tacit Agenda of a Literary Approach to the Bible". *Prooftexts* 27.2 (2007): 254–274.

Benjamin, Mara H. *Rosenzweig's Bible: Reinventing Scripture for Jewish Modernity*. Cambridge: Cambridge UP, 2009.

Bernstein, S[imon]. *The Seer from Frankfurt (On Franz Rosenzweig and His Life's Work)*. (Hebrew). New York: American Jewish Yearbook, 1939.

Bertolino, Luca. "Das Nichts und die Philosophie. Rosenzweig zwischen Idealismus und einer Hermeneutik der religiösen Erfahrung". *Franz Rosenweigs "neues Denken". Internationaler Kongreß Kassel 2004. Band I: Selbstbegrenzendes Deknken—im philosophos*. Ed. Wolfdietrich Schmied-Kowarzik. Munich: Karl Alber, 2006. 111–125.

Bertolino, Luca. "'Schöpfung aus Nichts' in Franz Rosenzweigs *Stern der Erlösung*". *Jewish Studies Quarterly* 13 (2006): 247–264.

Betz, John R. "Schelling in Rosenzweigs *Stern der Erlösung*". *Neue Zeitschrift für Systematische Theologie und Religionsphilosophie* 45.2 (2003): 208–226.

Biale, David. *The Demonic in History: Gershom Scholem and the Revision of Jewish Historiography*. Diss. University of California Los Angeles, 1977.

Biale, David. *Gershom Scholem: Kabbalah and Counter History*. 2nd ed. Cambridge MA: Harvard UP, 1982.

Bienenstock, Myriam. "Rosenzweig's Hegel". *Owl of Minerva* 23.2 (1992): 177–82.

Bienenstock, Myriam. "Recalling the Past in the Star of Redemption". *Modern Judaism* 23.3 (2003): 226–242.

Bienenstock, Myriam. "Auf Schellings Spüren im *Stern der Erlösung*". *Rosenzweig als Leser: Kontextuelle Kommentare zum "Stern der Erlösung"*. Ed. Martin Brasser. Tübingen: Niemeyer, 2004. 273–290.

Bienenstock, Myriam. *Cohen face à Rosenzweig. Débat sur la pensée allemande*. Paris: Vrin, 2009.

Bienenstock, Myriam. "How to do Philosophy by Writing Letters". Presidential Address. International Franz Rosenzweig Society Congress. University of Toronto. 2 Sep. 2012.

Blond, Louis. "Rosenzweig: Homelessness in Time". *New German Critique* 37.3 (2010): 27–58.

Bluhm, Heinz. "Luther's *German Bible*". *Seven-Headed Luther. Essays in Commemoration of a Quincentenary 1483–1983*. Oxford: Clarendon, 1983.

Bontas, Alin V. *Franz Rosenzweig's Rational Subjective System. The Redemptive Turning Point in Philosophy and Theology*. New York: Peter Lang, 2011.

Brasser, Martin. "'… nur das rechte blitzt'. Das Motiv des Angesichts und des Antlitzes im *Stern der Erlösung* von Franz Rosenzweig". *Faith Truth and Reason: New Perspectives on Franz Rosenzweig's 'Star of Redemption'*. Rosenzweigiana: Beiträge zur Rosenzweig-Forschung, Band 6. Eds. Yehoyada Amir et al. Freiburg: Karl Alber, 2012. 125–135.

Brasser, Martin et al. Eds. *Rosenzweig Jahrbuch I: Rosenzweig Heute*. Freiburg: Karl Alberg, 2006.

Breuer, Edward. *The Limits of Enlightenment: Jews, Germans, and the Eighteenth-Century Study of Scripture*. Cambridge MA: Harvard UP, 1996.
Britt, Brian. *Walter Benjamin and the Bible*. New York: Continuum, 1996.
Britt, Brian. "Romantic Roots of the Debate on the Buber-Rosenzweig Bible". *Prooftexts* 20.3 (2000): 262–289.
Brodersen, Momme. *Walter Benjamin: A Biography*. Trans. Malcolm R. Green and Ingrida Ligers. London: Verso, 1997.
Byrne, Brendan. "The Problem of Νόμος and the Relationship with Judaism in Romans". *Catholic Biblical Quarterly* 62.2 (2000): 294–309.
Casper, Bernhard. *Das Dialogische Denken. Eine Untersuchung der religionphilosophischen Bedeutung Franz Rosenzweigs, Ferdinand Ebners und Martin Bubers*. Freiburg: Herder, 1967.
Cohen, Richard A. *Elevations: The Height of the Good in Rosenzweig and Levinas* Chicago: Chicago UP, 1994.
Cohen, Richard A. "Franz Rosenzweig's *Star of Redemption* and Kant". *Philosophical Forum* 41.1–2 (2010): 73–98.
Comay, Rebecca. *Mourning Sickness. Hegel and The French Revolution*. Stanford CA: Stanford UP, 2011.
Cristuado, Wayne. *Religion, Redemption and Revolution: The New Speech Thinking of Franz Rosenzweig and Eugen Rosenstock-Huessy*. Toronto: University of Toronto Press, 2012.
Dagan, Hagai. "Franz Rosenzweig: Biography and Personal Philosophy". *The Journal of Jewish Thought and Philosophy* 10 (2001): 289–312.
Davidson, Herbert A. *Maimonides the Rationalist*. Oxford: The Littman Library of Jewish Civilization, 2011.
De Boer, Karin. "Hegel's Non-Revolutionary Account of the French Revolution in the *Phenomenology of Spirit*," *Epoché* 22.2 (Spring 2018): 455–468.
Di Cesare, Donatella. "Übersetzen als Erlösen: Über Walter Benjamins Theologie der Sprache". *Theologie und Politik: Walter Benjamin und ein Paradigma der Moderne*. Eds. Bernd Witte and Mauro Ponzi. Berlin: Erich Schmidt, 2005. 223–240.
Disse, Jörg. "Die Philosophie Immanuel Kants im *Stern der Erlösung*". *Rosenzweig als Leser: Kontextuelle Kommentare zum 'Stern der Erlösung'*. Ed. Martin Brasser. Tübingen: Niemeyer, 2004. 245–271
Ehrlich, Leonard H. "Rosenzweigs Begriff der Zeitigung aus den Quellen des Judentums". *Der Philosoph Franz Rosenzweig (1886–1929). Internationaler Kongreß – Kassel 1986. Band II: Das neue Denken und seine Dimensionen*. Ed. Wolfdietrich Schmied-Kowartzik. Freiburg: Alber, 1988. 731–744.
Elior, Rachel. "The Unknown Dimensions of the Feast of Weeks" (Hebrew). *And this is for Yehudah: Studies Presented to our friend, Professor Yehuda Liebes, on the Occasion of his Sixty-Fifth Birthday*. Eds. Maren R. Niehoff, Ronit Meroz et al. Jerusalem: The Bialik Institute and the Mandel Institute of Jewish Studies, 2012. 70–92.
Fabry, Heinz-Joseph & Helmer Ringgern. Eds. *Theologisches Wörterbuch zum Alten Testaments*. 10 Vols. Stuttgart: Kohlhammer, 1973–1996.
Faur, Jose. "The Biblical Idea of Idolatry". *Jewish Quarterly Review* 69.1 (1978): 1–15.
Finsterbusch, Karin. "Aufsummierte Tora. Zur Bedeutung von תורה als Bezeichnung für eine Gesetzsammlung im Pentateuch". *Journal of Ancient Judaism* 2 (2011): 1–28.

Fiorato, Pierfrancesco & Wiedebach, Hartwig. "Rosenzweig's Readings of Hermann Cohen's *Logic of Pure ognition*". *The Journal of Jewish Thought and Philosophy*. 12.2 (2012): 139–146.

Fishbane, Michael. *The Garments of Torah. Essays in Biblical Hermeneutics*. Bloomington & Indianapolis IN: Indiana UP, 1992.

Fishbane, Michael. *The Exegetical Imagination: On Jewish Thought and Theology*. Cambridge MA: Harvard UP, 1998.

Fishbane, Michael and Mendes-Flohr, Paul. Eds. *Texts and Responses: Studies Presented to Nahum N. Glatzer on the Occasion of his Seventieth Birthday by his Students*. Leiden: Brill, 1973.

Fisher, Cass *Contemplative Nation: A Philosophical Account of Jewish Theological Language*. Stanford CA: Stanford UP, 2012.

Flusser, David. "'He has planted it [i.e., the Law] as eternal life in our midst'" (Hebrew). *Tarbiz* 58.2 (1989): 147–153.

Fox, Everett. "Franz Rosenzweig as Translator". *The Leo Baeck Institute Yearbook* 34.1 (1989): 371–384.

Fraenkel, Carlos. Ed. *Traditions of Maimonideanism*. Leiden: Brill, 2009.

Franks, Paul. "What is the Context?" (review). *Jewish Quarterly Review* 96.3 (2006): 387–395.

Freund, Else. *Die Existenzphilosophie Franz Rosenzweigs. Ein Beitrag zur Analyse seines Werkes "Der Stern der Erlösung"*. 2nd ed. Hamburg: Felix Meiner, 1959.

Fuhrmans, Horst. *Schellings Philosophie der Weltalter. Schellings Philosophie in den Jahren 1806–1821. Zum Problem des Schellingschen Theismus*. Düsseldorf: L. Schwann, 1954.

Furstenberg, Yair. "The Rabbinic View of Idolatry and the Roman Political Conception of Divinity". *Journal of Religion* 90.3 (2010): 335–366.

Galli, Barbara E. "Rosenzweig and the Name for God". *Modern Judaism* 14.1 (1994): 63–86.

Galli, Barbara E. "Rosenzweig's All, Kabbalistically Reflected". *Franz Rosenzweigs 'neues Denken'. Internationaler Kongreß Kassel 2004. Band.2: Erfahrene Offenbarung—in theologos*. Ed. Wolfdietrich Schmied-Kowarzik. Freiburg: Karl Alber, 2006. 713–724.

Ganzel, Tova. "Transformation of Pentateuchal Descriptions of Idolatry". *Transforming Visions: Transformations of Text, Tradition, and Theology in Ezekiel*. Eds. William Tooman and Michael A Lyons. Eugene OR: Pickwick, 2010. 33–49

Gesenius, Wilhelm. *Hebräisches und Aramäisches Handwörterbuch über das Alte Testament*. Leipzig: Vogel, 1905.

Gibbs, Robert. "The Limits of Thought: Rosenzweig, Schelling, and Cohen". *Zeitschrift für philosophische Forschung*. 43.4 (1989): 618–640.

Gibbs, Robert. *Correlations in Rosenzweig and Levinas*. Princeton: Princeton UP, 1992.

Gibbs, Robert. "Gesetz in *The Star of Redemption*". *Rosenzweig als Leser: Kontextuelle Kommentare zum 'Stern der Erlösung"*. Ed. Martin Brasser. Tübingen: Niemeyer, 2004. 395–410.

Gilgen, Peter. "Rosenzweig's Thinking after Kant: A Reply to Richard A. Cohen". *Philosophical Forum* 41.1–2 (2010): 99–111.

Gillman, Abigail. "Between Religion and Culture: Mendelssohn, Buber, Rosenzweig, and the Enterprise of Biblical Translation". *Biblical Translation in Context*. Ed. Frederick Knobloch. Bethesda MD: University Press of Maryland, 2002. 93–114.

Gillman, Abigail. *A History of German Jewish Bible Translation*. Chicago IL: Chicago UP, 2017.

Glatzer, Nahum N. "Franz Rosenzweig". *YIVO Annual of Jewish Social Studies* I (1946): 107–133.
Glatzer, Nahum N. "Franz Rosenzweig: The Story of a Conversion". *Judaism* 1.1 (1952): 69–79.
Glatzer, Nahum N. *Franz Rosenzweig: His Life and Thought*. New York: Schocken, 1953.
Glatzer, Nahum N. "Franz Rosenzweig in His Student Years". *Paul Lazarus Gedenkbuch: Beiträge zur würdigung der letzten Rabbinergeneration in Deutschland*. Jerusalem: no publisher indicated, 1961. 143–153.
Glatzer, Nahum N. "Was Franz Rosenzweig a Mystic?" *Studies in Jewish Religious and Intellectual History Presented to Alexander Altmann*. Eds. Siegfried Stein and Raphael Loewe. Tuscaloosa AL: University of Alabama Press, 1979. 121–132.
Gordon, Peter Eli. "The Erotics of Negative Theology: Maimonides on Apprehension". *Jewish Studies Quarterly* 2 (1995): 1–38.
Gordon, Peter Eli. "Rosenzweig Redux: The Reception of German-Jewish Thought". *Jewish Social Studies* 8.1 (2001): 1–57.
Gordon, Peter Eli. *Rosenzweig and Heidegger: Between Judaism and German Philosophy*. Berkeley CA: University of California, 2003.
Greenberg, Gershon. "Franz Rosenzweigs zwiespältige Gottessicht: von der Zeit und in Ewigkeit". *Judaica* 34.1 (1978): 27–34.
Greenberg, Moshe. "Three Conceptions of Torah in Hebrew Scriptures". *Die Hebräische Bibel und ihre zweifache Nachgeschichte. Festschrift für Rolf Rendtorff zum 65 Geburtstag*. Eds. Erhard Blum et al. Neukirchen-Vluyn: Neukirchener, 1990. 365–378.
Greenspahn, Frederick E. "How Jews Translate the Bible". *Biblical Translation in Context*. Ed. Frederick Knobloch. Bethesda MD: University Press of Maryland, 2002. 43–49.
Greenstein, Edward. "Theories of Modern Bible Translation". *Prooftexts* 3.1 (1983): 9–39.
Grözinger, Karl Erich. "In Rosenzweigs Seele – die Kabbala". *Messianismus zwischen Mythos und Macht. Jüdisches Denken in der europäischen Geistesgeschichte*. Ed. Eveline Goodman-Thau and Wolfdietrich Schmied Kowarzik. Berlin: Akademie Verlag, 1994. 127–139.
Gruenwald, Itamar. *Apocalyptic and Merkavah Mysticism*. Leiden: Brill, 1980.
Grimm, Jacob and Wilhelm. *Deutsches Wörterbuch von Jacob und Wilhelm Grimm*. 16 Bde. In 32 Teilbänden. 1971. http://woerterbuchnetz.de/cgi-bin/WBNetz/wbgui_py?sigle=DWB&lemid=GA00001&mode=Vernetzung&hitlist=&patternlist=&mainmode=
Haberman, Joshua O. *Philosopher of Revelation: the Life and Thought of S.L. Steinheim: Including an annotated translation with a biographical and analytical introduction of the entire first volume of his four-volume work, The revelation according to the doctrine of Judaism, and selection from volumes 2,3 and 4*. Philadelphia PA: Jewish Publication Society, 1990.
Halbertal, Moshe and Margalit, Avishay. *Idolatry*. Cambridge MA: Harvard UP, 1992.
Harvey, Warren Zev. "The Return of Maimonideanism". *Jewish Social Studies* 42.3/4 (1980): 249–268.
Harvey, Warren Zev. "Why Philosophers Quote Kabbalah: The Cases of Mendelssohn and Rosenzweig". *Studia Judaica* XVI (2003): 118–125.
Heinemann, Isaac. *Reason for the Mitzvoth in the Literature of Israel. Part Two* (Hebrew). Jerusalem: Horev, 1993.

Hill Shevitz, Amy. "Silence and Translation: Franz Rosenzweig's Paralysis and Edith Rosenzweig's Life". *Modern Judaism.* 35.3 (2015): 281–301.
Hollander, Dana. *Exemplarity and Chosenness: Rosenzweig and Derrida on the Nation of Philosophy.* Stanford CA: Stanford UP, 2008.
Horwitz, Rivka. "From Hegelianism to a Revolutionary Understanding of Judaism: Franz Rosenzweig's Attitude toward Kabbala and Myth". *Modern Judaism* 26.1 (2006): 31–54.
Horwitz, Rivka. *Franz Rosenzweig: The Star and the Man. Collected Studies by Rivka Horwitz* (Hebrew). Ed. Aviezer Cohen. Be'er Sheva: Ben Gurion University Press, 2010.
Hyman, Arthur. "Maimonidean Elements in Hermann Cohen's Philosophy of Religion". *Hermann Cohen's Critical Idealism.* Ed. Reinier Munk. Dordrecht: Springer, 2005. 357–370.
Idel, Moshe. *Messianic Mystics.* New Haven CT: Yale UP, 1998.
Idel, Moshe. "On Aharon Jellinek and Kabbalah" (Heberw). *Pe'amim* 100 (2004): 15–22.
Idel, Moshe. "Franz Rosenzweig and Kabbalah". *Old Worlds, New Mirrors: On Jewish Mysticism and Twentieth-Century Thought.* Philadelphia: University of Pennsylvania Press, 2010. 159–167.
Idel, Moshe. "Multiple Forms of Redemption in Kabbalah and Hasidism". *Jewish Quarterly Review* 101.1 (2011): 27–70.
Iggers, Georg G. *The German Conception of History: The National Tradition of Historical Thought from Herder to the Present.* Middletown CT: Wesleyan UP, 1968.
Jacobson, Eric. *Metaphysics of the Profane: The Political Theology of Walter Benjamin and Gershom Scholem.* New York: Columbia UP, 2003.
Jay, Martin. "The Politics of Translation: Siegfried Kracauer and Walter Benjamin on the Buber-Rosenzweig Bible". *Leo Baeck Institute Yearbook* 21.1 (1976): 3–24.
Kaufmann, Yehezkel. *History of Israelite Faith.* Vol. 1. (Hebrew). Tel Aviv: Dvir, 1956.
Kavka, Martin. *Jewish Messianism and the History of Philosophy.* Cambridge: Cambridge UP, 2004.
Kavka, Martin. "Verification [Bewährung] in Franz Rosenzweig". *German Jewish Thought Between Religion and Politics: Festschrift in Honor of Paul Mendes-Flohr on the Occasion of His Seventieth Birthday.* Eds. Christian Wiese and Martina Urban. Berlin: De Gruyter, 2012. 174–183.
Kittel, Gerhard. Ed. *Theologisches Wörterbuch um neuen Testament.* 10 Vols. Stuttgart: W. Kohlhammer, 1957–1978.
Klein-Braslavi, Sara. *Maimonides as Biblical Interpreter.* Boston: Academic Studies Press, 2011.
Knohl, Israel. "The Bible's Treatment of Foreign Idolatry" (Hebrew). *Tarbiz* 64.1 (1995): 5–12.
Kohler, George Y. *Reading Maimonides' Philosophy in 19th Century Germany: The Guide to Religious Reform.* Dordrecht: Springer, 2012.
Kornberg Greenberg, Yudit. *Better than Wine: Love, Poetry and Prayer in the Thought of Franz Rosenzweig.* Atlanta GA: Scholars Press, 1996.
Kracauer, Siegfried. "Die Bibel auf Deutsch: zur Übersetzung von Marin Buber und Franz Rosenzweig". *Frankfuter Allgemeine Zeitung* 27/28 April, 1926; reprinted in idem, *Das Ornament der Masse.* Frankfurt a. M.: Suhrkamp, 1963. 173–186.
Kracauer, Siegfried. "The Bible in German: On the Translation by Martin Buber and Franz Rosenzweig". *The Mass Ornament: Weimar Essays.* Trans. Thoman Y. Levin. Cambridge MA: Harvard UP, 1995, 189–201.

Lambrianou, Nikolas. "'A Philosophy and Theology of Hyphenation': Walter Benjamin, Weimar and New Thinking". *Journal for Cultural and Religious Theory* 5.2 (2004): 78–98.
Levy, Zeev. *A Precursor of Jewish Existentialism: The Philosophy of Franz Rosenzweig and its Relationship to Hegel's System* (Hebrew). Tel Aviv: Sifriyat Poalim, 1969.
Licht, Ya'akov Shalom. "מקרא קדש" (Hebrew). *Biblical Encyclopaedia. The Wealth of Knowledge on the Miqra and its Era. Vol. 5: ממוכן-סתרי*. Eds. Moshe David Cassuto et al. Jerusalem: Mosad Bialik, 1978. 437–440.
Liddell, Henry George and Scott, Robert. *Greek–English Lexicon*. 7th ed. New York: Harper & Brothers, 1883.
Liska, Vivian. *German–Jewish Thought and Its Afterlife. A Tenuous Legacy*. Bloomington IN: Indiana UP, 2017.
Lorberbaum, Menachem. *Dazzled by Beauty: Theology as Poetics in Hispanic Jewish Culture* (Hebrew). Jerusalem: Ben-Zvi Institute, 2011.
Losch, Andreas. "What is Behind God's Name? Martin Buber's and Franz Rosenzweig's Reflections on the Name of God". *Leo Baeck Institute Yearbook* 60 (2015): 91–106.
Lowenstein, Steven. "Religious Life". *German–Jewish History in Modern Times. Volume 3: Integration in Dispute 1871–1918*. Ed. Michael Brenner. New York: Columbia UP, 1997. 103–124.
Lucca, Enrico. "Gershom Scholem on Franz Rosenzweig and the Kabbalah. Introduction to the Text". *Naharaim* 6.1 (2012): 7–19.
Lucca, Enrico and Wygoda, Ynon. "A Goy Who Studies Torah. Two Unpublished Sources by Ernst Simon and Gershom Scholem on the Spiritual Legacy of Franz Rosenzweig". *Naharaim* 12.1–2 (2018): 197–224.
Mach, Dafna. "Franz Rosenzweig als Übersetzer jüdischer Texte. Seine Auseinandersetzung mit Gershom Scholem". *Der Philosoph Franz Rosenzweig (1886–1929). Internationaler Kongreß – Kassel 1986. Band I: Die Herausforderung jüdisches Lernes*. Ed. Wolfdietrich Schmied-Kowartzik. Freiburg: Alber, 1988. 251–272.
Meineke, Stefan. "A Life of Contradiction: The Philosophy of Franz Rosenzweig and His Relationship to History and Politics". *Leo Baeck Institute Year Book* 36 (1991): 461–89.
Meir, Ephraim. *Letters of Love: Franz Rosenzweig's Spiritual Biography and Oeuvre in Light of the Gritli Letters*. New York: Peter Lang, 2006.
Mendes-Flohr, Paul. "Franz Rosenzweig and the Crisis of Historicism". *The Philosophy of Franz Rosenzweig*. Ed. Paul Mendes-Flohr. Hanover: Brandeis UP, 1988a. 138–161.
Mendes-Flohr, Paul. "Franz Rosenzweig and the German Philosophical Tradition". *The Philosophy of Franz Rosenzweig*. Ed. Paul Mendes-Flohr. Hanover: Brandeis UP, 1988b. 1–19.
Mendes-Flohr, Paul. "Franz Rosenzweig's Concept of Philosophical Faith". *Leo Baeck Yearbook* 34.1 (1989a): 357–369.
Mendes-Flohr, Paul. "Law and Sacrament: Ritual Observance in Twentieth-Century Jewish Thought". *Jewish Spirituality From the Sixteenth-Century to the Present*. Ed. Arthur Green. New York: Crossroad, 1989b. 317–345.
Mendes-Flohr, Paul. *Divided Passions: Jewish Intellectuals and the Experience of Modernity*. Detroit MI: Wayne State UP, 1991a.
Mendes-Flohr, Paul. "'Knowledge as Service?': An Appreciation of Nahum N. Glatzer". *Jewish Studies* 31 (1991b): 25–46.

Mendès-Flohr, Paul. "'The Stronger and the Better Jews': Jewish Theological Responses to Political Messianism in the Weimar Republic". *Jews and Messianism in the Modern Era: Metaphor and Meaning*. Ed. Jonathan Frankel. Oxford: Oxford UP, 1991c. 159–185.

Mendès-Flohr, Paul. "Scholarship as a Craft: Reflections on the Legacy of Nahum Glatzer". *Modern Judaism* 13.2 (1993): 269–276.

Mendès-Flohr, Paul. "Martin Buber: A Builder of Bridges". *Jewish Studies Quarterly* 14 (2007): 101–119.

Mendès-Flohr, Paul. "Between sensual and heavenly love: Franz Rosenzweig's reading of the Song of Songs". *Scriptural Exegesis: The Shapes of Culture and the Religious Imagination. Essays in Honour of Michael Fishbane*. Eds. Deborah A. Green and Laura S. Lieber. Oxford: Oxford UP, 2009. 310–318.

Mendès-Flohr and Reinharz, Jehuda. "From Relativism to Religious Faith: The Testimony of Franz Rosenzweig's Unpublished Diaries". *Leo Baeck Institute Yearbook* 22.1 (1977): 161–174.

Mosès, Stéphane. "Walter Benjamin and Franz Rosenzweig". *The Philosophical Forum* 15.1–2 (1983–1984): 188–205. Reprinted in Gary Smith. Ed. *Benjamin: Philosophy, History, Aesthetics*. Chicago: Chicago UP, 1989. 228–246.

Mosès, Stéphane. "Politik und Religion. Zur Aktualität Franz Rosenzweigs". *Der Philosoph Franz Rosenzweig (1886–1929). Internationaler Kongreß – Kassel 1986. Band II: Das neue Denken und seine Dimensionen*. Ed. Wolfdietrich Schmied-Kowartzik. Freiburg: Alber, 1988. 855–875.

Mosès, Stéphane. *System and Revelation: The Philosophy of Franz Rosenzweig*. Trans. Catherine Tihanyi. Detroit MI: Wayne State UP, 1992.

Mosès, Stéphane. *The Angel of History: Rosenzweig, Benjamin, Scholem*. Trans. Barbara Harshav. Stanford CA: Stanford UP, 2009.

Moyn, Samuel. "Is Revelation in the World?" *Jewish Quarterly Review* 96.3 (2006): 396–403.

Murakoa, T. *A Greek–English Lexicon of the Septuagint*. Louvain: Peeters, 2009.

Myers, David N. *Resisting History: Historicism and its Discontents in German–Jewish Thought*. Princeton NJ: Princeton UP, 2003.

Navarette Alonso, Roberto. "'Der Jude, der in deutschem Geist Macht.' Das Hegelbuch Franz Rosenzweigs und seine Wirkung". *Naharaim* 10.2 (2016): 273–302.

Niehoff, Maren Ruth. "The Buber-Rosenzweig Translation of the Bible within Jewish-German Tradition". *Journal of Jewish Studies* 44.2 (1993): 258–279.

Niehoff, Maren Ruth. "Jellinek's Conception of *Aggadah*" (Hebrew). *Jewish Studies* 38 (1998): 119–127.

OED Online. Oxford University Press. http://www.oed.com.

Pines, Shlomo. "The Limitations of Human Knowledge According to Al-Farabi, ibn Bajja, and Maimonides". *Studies in Medieval Jewish History and Literature*. Ed. Isadore Twersky. Cambridge, MA: Harvard UP, 1979. 82–109.

Plaut, W. Gunther. *German–Jewish Bible Translations: Linguistic Theology as a Political Phenomenon*. New York: Leo Baeck Institute, 1992.

Pöggeler, Otto. "Rosenzweig und Hegel". *Der Philosoph Franz Rosenzweig (1886–1929). Internationaler Kongreß – Kassel 1986. Band II: Das neue Denken und seine Dimensionen*. Ed. Wolfdietrich Schmied-Kowartzik. Freiburg: Alber, 1988. 839–853.

Pöggeler, Otto. "Between Enlightenment and Romanticism: Rosenzweig and Hegel". *The Philosophy of Franz Rosenzweig*. Ed. Paul Mendes-Flohr. Hanover: UP of New England, 1988. 107–123.
Pollock, Benjamin. *Franz Rosenzweig and the Systematic Task of Philosophy*. Cambridge: Cambridge UP, 2009.
Pollock, Benjamin. "On the Road to Marcionism: Franz Rosenzweig's Early Theology", *Jewish Quarterly Review* 102.2 (2012a): 224–255.
Pollock, Benjamin. "'Within Earshot of the Young Hegel': Rosenzweig's Letter to Rudolph Ehrenberg of September 1910". *German Jewish Thought Between Religion and Politics: Festschrift in Honor of Paul Mendes-Flohr on the Occasion of His Seventieth Birthday*. Eds. Christian Wiese and Martina Urban. Berlin: De Gruyter, 2012b. 185–208
Pollock, Benjamin. *Franz Rosenzweig's Conversions: World Denial and World Redemption*. Bloomington IN: Indiana UP, 2014.
Ravitzky, Aviezer. "The Secret Teachings of the *Guide of the Perplexed:* Commentary in His and Our Generations" (Hebrew). *Al Da'at HaMakom: Studies in Jewish Thought and its History*. Jerusalem: Keter, 1991. 142–181.
Reichert, Klaus. "'It is Time': The Buber-Rosenzweig Translation in Context". *The Translatability of Cultures: Figurations of the Space Between*. Eds. Sanford Budick and Wolfgang Iser. Stanford: Stanford UP, 1996. 169–185.
Reinharz, Adele. "The meaning of nomos in Philo's Exposition of the Law". *Studies in Religion* 13.3 (1986): 337–345.
Richardson, Peter. "Editorial: Torah–Nomos, A seminal question". *Studies in Religion* 13.3 (1986): 3–4.
Robinson, James T. Ed. *The Cultures of Maimonideanism: New Approaches to the History of Jewish Thought*. Leiden: Brill, 2009.
Rosen-Zvi, Ishay. "'Utterly Destroy all the Places'. The Polemic on the Injunction to Destroy Idolatrous Worship in Tannaitical Literature" (Hebrew). *Resheet* 1 (2009): 91–115.
Rosenberg, Shalom. "On Biblical Interpretation in the *Guide*" (Hebrew). *Jerusalem Studies in Jewish Thought* I. Jerusalem: Magnes, 1981. 85–157.
Rosenberg, Shalom. "The Philosophical Interpretation of Song of Songs – Introductory Comments" (Hebrew). *Tarbiz* 59.1–2 (1990): 133–152.
Rosenwald, Lawrence. "On the Reception of Buber and Rosenzweig's Bible". *Prooftexts* 14.1 (1994): 141–165.
Samuelson, Norbert. "The Comparative Maps of the Human". *Zygon* 31.4 (1996): 695–710.
Samuelson, Norbert. "Exploring Rosenzweig's Sources – The God of Maimonides". *Rosenzweig Jahrbuch 1: Rosenzweig heute*. Eds. Martin Brasser et al. Freiburg: Karl Alber, 2006. 155–165.
Samuelson, Norbert. Rev. of *Franz Rosenzweig and the Systematic Task of Philosophy* by Benjamin Pollock. *Journal of the American Academy of Religion* 78.2 (2010): 573–576.
Sander, Eric. *Paul, the Law, and the Jewish People*. Philadelphia PA: Fortress, 1983.
Sauter, Caroline. *Die virtuelle Linearversion. Walter Benjamins Übersetzungstheorie und -praxis*. Heidelbeg: Universitätsverlag, 2014.
Sax, Benjamin. *Language and Jewish Renewal: Franz Rosenzweig's Hermenuetic of Citation*. Diss. University of Chicago, 2008.
Sax, Benjamin. "Das geflügte Wort: Franz Rosenzweig as Post-*Goethekenner*. *Naharaim* 5 (2011): 115–149.

Sax, Benjamin. "*Wissenschaft* and Jewish Thought: Ismar Elbogen's Early Influence on Franz Rosenzweig." *Pardes* 24 (2018): 191–216.
Schäfer, Peter. "New Testament and Hekhalot Literature: The Journey into Heaven in Paul and in Merkavah Mysticism". *Hekhalot-Studien*. Tübingen: Mohr-Siebeck, 1988. 234–249.
Scharf, Orr. *Thinking in Translation: Scripture and Redemption in Franz Rosenzweig's Thought*. Dissertation. The University of Haifa, 2014a.
Scharf, Orr. "'If one translates a verse literally, he is a liar': On dual loyalties in the Buber-Rosenzweig translation of the Bible." *"Theocracy" and "Nation" in Jewish Thought: Past and Present: Proceedings of the Second International Symposium of the Project of Young Scholars*. Doshisha University, 2014b.
Scharf, Orr. "Exile in the Land of the Bible – Martin Buber and the Completion of the Translation of the Bible into German in Jerusalem" (Hebrew). *Chidushim* 17.1 (2015): 83–112.
Scharf, Orr. "Clandestine Scholarship: The Septuagint as a Key into Marin Buber's and Franz Rosenzweig's Bible Translation". Eds. Andreas Losch et al. *"Alles in der Schrift ist echte Gesprochenheit". Martin Buber und die Verdeutschung der Schrift*. Lich: Edition AV, 2016. 120–129.
Scharf, Orr. "Von 'Ecclesia et Synagoga' zu 'Zwei Glaubenweisen': Martin Bubers Vorlesungen über Judentum und Christentum". Martin Buber. *Martin Buber Werkausgabe 5. Vorlesungen über Judentum und Christentum*. Herausgegeben, eingeleitet und kommentiert von Orr Scharf. Gütersloh: Gütersloher Verlaghaus, 2017. 11–49.
Scharf, Orr. Bleakness in the Age of Google: Walter Benjamin and the Possibility of Redemptive Translation". Eds. Madeleine Kasten et al. *Benajmin's Figures: Dialogues on the Vocation of the Humanities*. Nordhausen: Traugott Bautz, 2018a. 237–258.
Scharf, Orr. "Whose Bible is it Anyway? The Buber-Rosenzweig Translation as a Bible for Christian Readers". Eds. Magdalena Waligórska and Tara Kohn. *Jewish Translation, Translating Jewishness*. Berlin: De Gruyter, 2018b. 39–66.
Schindler, Renate. "Gesetz und Gebot in Franz Rosenzweig's *Stern der Erlösung*". *Torah – Nomos – Ius. Abendländischer Antinomismus und der Traum vom herrschaftsfreien Raum*. Eds. Gesine Palmer et al. Berlin: Vorwerk 8, 1999. 285–303.
Schmied-Kowarzik, Wolfdietrich. *Franz Rosenzweig. Existentielles Denken und gelebte Bewährung*. Freiburg: Karl Alber, 1991.
Schmied-Kowarzik, Wolfdietrich. "Cohen und Rosenzweig: zu Vernunft und Offenbarung". *Revista Portugesa de Filosophia* 62.2/4 (2006a): 511–533.
Schmied-Kowarzik, Wolfdietrich. *Rosenzweig im Gespräch mit Ehrenberg, Cohen und Buber*. Rosenzweigiana: Beiträge zur Rosenzweig-Forschung Band. 1. Freiburg/Munich: Karl Alber, 2006b.
Schnädelbach, Herbert. *Philosophy in Germany 1831–1933*. Trans. Eric Matthews. Cambridge: Cambridge UP, 1984.
Scholem, Gershom. *Franz Rosenzweig and his Book* The Star of Redemption. *Eulogy Delivered at the Hebrew University on the 30th Day to His Death* (Hebrew). Jerusalem: Book Publishing House near the Hebrew University, 1930.
Scholem, Gershom. *Jewish Gnosticism, Merkabah Mysticism, and Talmudic Tradition. Based on the Israel Goldstein Lectures, Delivered at the Jewish Theological Seminary of America, New York*. New York: Jewish Theological Seminary of America, 1965.

Scholem, Gershom. *The Messianic Idea in Judaism and Other Essays on Jewish Spirituality*. New York: Schocken, 1971.

Scholem, Gershom. "Reflections on Jewish Theology". *On Jews and Judaism in Crisis. Selected Essays*. Ed. Werner J. Dannhauser. New York: Schocken, 1976. 261–297.

Scholem, Gershom. *Walter Benjamin: The Story of a Friendship*. Trans. Harry Zohn. New York: Schocken Books, 1981.

Scholem, Gershom. "Ein offene Wort über die wahren Absichten meines Kabbalastudiums". Biale, David. *Gershom Scholem: Kabbalah and Counter History*. 2nd ed. Cambridge MA: Harvard UP, 1982. 155–156.

Scholem, Gershom. "Franz Rosenzweig and His Book *The Star of Redemption*". *The Philosophy of Franz Rosenzweig*. Ed. Paul Mendes-Flohr. Hanover: Brandeis UP, 1988.

Scholem, Gershom. "On Franz Rosenzweig and His Familiarity with Kabbala Literature". *Naharaim* 6.1 (2012): 1–6.

Schreiner, Klaus. "Messianism in the Political Culture of the Weimar Republic". Eds. Peter Schäfer and Mark Cohen. *Toward the Millennium: Messianic expectations from the Bible to Waco*. Leiden: Brill, 1998. 311–361.

Schwarcz, Moshe. *Language, Myth, Art* (Hebrew). Tel Aviv: Schocken, 1966.

Schwarcz, Moshe. "Introduction: Franz Rosenzweig's Place in Jewish Philosophy" (Hebrew). *Kochav Ha-Ge'ula* Trans. Yehoshua Amir. Jerusalem: Mosad Bialik, 1971. 9–42.

Schwarcz, Moshe. "Atheism and Modern Jewish Thought". *Proceedings of the American Academy for Jewish Research* 44 (1977): 127–150.

Schwarcz, Moshe. *From Myth to Revelation* (Hebrew). Tel Aviv: Hakibbutz Hameuchad, 1978.

Schweid, Eliezer. "Spiritual Reorientation as System of Thought" (Hebrew). *Israel Efrat: Poet and Thinker*. Eds. Yitzhak Orpaz et al. Tel Aviv: Tel Aviv University, 1981. 231–257.

Schweid, Eliezer. "Franz Rosenzweig as Philosophical Interpreter of the Bible". *Milet: Everyman's University Studies in Jewish History and Culture*. Eds. Shmuel Ettinger, Yitzhak D. Gilat, Shmuel Safrai. Tel Aviv: Open University, 1985. 299–322.

Seeskin, Kenneth. *Searching for a Distant God: The Legacy of Maimonides*. Oxford: Oxford UP, 2000.

Segal, Alan F. "Torah and *nomos* in recent scholarly discussion". *Studies in Religion* 13.3 (1986): 19–27.

Seidman, Naomi. *Faithful Renderings: Jewish–Christian Difference and the Politics of Translation*. Chicago IL: University of Chicago Press, 2006.

Sheppard, Eugene R. "'I am a Memory Come Alive': Nahum Glatzer and the Legacy of German Jewish Thought in America". *JQR* New Series 95.1 (1994): 123–148.

Sommer, Benjamin D. *Revelation and Authority. Sinai in Jewish Scripture and Tradition*. New Haven CT: Yale UP, 2015.

Stahmer, Harold. "'Speech Letters' and 'Speech-Thinking': Franz Rosenzweig and Eugen Rosenstock-Huessy". *Modern Judaism* 4.1 (1984): 57–81.

Stahmer, Harold. "The Letters of Franz Rosenzweig to Margit Rosenstock-Huessy: 'Franz', 'Gritli', 'Eugen' and 'The Star of Redemption'. *Der Philosoph Franz Rosenzweig (1886–1929). Internationaler Kongreß – Kassel 1986. Band I: Die Herausforderung jüdisches Lernes*. Ed. Wolfdietrich Schmied-Kowartzik. Freiburg: Alber, 1988. 109–137.

Steiger, Johann Anselm. *Fünf Zentralthemen der Theologie Luthers und Seiner Erben. Communicatio – Imago – Figura – Maria – Exempla. Mit Edition zweier christologischer Frühschriften Johann Gerhards*. Leiden: Brill, 2002.

Stern, Josef. "The Maimonidean Parable, the Arabic *Poetics*, and the Garden of Eden". *Midwest Studies in Philosophy* 33 (2009): 209–247.
Stern, Sacha. *Calendar and Community: a History of the Jewish Calendar, Second Century BCE –Tenth Century CE*. Oxford: Oxford UP, 2001.
Stern, Sacha. *Time and Process in Ancient Judaism*. Oxford: The Littman Library of Jewish Civilization, 2003.
Talmage, Frank. "Apples of Gold: the Inner Meaning of Sacred Texts in Medieval Judaism". *Jewish Spirituality (Vol.1): From the Bible through the Middle Ages*. Ed. Arthur Green. New York: Crossroad, 1986. 313–355.
Taubes, Jacob. *Abendländische Eschatologie*. Bern: A. Francke AG, 1947.
Turner, Joseph. "A Reading of Psalm 90 in Light of Franz Rosenzweig's Notion of Time". *Rosenzweig als Leser: Kontextuelle Kommentare zum 'Stern der Erlösung"*. Ed. Martin Brasser. Tübingen: Niemeyer, 2004. 499–507.
Uffenheimer, Benjamin. "Martin Buber: Master of Biblical Interpretation" (Hebrew). *Molad*, 16 (1958): 48–54.
Urbach, Ephraim E. *The Sages: Their Concepts and Beliefs* (Hebrew). Jerusalem: Magnes, 1969.
Vermes, Geza. *Scripture and Tradition in Judaism. Haggadic Studies*. 2nd ed. Leiden: Brill, 1973.
Vermes, Geza. "The Genesis of the Concept of 'Rewritten Bible'". *Rewritten Bible after Fifty Years: Texts, Terms, or Techniques? A Last Dialogue with Geza Vermes*. Ed. Zsengellér, József. Leiden: Brill, 2014. 3–9.
Vogel, Manfred H. *Franz Rosenzweig on Secular/Profane History*. Atlanta: Scholars Press, 1996.
Weintraub, Ze'ev. *The Translations of the Torah into German* (Hebrew). Chicago IL: Chicago's College of Jewish Studies, 1967.
Westerholm, Stephen. "Torah, nomos, and law: A question of meaning". *Studies in Religion* 13.3 (1986): 327–336.
Wiener, Leon Dow. *And Walking on Thy Journey. A Theory of Halakhah Based on the Teachings of Franz Rosenzweig* (Hebrew) Raman Gan: Bar Ilan UP, 2017.
Wiese, Christian. *Challenging Colonial Discourse: Jewish Studies and Protestant Theology in Wilhelmine Germany*. Trans. Barbara Harshav and Christian Wiese. Leiden: Brill, 2005.
Wolfson, Elliot R. "Facing the Effaced: Mystical Eschatology and the Idealistic Orientation in the Thought of Franz Rosenzweig". *Journal for the History of Modern Theology* 4.1 (1997): 39–81.
Wolfson, Elliot R. "Light Does not Talk but Shines: Apophasis and Vision in Rosenzweig's Theopoetic Temporality". *New Directions in Jewish Philosophy*. Eds. Aaron Hughes and Elliot R. Wolfson. Bloomington, IN: Indiana UP, 2010. 87–148.

Index of References

Hebrew Bible

Genesis:

1:1   79, 139
1:2   84, 137, 155, 156, 157
1:14–18   94
1:27   73
1:28   137
2:1–3   94
2:19   137
8:22   94
16:13   15, 71
20:5   121,

Exodus:

3:14   XI, 88, 89, 91, 167
4:15   XI, 161,162
12:16   101
12:49   XI, 162
19:1   XI, 158, 167
19:2   159
20   87
20:1   91, 95
20:2   19, 87, 95
33:11   127,

Leviticus:

17:10   123,
19:2   34
19:4   117
20:6   71
20:26   19
23   96,167
23:2   101
23:32   100
23:43   101
25:2—8   72

Numbers:

6:25   74, 112,125

6:26   112
28–29   XI, 96, 97, 167
28:2   97
28:9   97
28:11   97
28:16–18   97
28:26   97
29:1   97

Deuteronomy:

4:9   112
4:12   112
5:3   99, 157
5:4   95
5:5   96
5:14
5:15   96
8:2   58
13:4   58
31:13   58
32:1–43   160
32:4   56
32:7   39
32:11   155, 156
32:16   160

II Samuel

15:11   121

Isaiah:

2:2   106
2:8   117
25:8   xi, 79–83, 85, 88, 91
44:6   53, 111
55:8   71

Jeremiah:

10:10   113, 114, 116, 117–118

https://doi.org/10.1515/9783110476897-013

23:20   106
30:24   106
48:47   106
49:39   106

Ezekiel:

10:22–11:1   129, 131
38:16   106

Jonah:

2:3–4   xi, 83–86

Micah:

6:8   119–123

Zephaniah:

3:9   66, 71, 141, 146

Zechariah:

14:9   141

New Testament

Matthew:

5:29   126
6:22   122
25:40   18, 122

Luke:

11:34   122

John:

1:1   82, 139
1:46   67

Psalms:

45:5   107, 113, 118–119
73:23   170
89:9–10   85
89:12   106
96:5   117
115   78, 114
115:9   114
116:6   121
Psalms 119   160
119:6   121
119:130   121

Song of Songs:

8:6   37

Daniel:

11:14   xi, 16, 17, 66

Romans:

12:8   122
16:19   122

I Corinthians:

15:28   66, 67, 122
15:55   79

Revelation:

1:8   53
21:7   53
22:13   53

Index of Names

Aeschylus 7
Aligheri, Dante 46
Althusser, Louis 46
Altmann, Alexander 13, 23f., 65–67
Amir, Yehoshua 38, 160
Amir, Yehoshua 74, 79, 121, 160
Amir, Yehoyada 38, 50, 79
Aquinas, Thomas 59
Aristotelian-Averrosian 59
Aristotle 15, 50, 59, 62, 106
Avineri Shlomo 28, 29, 47

Badt-Strauss, Bertha 26
Baeumer, Max L. 69
Batnitzky, Leora 11, 50, 76, 87, 122, 135, 141
Baudelaire, Charles 135, 138, 142–144, 146, 166
Bauer, Anna Elisabeth 76, 89, 148
Beckwith, Roger T. 97
Ben Bezalel, Judah Loew (Maharal) 154
Ben Yehuda, Eliezer 101f.
Ben Zoma, Simeon 156
Benjamin, Mara H. 5, 76, 93, 95, 119, 142, 145, 151, 153, 161
Benjamin, Walter 4, 7, 9, 133f., 142f., 145f., 166f.
Bernstein, S[imon] 3, 133
Bertolino, Luca 78, 128
Betz, John R. 67
Biale, David 4
Bienenstock, Myriam 28, 40, 67, 110
Bloch, Ernst 2
Bluhm, Heinz 163
Brasser, Martin 123, 125f.
Breuer, Edward 151
Breuer, Isaak 93
Britt, Brian 135
Brodersen, Momme 135, 146
Buber, Martin 3–7, 9, 11, 21, 50, 88f., 103, 107–109, 112, 114, 123–125, 129, 132–135, 141, 143, 145, 147–159, 161–165, 167, 169

Buddah 7
Byrne, Brendan 163

Calvin, John 165
Casper, Bernhard 78, 89f.
Cocteau, Jean 144
Cohen, Hermann 7, 31, 50f., 64, 68, 78, 82, 96, 107, 109f., 116f., 122, 132, 165, 167, 169
Cohen, Richard 123, 128
Cohn, Emil 27, 142
Comay, Rebecca 47f.
Cristuado, Wayne 79

Dagan, Hagai 10
Davidson, Herbert A. 65
Descartes, Rene 53
Di Cesare, Donatella 135

Eckhart, Meister 59
Ehrenberg, Hans 15, 24f., 52f, 67, 73, 145
Ehrenberg, Rudolph 1, 12f., 22, 25f, 67f., 134
Ehrlich, Leonard H. 92, 95, 102
Einstädter, Heinrich 105
Elbogen, Ismar 31, 50, 79, 93, 116, 129
Elior, Rachel 100

Fabry, Heinz-Joseph & Helmer Ringgern 121
Faur, Jose 86
Fichte, Johann Gottlieb 53
Finsterbusch, Karin 160
Fiorato, Pierfrancesco 110
Fishbane, Michael 79, 83
Fisher, Cass 50
Flusser, David 105
Fox, Everett 76
Fraenkel, Carlos 64
Franks, Paul 38, 51
Freund, Else 10, 25, 79, 109, 124
Fuhrmans, Horst 40
Furstenberg, Yair 87

Index of Names

Galli, Barbara E.   32, 74, 89, 91, 111, 121, 128, 141
Ganzel, Tova   86
Gesenius, Wilhelm   153
Gibbs, Robert   110, 160
Gillman, Abigail   151
Glatzer, Nahum N.   9–11, 13, 15f., 20–22, 26, 33, 52f., 55, 67, 78, 83, 99, 128, 131, 142
Goethe, Johann Wolfgang von   5f., 8f., 11, 14, 20–22, 28, 31, 33, 72, 84f., 153, 165
Gordon, Peter Eli   10, 28, 47, 50, 78, 135, 155
Graetz, Heinrich   79, 129
Greenstein, Edward   161
Grimm, Jacob and Wilhelm   121, 123, 132
Gruenwald, Itamar   129

HaCohen, Ran   148
Halbertal, Moshe   87
Halevy, Yehudah   1, 50, 65, 89, 105, 133, 135, 141f., 147, 169
Hallo, William   60, 73f., 111
Halvey, Yehudah   9
Harvey, Warren Zev   50, 64, 132
Hegel, Georg Wilhelm Friedrich   1f., 6, 8f., 20, 22–26, 28, 31–33, 35f., 40, 42–55, 59f., 68f., 72–74, 82, 106, 152, 167
Heinemann, Isaac   160
Herder, Johann Gottfried   53, 153, 165
Hill Shevitz, Amy   148
Hirsch, Samson Raphael   103
Hobbes, Thomas   2
Hölderlin, Johann Christian Friedrich   68
Hollander, Dana   11
Horrnefer, August   15
Horwitz, Rivka   8, 10, 56, 66, 128, 159
Hyman, Arthur   64

Ibn Gabirol, Shlomo   59
Ibn Paquda, Bahya   166
Ibn Tibbon, Shmuel   56, 57, 165, 166
Ibn Tibbon, Yehuda   166
Idel, Moshe   2f., 128, 130, 132
Iggers, Georg   12

Jacobson, Eric   135f.
Jay, Martin   135, 145f.
Jellinek, Aharon Adolph   129–131
Jephcott, Edmund   136

Kafka, Franz   145f.
Kant, Immanuel   8, 11, 18, 20–22, 28, 32–35, 53, 65, 72, 116, 152, 159f., 167
Kaufmann, David   55
Kaufmann, Yehezkel   86
Kautzsch, Emil   16, 80, 84, 117, 121, 153
Kavka, Martin   50, 78, 107
Klein-Braslavi, Sara   61
Knohl, Israel   86
Kohler, George Y.   64
Kornberg Greenberg, Yudit   128, 135
Kracauer, Siegfried   135, 145

Lambrianou, Nikolas   135
Leibniz, Gottfried Wilhelm   2, 53
Lessing, Johann Gotthold   53, 69
Licht, Ya'akov Shalom   101, 103, 129, 131
Liddell, Henry George and Scott, Robert   139
Liska, Vivian   147
Lorberbaum, Menachem   58
Losch, Andreas   89
Lucca, Enrico   132
Luria, Isaac   7, 78
Luther, Martin   5, 16, 18f., 80, 82–85, 90, 114, 117, 121–123, 127, 137, 149, 151, 153, 155, 162f., 165, 167

Mach, Dafna   76
Maimonides   50f., 57, 66, 71f., 74
Maimonides (Moshe son of Maimon)   4, 6, 9, 11, 16, 33, 50–52, 55–62, 64–68, 70–72, 78, 95, 109, 118, 122, 165
Marcion of Synope   11, 25
Margalit, Avishay   87
Mayer, Eugen   26f, 51, 107f., 123, 132
Mayer, Hermann   107
Meinecke, Friedrich   1, 8, 12, 22, 24
Meineke, Stefan   2, 29
Meir, Ephraim   122
Mendelssohn, Moses   19, 69, 84, 88–91, 103, 154, 158, 167

Index of Names

Mendes-Flohr, Paul 2, 11f., 20–22, 24, 29, 37, 52, 78, 148, 157
Michelangelo 146
Mosès, Stéphane 21, 95, 108f., 113, 116, 120, 128, 134f.
Murakoa, T. 163
Myers, David 12, 24

Navarette Alonso, Roberto 46f.
Niehoff, Maren Ruth 130, 155f.
Nietzsche, Friedrich 5f., 8f., 15, 20f., 28, 32, 127, 167

Oppenheim, Gertrude 14, 27, 51, 57, 106, 144

Philippson, Ludwig 16, 80, 83f., 114, 121
Philo of Alexandria 31
Pines, Shlomo 56f., 65
Plato 59, 62, 90, 106, 111, 144, 146, 166f.
Plaut, W. Gunther 151
Pöggeler, Otto 23, 28
Pollock, Benjamin 10–13, 24–28, 34, 46, 50, 54, 66, 78f.
Prager, Joseph 13, 26f.
Proust, Marcel 135, 143f., 146, 166

Reichert, Klaus 151
Reinharz, Jeudah 11f., 20–22, 24, 163
Richardson, Peter 163
Rickert, Heinrich 12
Robinson, James T. 64
Rosen–Zvi, Ishay 87
Rosenberg, Shalom 57, 64
Rosenwald, Lawrence 135, 141
Rosenzweig, Adele 22, 46f
Rosenzweig, Edith (nee Hahn) 148
Rosenzweig, Franz 1–62, 64–123, 125–135, 139–169, 171
Rousseau, Jean-Jacques 20, 45

Samuelson, Norbert 50, 56, 75, 113f., 123
Sander, Eric 163
Sauter, Caroline 145
Sax, Benjamin 20, 50, 79, 93
Schäfer, Peter 129

Scharf, Orr 32, 135, 143, 148, 151f., 169
Schelling, Friedrich Wilhelm Joseph 2, 9, 20, 31–33, 35, 40, 50f., 53f., 57–59, 66–70, 72, 82, 126, 167
Schiller, Friedrich 72, 79
Schindler, Renate 160
Schmied-Kowarzik, Wolfdietrich 110
Schnädelbach, Herbert 23
Scholem, Gershom 3f., 128f., 132, 134f., 145, 169
Schottlaender, Rudolph 146
Schreiner, Klaus 2
Schwarcz, Moshe 30, 34f., 38–42, 51, 54, 58, 66, 70, 140
Schweid, Eliezer 38, 40–42, 93
Seeskin, Kenneth 50
Sheppard, Eugene 10
Sommer, Benjamin 42, 153f., 158
Spengler, Oswald 2
Spinoza, Baruch Benedict 2, 53, 69, 144
Steinheim, Salomon Ludwig 38f.
Strauss, Bruno 26
Susman, Margarete 27

Taubes, Jacob 2
Tillich, Paul 67
Tramer, Hans 25–27

Uffenheimer, Benjamin 155

Weibel, Alois Adalbert 84
Wellhausen, Julius 153
Westerholm, Stephen 163
Wiedebach, Hartwig 110
Wiener, Leon Dow 42, 99
Wiese, Christian 151
Wittgenstein, Ludwig 51, 65
Wolfson, Elliot R. 109, 123, 128
Wygoda, Ynon 132

Yitzhaki, Shlomo (Rashi) 90, 101, 105, 111, 156

Zunz, Leopold Yom Tov Lippmann 15f., 19, 79f., 83f., 93, 103, 114, 121, 129

Index of Subjects

Ages of the World   40, 66, 167
Á la recherché du temp perdu   135, 144
Alles in allem   see All in All
All in All   66–70, 74
Angesicht   see Divine Face
Anthropomorphic   see Anthropomorphism
Anthropomorphism   51, 61
Antlitz   see Divine Face
Avoda zara   see Idolatry

Baden-Baden conference   12, 2–24, 29, 31, 36, 52, 53
Be'ur   90, 154,
Bible
– as artefact   103
– as repository of truths   5–4, 75, 93, 113
– and philosophical system   4, 33, 70, 88, 92109, 120, 168
– Interpretation of   5, 33, 37–39, 55, 57–58, 64, 151–153
– Relation to idolatry   79, 87, 117
– Rosenzweig's interest in   15, 26–27, 84

Christianity
– Appropriation of Bible   134, 151–153
– Calendar   93
– in Hegel   48, 50,
– in Schelling   66–70
– Redemptive role   18–19, 53, 67, 69,
Cosmology   92, 94–96
Creation
– and nothingness   78, 82–83
– Double negation   59–61
– Ex nihilo   60–62, 110

Da-Sein   see Name of God
Das älteste Systemprogramm des deutschen Idealismus   12, 50, 53–54, 58, 66
Death   37, 79–86,88, 100, 107–108, 111, 169
Der Ewige   see Name of God
Der Tischdank   76, 122
Die Schechina   25

Die Schrift
– and rabbinic Judaism   152–155
– Approach to translation   149–152
– Critiques of   145–146
– Edith Rosenzweig's contribution to   148–149
– *Geist*   152, 155–157
– *Gesetz*   159–164
– History of   147–152
– *Nomos*   159–164
Divine Face   17, 108, 123–128
Divine trial   56, 58

Ec-static   see Ek-stasis
Eheye   see Name of God
Ek-stasis   39, 74
End of Days   see Eschatology
Eschatological   see Eschatology
Eschatologie   see Eschatology
Eschatology   67, 72, 74
Eternal life   19, 74, 103–106

Faust   14

Geist   see *Die Schrift*
German Idealism   24, 28–29, 31–33, 50
– Critique of   34–36, 42–43
Gesetz   see *Die Schrift*
Gesprochenheit   153, 158
Gnosis   25, 28
Gnosticism   see Gnosis
Guide of the Perplexed   4, 51, 55–56, 63, 70, 165

Halbhundredtag   25
Halakhah   93, 99, 154, 157–159
Hegel und der Staat   1, 22, 28, 44–48
Hegelianism
– and paganism   50, 53–54, 58–60, 78
– and trauma   46–49
– Critique of   23, 32, 34–36, 42, 44–47, 53–55, 72, 78
– Revolution   43–49

Hekhalot literature   129–131
Hen kai pan   68–69
Heutigkeit   99, 101,157–159

Idolaters   see Idolatry
Idolatrous   see Idolatry
Idolatry
– Asian   78, 85–86
– *Avodah zara*   87
– Greek   78–79, 86
– The Bible's relation to   86–87, 117
Idols   see Idolatry
Islam   50, 70

Jewish Calendar
– and worship   92–93, 96–101, 127–129
– Rosh Hashanah   97–100
– Sabbath   94–96, 97, 99–101, 104
– Shavuot   96–100
– Sukkot   97–100
– Time Reckoning   92–96
– Yom Kippur   10, 27, 31, 50, 53, 67–68, 98–100, 128–129

Kabbalah   see Mysticism

Law   see Bible
Legende (Goethe poem)   84–85
Lehranstalt für die Wissenschaft des Judentums   31, 50–51, 64, 68, 76, 110, 116, 122, 129,
Leipziger Nachgespräch   9, 13, 25–27, 31

Ma'aseh Beresheet   57, 156, 157
Ma'aseh Merkavah   57, 156
Mashal   see Parable
Messiah   see Messianism
Messianic   see Messianism
Messianism   2, 3, 16, 20–23, 56, 66, 70–72, 145–147
Merkavah mysticism   see Mysticism
Mikra kodesh   101–106
Mishnah   98, 100, 102, 159, 166
Mishneh Torah   16, 56, 57, 65–66, 68, 70–71, 118
Monism   34–35

Mysticism
– and Maimonides   58, 64–66
– and Rosenzweig   128–129
– Kabbalah   2–3
– Merkavah mysticism   129–131,156
Myth   32, 39, 54,56–58, 77–81, 83–88

Name of God   19, 77, 80–81, 86–91, 100, 104, 162
Negative theology   56, 64
New Testament   18, 66, 67, 79, 82, 122, 139, 152, 163
New Thinking
– Concept   32, 41
– Essay   108,113, 133,169
Nomos   see *Die Schrift*

Offenbarungsglaube   29, 31, 52
"On Language as Such and the Language of Man"   134, 136–138, 139

Pagan   see Idolatry
Paganism   see Idolatry
Parable   56–59
Phenomenology of Spirit   35, 44, 45, 47–49

Relativism   2, 3, 6, 9–13, 23, 25, 29
Redemption
– Models of   2–3
– Translation as   134–147
Religion of Reason out of the Sources of Judaism   7, 107, 109–110, 116–120
Revelation
– and Sinai   19, 100, 154, 157–159, 161
– and Reason   55, 64–66, 106
Revolution   see Hegelianism
Rosh Hashanah   see Jewish Calendar

Sabbath   see Jewish Calendar
Schechina (sonnet cycle)   25
Scholasticism   53, 60, 61
Septuagint   139, 145, 149, 151, 152, 163–164, 169
Shavuot   see Jewish Calendar
Shechinah (hypostasis)   131
Song of Songs   5, 37, 57, 58, 88

Sprachdenken 76, 141
Stuttgart Private Lectures 66–67
Sukkot   see Jewish Calendar
Synagogue   27, 75, 92, 93

Tableaux Parisiens   135, 138, 143–144
Talmud   51, 64, 83, 90, 100, 122, 146, 154, 156, 159, 166, 167,168
Temple   72, 99, 100, 103, 108, 123, 128–131, 154, 167
Tetragrammaton   see Name of God
"The Builders"   99, 157, 161
The Origin of German Tragic Drama   135
The Star of Redemption
– as Jewish book   113–114, 120, 128
– Gate   37, 73, 108, 111, 123, 129–131
– "Into life"   37, 73, 107–110, 132, 150, 152,
– Martin Buber's interpretation of   111–114

– Moto of   107–108, 111–114
– Structure of   36–37, 77–79, 88, 91, 115, 140
– Threshold   72–74, 104, 123
"The Task of the Translator"   138–140, 143–144, 147
Truth
– In Rosenzweig   110–115
– In Hermann Cohen   116–120

Urzelle des Stern der Erlösung   126

Volks Bilder Bibel   84
Vulgate   149, 152, 162

Yom Kippur   see Jewish Calendar

Zweiundneunzig Hymnen und Gedichte des Jehuda Halevy   135, 141, 142, 147, 169

www.ingramcontent.com/pod-product-compliance
Lightning Source LLC
Chambersburg PA
CBHW030653230426
43665CB00011B/1072